PRAISE FOR
CHRISTIANITY REIMAGINED

From a deeply committed religious man:

Is it possible to experience the profound depth of the Divine Presence through the pages of a book? The answer...a resounding *yes*. This is more than a book—it's a seismic shift for your Soul: a spiritual earthquake that cracks open the ordinary to reveal the extraordinary. More than a read, it's a revelation. Dr. Forman makes a couple of points with which I do not agree, yet he never asks me to drop my religious view, but rather to see it with a new kind of depth: not either/or but both/and. This is vital, given what this book is opening up. Prepare to be catapulted into the transcendent Divine. This book is *tectonic*!

—Martin Rutte, coauthor, *The New York Times* Business Bestseller *Chicken Soup for the Soul at Work*; founder: Project-HeavenOnEarth.com

From committed Christians with doubts:

I have spoken with many, many people as a spiritual director. The people that Forman has interviewed are much the same kind of people that I've been talking to over the years, especially in the way they've tried to weave together science and religion. They know that Christianity isn't quite a fit, but they stay in the church because it gives them a sense of the holy. But most of them have not got the words for what they struggle with or how to resolve their dilemma. The book is not saying you have to reject Christianity or leave it, but instead, it reimagines Christianity in a way that makes sense. People in the parish are hungry for this: the world needs this kind of reimagining of the Divine. I hope every parish gets a copy and reads / discusses.

—Mary Meader, Episcopalian, cofounder, Bethany House of Prayer

As a priest and a "child of the church," I can only say that Forman's orientation is long overdue. His poignant examples of people with spiritual experiences will help to open hearts to explore the inner dimension of Being. The contemporary interest in human subjectivity (i.e., consciousness) testifies to the need for a Phenomenological Theology like his. I hope that Forman's "inner pilgrimage" gets the attention that it deserves.

—Edward Harris, Lutheran Priest, Stockholm

From a former conservative believer:

Has church lost some (or all) of its meaning for you? Dr. Forman's powerfully engaging new book offers an inspiring reimagining of Christianity that may very well work for you. It addresses our culture's deep hunger for authentic relationship and community within a spiritual context. I hope that Christians and non-Christians alike read this in order to ignite new possibilities for Christianity in a time of great need for connection with the Divine and with others.

—Melissa West, Psychotherapist and author of *Exploring the Labyrinth*

From the "spiritual but not religious":

For decades, scholars, pollsters, and clergy alike have been asking why people have been leaving churches in droves. Robert Forman asks a more salient question: Why do so many keep showing up—especially those who no longer believe in core doctrinal tenets? The surprising answers he came up with deserve the close attention of everyone who cares about the future of religion.

—Philip Goldberg, Interfaith Minister and author of *American Veda* and *Spiritual Practice for Crazy Times*

I couldn't put this book down. Forman's vision is so wide yet deep! It is centered on the living and universal core of spirituality that cuts across religions but also on Christianity's unusual emphasis on relationship. I was especially moved by his notion of "Sacramental Conversations." It has tremendous implications for people to reach one another at depths while at the same time unifying the religions. In this he is not asking people to give up anything of Christianity, but rather change their emphasis to the living, experiential volcano that was in Christianity's beginning and still lives today.

—Doug Kruschke, Founder, InSynergy

From Christians who fell away:

I was raised in a family for which the Congregational Church was a central feature of our lives. However, as an adult and a biomedical scientist, I grew apart from the church. Forman, in this book, offers a very personal account of his own recent entry into a church. He writes with clarity about how church works for him, about the dilemmas posed by some church doctrines and with concern for others' journeys. Reading this book has rekindled my interest in exploring church once again.

—Livingston Van De Water, Professor Emeritus, Albany Medical College

Imagine a secular Jew, a professor of religious studies and a long-term student of mysticism walking into an Episcopal Church and being so moved that he cries. Not once but every time he attends one of these services in churches around New England for the next eight years. Wouldn't you want to understand why you, and the many others in a similar boat, were so moved, what combination of song, ritual and good fellowship moved your heart? And wouldn't you also want to make sense of Church teachings and doctrines in ways that could speak to your modern sensibilities? This is what Robert Forman does in this fascinating and moving account of his journey, and that of others like him, to insight, community and greater connection to the ground of being.

—Christopher Schaefer, Ph.D., author, international community development advisor, adult educator, and student of Anthroposophy

CHRISTIANITY REIMAGINED
A MYSTICAL APPROACH FOR DOUBTERS AND THE DUBIOUS

ROBERT K.C. FORMAN

APOCRYPHILE
PRESS

Apocryphile Press
PO Box 255
Hannacroix, NY 12087
www.apocryphilepress.com

Copyright © 2024 by Robert K.C. Forman
Printed in the United States of America
ISBN 978-1-965646-05-2 | paper
ISBN 978-1-965646-06-9 | ePub

No part of this book may be reproduced, stored in a retrieval system, or transmitted in any form or by any means—electronic, mechanical, photocopy, recording, or otherwise —without written permission of the author and publisher, except for brief quotations in printed reviews.

Please join our mailing list at www.apocryphilepress.com/free. We'll keep you up-to- date on all our new releases, and we'll also send you a FREE BOOK. Visit us today!

CONTENTS

Introduction   xi

PART ONE
FIRST ENCOUNTERS

1. The Crack Through Which the Light Got In   3
2. Discovering Path Mates   19

PART TWO
THE HORIZONTAL SPIRITUAL POWER REIMAGINED

3. The Crack Widens   31
4. They are My Family Now   41
5. "More Willing to Be Vulnerable There"   58
    Ruminations on the Horizontal   69

PART THREE
THE VERTICAL SPIRITUAL POWER REIMAGINED

6. "Being and At-Oneness"   73
7. Electrons, Quarks, The Omnipresent Field and Love   99
    Ruminations on the Vertical   115

PART FOUR
JESUS REIMAGINED

8. Jesus of Nazareth   121
9. Resurrection Reimagined   135
    Ruminations on the Story of Jesus   147

PART FIVE
CHRISTIANITY'S COMPONENTS REIMAGINED

10. Reimagining Sin and Salvation   155
11. Reimagining Ethics   169
12. Reimagining Prayer   180

13. Reimagining Being Called	193
14. Reimagining the Afterlife	202
Ruminations on Christianity	209

PART SIX
FINAL REIMAGININGS

15. Translating Traditional Language	217
16. Final Ruminations	223
Epilogue	243
Gratitude	255
Works Cited	257

*For Ezra, Phoebe, Silas, Emme, Pia and Otto,
my beloved family, community, and hyperbrain.*

Last year's words belong to last year's language
And next year's words await another voice.
— T.S. Eliot "Little Gidding"

INTRODUCTION

What you are holding in your hands is nine years' worth of head-scratching, belly-dropping and heart-palpitating ponderings and discoveries. It is the product of more than 60 long interviews with thoughtful churchgoers, and of account after account of the religious life that I heard from more than 2000 patients as a board-certified chaplain. It has been shaped as well by my lifetime in academia: a Ph.D. in religion, many academic books and articles, and 20 years of university teaching.

It also comes from the discoveries of people like Mark Hogan. Mark, a smiling and roundish sixty-something, grew up a committed Catholic, served on the altar, became a deacon, and had numerous friends there. In his 40's, Mark just could no longer accept the ethics of the whole priesthood and became an Episcopalian. Though he feels more comfortable there, and still goes to church regularly, the virgin birth, the water-walking and the claims about the resurrection just don't add up for him. He's struggling to make sense of it, or struggling to believe it all. That is, he's been struggling to make a new kind of sense of the confusing and ambiguous gift that is his religion.

It is also the product of people like Anna Christina Sundgren. As a child on an island in the Swedish archipelago, she attended the Swedish Lutheran church. But her spiritual life was centered on connecting with nature, and she pulled away from the church as an adolescent. However, once she became a therapist and saw the value of its deep relational bonds, she rediscovered religion, which led her into a Lay Franciscan community in which members often open up to one another and feel "part of something bigger" together.

Many, many people like Mark, Anna Christina and me—who are actively Christian but "doubt" what they hear from the pulpit—have been reimagining this ancient religion. We've been making new sense of its antique doctrines, its obscure liturgy and of its very old way of thinking. We've been rethinking the old bugbears like sin, salvation, water-into-wine and the whole Jesus narrative. What we've come up with makes new and damn good sense. And I, as well as the fifty-plus people that I interviewed and the 2000 patients that I chaplained, are sure that we are better off going to church on Sunday mornings than just staying home with bagels and newspapers. It is to the doubters that I am writing this book.

I am also writing to people like George Case. George was raised in a traditional Christian denomination. His parents were missionaries and he was brought up to believe it all. But when he was a teenager, he began to resent the control, resent the behavioral pressures, especially around sex, and resent that he was supposed to believe the whole system. At this point, he is just plain dubious of the whole enterprise, dubious of the claims about Jesus, about the community, about the whole mess, as he put it. He is part of the fastest growing religious groups today, the "spiritual but not religious" or the religious "nones." I am writing as well to the dubious.

God knows that in suggesting that church might actually help Mark, Anna Christina, George and me, and the countless others like us, I am very conscious that I'm swimming against a

INTRODUCTION

powerful cultural current. Among educated people—especially the liberal and perhaps the "spiritual but not religious"—respect for Christianity has plummeted. With all the misogyny, pedophilia and antisemitism of much of the institution, with all the judgmental, anti-intellectual and self-righteous "Christian Nationalists'" and with all the institution's crusades, witch hunts and heresy trials, one can't help but wonder how anyone could explore such an institution without gagging?

But the Christianity that makes liberal and educated souls gag is not the Christianity in which we participate. The churches that people like Anna Christina, Mark and I choose to attend are among the 52% of denominations that are more or less liberal, that are welcoming, open-hearted and non-cultish (Lipka, 2016).[1] None of the leaders of our churches have ever insisted that we dress, act, think or talk in a certain way. Nor have any of them told us whether we can have an abortion, when we can have sex nor whom we can love.

Without offering too much of a spoiler, I've come to see that, at its core, Christianity is talking about, capitalizing on, and giving rise to important religious or spiritual *experiences*.

To get a sense for the kinds of experiences that we're talking about, I want to ask you, the reader, to consider two questions.

1. What were your deepest, most meaningful experiences like? Some might call them spiritual experiences, or "non-ordinary experiences" in which you were seeing yourself, another or the world in a way that was above and beyond how you "normally" see? Perhaps one came at a time when you were just overwhelmed with beauty? Perhaps it was a few moments when time seemed to disappear? Maybe you caught a glimpse of the beauty, peace and power that seemed to flow through the landscape, like a current through a wire.

INTRODUCTION

Or when you were suddenly overcome with love? Perhaps it came when you were on a walk in the woods, when you were struck with the sounds of the birds or the beauty of the dappled sunlight? Perhaps childbirth was your deepest and most meaningful experience, when you felt not only connected with your baby but at one with some holy energy or at one with the world?

Here's how the Rev. Stephanie Bradbury, a sixtyish Episcopal Priest from Lowell, Massachusetts described hers: sometimes in church, she told me, "something transcendent comes."

> I've also experienced it in solitary walks in the woods, where the trees and I are connecting in some way. In these moments I'm connecting with what's real, what's alive. I go deep, soul deep. Life seems as slick as glass.

In such experiences all your anxieties and concerns seem to just drop away, time seems to evaporate and you're *there*, fully *there*. Such "spiritual experiences" can happen in church. Or they can happen in an unlikely place, entirely non-conducive to spirituality.

Such experiences used to happen to me most often on meditation retreats, when I found myself wide open to a sense of a "vastness." Recently such "non-ordinary experiences" have bubbled up in church, as you'll see, when I find myself affected so intensely that I just weep. Sometimes they've happened when I'm riding my motorcycle around a graceful curve, the branches on either side arching over the macadam, and a farmhouse at the far end of field shining in the sunlight. At these moments I'm "there," really "there," and somehow expanded into something non sensory but wide. It's like I'm somehow stretching out, becoming a vast ocean. Generally, these times

INTRODUCTION

come when I'm not talking. Sometimes though they come during intimate conversations, when we're feeling our way towards some deeper truths about what we really feel or who we really are. At those times, the walls of the room around us seem to fall away and we find ourselves amid something wide and sweet. Tears or no tears, in church or not, these times carry a quiet and pervasive joy. These moments are holy.

When you think back over your lifetime, can you think of any such non-ordinary moments? What are they like for you?

2. Have you ever undergone a period of inner growth? That is, have you gone through a process after which you became less obsessed or fixated on something? Have you ever worked through the pain of a childhood trauma, for example? Or become conscious of your tendency to deny or shade the truth? Perhaps you came to terms with how you had been causing your spouse or your child pain, and then fixed that tendency in you? In other words, can you think of any times in which you became a bigger person?

Such growth comes in two forms, I think: psychological and spiritual. I'm a fan of both. Psychotherapy helps us identify what happened to us when we were kids, hopefully helping us resolve some of our hurt, guilty or angry feelings. Therapy can help us understand our families' dysfunctions, release some of our adult neuroses and resolve many of our long-standing issues. Perhaps you've seen how amazing a tool it can be when it works.

Growth I think of as "spiritual," on the other hand, points to the maturation of spirit. It may be an increasing ability to sense a non-sensory reality, or to delve into a religious text with new eyes. Spiritual growth is about being more present than before, both to yourself and to others. With attention, with meditation, with the willingness to open up to ourselves, to others and to spirit, it can help us mature in our ability to love.

These two forms of growth are related, but not quite the same (but that's an issue for another book).

When you think back over your journey, can you think of any times in which you went through such inner growth? What were they like for you?

I bring up these two kinds of phenomena—the waves of ecstasy that sometimes wash over us and the inner growth towards spiritual connection—because they stand both at the beating heart of our religious lives and as the cornerstone of this book. I've come to see that whether we are progressive, liberal or fundamentalist, there are similar deep experiences at the core of our spiritual lives. Christianity is all about encouraging, fostering and talking about such deeply centered experiences. As we will see in the chapters below, they live as the quivering core of terms like "God," "Christ," "The Lord" or "salvation."

Christianity then swirls around experiences like yours which touch on something Infinite, maturing in the light of such experiences within you as a human being and as part of a community, and teaching us how better to love. Rumbling below the ancient words and models are references to experiences and spiritual shifts like yours. Speaking about and out of these experiences is one place we can meet below the seemingly intractable differences between fundamentalists, Catholics and liberal Christians. We can hear such whispers, whether we believe in the ancient claims and doctrines or not. Beneath the liturgy, language and ritual of the countless forms of the religion are spiritual experiences and life transformations much like your own.

INTRODUCTION

In other words, we will see how the various doctrines, denominations, sects and models of Christianity all swirl around and point towards experiences like yours and mine.

I say this, but offer two words of caution. First, some have complained to me that they've never had a spiritual experience. They struggle with knowing what experiences they've had or have struggled with recognizing them. If you're in this boat, I suggest that as you read this book you may realize, "Oh, I've sensed something like that." Most people probably have had plenty of such experiences, but just haven't recognized them. The experiences we're talking about don't come with flashing neon lights. Most are quiet and subtle: the feeling of connection with someone or something, the vague sense that there's something deep but unnamed here, or the like. In other words, you may very well recognize more than you know. If you're *sure* you've never had any such deep or connective experiences, I suspect the book will not feel very relevant to you.

The other thing I want to warn you, especially my readers who do believe in the traditional doctrines and models, is that the book offers a *Reimagined* Christianity. We'll be reimagining virtually everything—the phrases, the rituals and the approaches which have been a gift to millions of believers. I ask you to be willing to drop, just for a while, your assumptions and your habits of thought about Christianity and bear with me. I will ask you to do so for, as you'll see, I'll not be asking you to *drop* any of your beliefs, understandings or rituals but rather to deepen them! By the end, I hope that you will see that this approach enriches the words and models that have worked for you for so long. We're about both/and, not either/or. But to do so, I will ask you to be willing to set aside for now your habits of thought about what the models and terms mean.

I want to stress this: I am not asking you to *drop* any beliefs or thoughts, but rather to use this book to deepen them. If on the other hand you see this approach as threatening, I would love for you to explore this response with your friends and, if possible, with me. I only ask that you do so in the spirit of Jesus's commandment to "love thy neighbor." We have all experienced how easy it is to repudiate someone when we don't agree with them, but it is my hope that we can examine our differences through what we will call below a "sacramental conversation." That means speaking with honesty and teasing out the others' and our own heartfelt needs and longings which stand beneath our positions. It means listening instead of reacting, reaching out instead of recoiling and looking not for the flaws but for the beauty in the other's thoughts. I hope that together we might explore our differences as an element of finding ways to connect. And thereby fulfill the essence of Christianity.

Now, I believe I am in a unique position to *Reimagine Christianity*. I've come to Christianity with less of the baggage that a life-long Christian might carry and more of the mystical: I didn't grow up Christian but a Reform Jew, which I abandoned during college. I have practiced Transcendental Meditation every day for some 55 years. Based on this practice and the rich spiritual life it led to, I wrote *Enlightenment Ain't What It's Cracked Up To Be* (Forman, 2011). I also bring substantial academic credentials to the task: my Ph.D. in the study of religion had a focus on religious and spiritual experiences of every sort. As a university professor, I became a leading figure in one of the longest-standing debates in the field of religious studies, the so-called "Katz-Forman debates" about the nature of spiritual experiences. Many of my twelve books and forty some articles grew out of those conversations. Those books and the larger debates are, even 35 years later, still being discussed in Ph.D.

INTRODUCTION

dissertations and journal articles. I founded an ecumenical organization of spiritual leaders and teachers, *The Forge Institute for Spirituality and Social Change*, through which I became aware of the kinds of experiences this book talks about in virtually every spiritual tradition. I don't think I'm being immodest to say I bring a deep knowledge of the issues and the phenomena.

But that's only about my understanding and writing. This book is also about the emotional and spiritual effects of Christianity, and here I write as a man who has been deeply touched in church week after week. Indeed, I wept or cried in church every Sunday for 8 ½ years! Although I remain, like most Mystics, on the Margins, highly dubious about Christianity's terms, models and claims, I continue to have a real love of the tradition, especially its weekly ritual.

In other words, I come as a man who is both spiritual and secular, emotional and intellectual, convinced first-hand of Christianity's power yet also highly skeptical of its models. That means I stand astride what I see as the principal pros and cons of the religion: the doubt and the respect, the skepticism and the commitment, the nays and the yeas.

Despite my ambivalence, the bottom line is that I value Christianity. Deeply. I have been profoundly enriched by it. I have more and deeper connections than I might otherwise have had, more sense of meaning, more open heart and positivity, and, yes, more of a felt-connection with something deep and transcendent. As you'll see in the Epilogue, it's helped me resolve one of my most intractable life issues. And I am encouraged by the studies that have found a significant relationship between religiosity, well-being and mental health, and that churchgoers have better mental health and more positive emotions.[2] I am personally encouraged by the number of studies that have discovered that people who go to church tend to live longer: Middle-aged adults—both men and women—

INTRODUCTION

who attend church or other houses of worship have a 55% lower risk for mortality from any source (Marino).

I owe an enormous debt of gratitude to the wonderful people with whom I have had the privilege of conversing these eight and a half years. I conducted more than sixty long interviews with some of the wisest people I've ever. It was an honor to hear so many people's deep personal sharings and the wisdom they bring to their experiences and their religion. The commitment of time I asked of my interviewees was substantial and I am incredibly thankful.

As a hospital chaplain I talked with several thousand patients. I wish to thank those patients, many of whom were wonderfully open and forthright with me about their experiences of their religion and their connections with the Divine, even as they faced pain and death. While in the following chapters you will see the thoughts and understandings of all these people about their sense of the transcendent, about their commitments, about their communities, about their thoughts about life, death, the resurrection and more, I could not possibly represent the richness of any one of them, much less all of them. I can only hope that I have done them justice.

In other words, as I've tried to understand the reimagined version of this strange, frustrating and inspiring religion, I have been helped enormously. But I have also continued to think about and research what I have been hearing from others and encountering in church week after week. Though in most of this book I quote and summarize much of what I heard from my patients and interviewees, I have also come up with my own ways of thinking, especially scientific ways. Honestly, if you find those chapters (end of Chapter 5 and Chapter 7) jarringly

INTRODUCTION

heady, please feel free to skip or skim them; you will still understand the book.

The upshot is that this Reimagined Christianity is a far more beautiful, benevolent and beneficial path of love than any of us might imagine.

---

1. Of the 23 denominations listed in the 2016 Pew survey of churches politics, 12 of them, 52%, lean Democratic as opposed to Republican.
2. Harold G. Koenig, professor of psychiatry at Duke University School of Medicine concluded: "A large volume of research shows that people who are more R/S [religious/spiritual] have better mental health and adapt more quickly to health problems compared to those who are less Religious / Spiritual." Frank Newport, Dan Witters, Sangeeta Agrawal wrote, "The very religious rate their lives more positively, are less likely to have ever been diagnosed with depression, and experience fewer daily negative emotions." (Thornhill

PART ONE
FIRST ENCOUNTERS

CHAPTER 1

THE CRACK THROUGH WHICH THE LIGHT GOT IN

BREAKTHROUGH

Eight and a half years ago, Lauren, a friend in my chaplaincy training program, invited me to witness her installation as a priest in Mahwah, New Jersey. Though it was some 200 miles away, she was a dear friend and I wanted to support her.

When the day came, however I was in no mood to go. I had recently separated from my wife of 40 years and was afraid I'd made a huge mistake. (We've since reconciled, happily.) My training as a chaplain had not yet led to a job and I saw no prospects for one. I felt very fragile, very much on my own and very scared. I had visions of dying broke and alone in some nursing home reeking of urine, abandoned by my family and forgotten by my friends. And her installation was happening some 200 miles away. No, I was *not* in the mood!

But I had promised Lauren. So I went.

Though I was feeling grumpy and scared, when I walked into the enormous Cathedral in Mahwah, with its stone walls, dark windows and high oak rafters, I was actually struck by the quiet of the space. The church felt settled and cool, and it smelled of candle wax and frankincense.

The service went on for 2 ½ hours. I had no idea that ordaining priests would take soooo long! I spent the first hour or so thinking grumpy thoughts about how old fashioned their ideas of God and Christ were and about how mindless were the sheep in the pews. This whole way of thinking is so outdated, I thought, so Iron Age! All those "I believes" and "we sinners" and "angels this" and "evil one that."

Some of my criticism came from what I knew of physics, astrophysics, biology and the like: Where does a God who created the world fit in with electrons, quarks and neutrinos? Given black holes and supernovas and cosmic dust clouds and galaxy clusters so far away that their light takes billions of years to arrive, where might a quasi-human "Maker" of heaven and earth fit? And where did He sit? Did he point his finger some 13.8 billion years ago, I thought, and shout "bang?" Did he intentionally stretch time and space like a wad of faster-than-the-speed-of-light gum? Did he mutter, "Let there be black holes?"[1]

Then I found myself thinking about how supposedly benevolent this God was. How could a good God have allowed world wars and the holocaust and Hiroshima and tsunamis and earthquakes that kill 20,000 children? Or why had He taken my friend Nadine at 32, who had two small kids?

What about Jesus, Joseph and Mary, I continued thinking? Was Mary a virgin? Really? How can we be sure that she hadn't gotten raped or...um...playful and was too ashamed to tell? Or maybe this was just a touching story that some early Christians cribbed from the Egyptian myths of fatherless gods like Net and Horus? And in what sense might the death of a carpenter from Nazareth 2000 years ago save some Hindu farmer that never heard of him?

Then there was the tale of the resurrection. If he had been

dead for three days, did his blood un-coagulate? Did the maggots scatter? And how was his undying supposed to help me with my anxieties or my lack of job prospects?

Next Darwin came to mind. I just couldn't picture some Divine Dude in the sky whittling all the dinosaurs and kangaroos and wooly mammoths and cockroaches and fur-free humans into existence, fully formed, ZAP! And why, by the way, did he then kill off all the dinosaurs and the wooly mammoths? Do Divine Dudes take do-overs? No, it made a whole lot more sense to me that micro-organisms and multi-celled sponges and sea-floor creatures and amphibious crocodiles and eventually apes and human beings all evolved through millions of years of natural selection.

While I was busy thinking these heretical thoughts, readers were up there asking us to recite the "creed" with its lines about a "maker of heaven and earth" and a babe born of a virgin. Talk about cognitive dissonance!

Nonetheless, I had to admit that the whole ceremony was lovely, and Lauren looked radiant. The church felt tranquil, and I liked the smell of frankincense and flowers. With all the pomp and incense and bells and gold-embossed robes, these people knew how to throw a ritual! The large choir, their white robes pressed sharply, was damned good. The woman "cantor" had an especially angelic voice. With the cool stone walls, the dark rafters, the smells, the music, the hush and the bowing, it all felt downright medieval.

And then something struck me. To explain I'll need to put on my "Professor of Religions" hat, because it's something that I've taught to countless college students.

Every system of thought—be it religious, secular, communist, scientific, old or new—draws a map of the world. A group's map includes everything it thinks there is. The Christian map, for example, includes churches, good and evil, God, the Devil, sin, salvation, priestly vestments, messiahs, and so on. Their map also includes more mundane things like communion wafers, pews, church suppers, Easter Bunnies, altar cloths, Christmas trees and Santa Claus. All these things and images and words and feelings make up what we professors call the Christian "world view."

Based on its map of what there is in the world, every system of thought then goes on to tell its people what they are to do. Christianity, to continue with our example, posits that there is something in the world called "sin." It holds that sin is a bad, bad thing and if someone does a sin, they'll go to a nasty place after they die, forever. So, they pose their version of life's problem: "Doesn't that sound awful?!"

Then they offer the cure to the problem they've named. The various denominations tell their people to "have faith in Jesus," "confess your sins," "perform the sacraments," "do good moral deeds" or some such. The various actions they prescribe become part of what we call its "ethos." These two are connected: Christianity (or any system of thought) posits the problem of life (there is sin, which leads to trouble after death), frames the question (how can we cure sin?) and then supplies activities that answer the question (have faith, perform a sacrament, etc.).

Every system of meaning—be it religious, cultural, political, scientific, communist or even atheist—does this trick. With something like a conceptual sleight of hand, every system of meaning states what there is, frames its question, and then answers it.

A people's worldview plus their ethos, along with the incredibly complicated web of words and activities and hopes and foibles to which they give rise, is its "framework."

Having a worldview and ethos is not a bad thing. We all need to make sense of our world, know how to act, answer life's questions and live in a world that seems to make sense. Without a framework, we'd have no way to orient our lives, know with confidence what to do, etc. We all need frameworks.

OK I'll take my professor's hat off now.

Here's the revelation of that morning: All the readings and sermons and prayers and songs I was hearing *seemed* to be about (or perhaps from) God or Jesus. But my insight was that I was witnessing a group of people who *thought* it was about God. If I stopped asking whether that God created the world in six days or if Jesus actually rose from the dead, what I was actually seeing was a group of human beings, each more or less like me, who *tell* one another the story of a Great Maker in the Sky and of his wondrous Son. They tell one another how Jesus had a wondrous birth and grew up in Nazareth and how, some thirty years later, he died and then emerged from his tomb and lived. I was seeing their *worldview*. When they eat the bread and drink the wine and whisper that it's the "body of Christ," I was seeing their *ethos*. And when they tell each other these things and do their ritual actions, they may *feel* something larger. Maybe they even have ecstatic experiences or become radiant, like Lauren.

"It's just these people's worldview," I thought to myself. "This whole system is all the work of human beings, much like me."

"Good Grief," I thought so loudly that my neighbors nearly heard, "It's just us!"

"It's always been us," I thought. No miraculous writers took dictation from a Divine angel. No Father out there sculpted the planets. No supermen. It's all been us. With our human minds and feelings, our mystical sense, it's all been our human handiwork. It's the thoughts that people think, the feelings that people feel in the communities that people build. It's always been us. These human beings have been giving voice to their fears and hopes, trying to answer their very human hurts and needs, and they've used this particular language. All those centuries of books and rituals and wars and theologizing—Christianity has all been the handiwork of human beings like me, like everyone sitting, thinking and feeling in the pews around me. It's just us.

But this doesn't mean, I realized immediately, that what's here is *meaningless*. It's quite meaningful, just not in the way that math or astrophysics or cell biology is. We human beings are blessed with all kinds of sensations, feelings, abilities and hopes. These people are trying to express in their language the kinds of feelings and sensations that we human beings sometimes have. Over the years some Christians have written beautiful poetry, sung glorious oratorios and painted gorgeous chapels. Some of them wrote the Magnificat and the Messiah and Gospel Music. They've etched some amazing stained-glass windows and painted chapels like the Sistine. They've built countless buildings of oak and stone like Notre Dame and Chartres and, well, this one. It's all been people, framing human fears and giving voice to human hopes. Some of these people have inspired others to tears and led one another to insights or fleshed out their mythology or began wars. And some of them have also mystically sensed, however vaguely and ineffably, "something more" and tried to express it. I doubt that there's a God-man up there making all this happen, but there certainly is an "us" down here, sitting in pews we've carved, expressing hopes in songs we've written and offering each other smiles.

There's only us. We may not be as perfect or as pretty as Hermes or Thor or Athena or Jesus or Sarasvati. We may not be eternal. But taken all in all, the emotions and sensations that they're stimulating and expressing are quite real.

That was my first insight—"It's just us." As I thought it, I relaxed a bit. I could stop my infernal mouse-wheel of griping about whether there's a heaven or hell or a supernatural Son. I went from Mr. Grumpy-Pants, fighting with the theologians in my head, to just sitting in a pew with other feeling people. They may live in a different worldview and believe some things that I don't—like Jesus walking on water or a God's creating the cosmos in 6 days—but I suspect their feelings and longings are much like my own. "It's just us!"

Then came a second "ah ha" moment. Because of this people's worldview and framework, something in their lives *changes*. They *help* one another more. When a fellow church member gets sick, some of these folks might actually bring her dinner, even if they don't know her well. When a parishioner loses his mom, his church mates might go to her funeral. Some might take food to a homeless shelter, build a house for a poor family or sing in a hospital to kids with cancer. Of course, non-church members do these things as well, as do meditators and more secular "religious nones." But because these people express their feelings and longings through this particular framework, they're more likely to do such actions and to help each other than, well, a secular, scientific or spiritual fellow like me. (I was right. I've since learned that 30.5% of liberal churches engage in charity work of some kind, whereas only 21.7% of non-Christian groups do.[2]

An image from the movie *Titanic* came to mind. These church members are like people in a rowboat reaching down to pull drowning people out of the frigid ocean. They pull each other up. They help one another.

I, like many of the secular, scientific or meditative types I know, often feel that I'm pushing my rock up my hill pretty much on my own. I certainly help others sometimes. But if I'm honest with myself, I thought, I'm a little self-involved. I don't know many people who would pull me up into their rowboat.

As I continued to think about it, I realized that the great

stone walls and oak rafters of that very church got built because something in their beliefs encouraged them to cooperate and to build it. Some Christians glazed the stained glass, cut the stone.[3] Others wrote the music, joined the choir, baked the muffins for the coffee hour, bought and arranged the flowers and laid out the green and gold altar cloth. Again, we spiritual or we secular people also do these things. But the folks here are, frankly, more likely than we merely secular / spiritual folks to start a day care in a church basement, inoculate children in Africa or feed the homeless.[4] Unlike most of us ambitious types who are so focused on making our way up the success ladder, and unlike most of us spiritual folks who sit on our solitary Zen cushions, these folks have, or are supposed to have, each other's backs.

Christianity *looks* like it's all about *believing* in something or some person, I thought to myself. It *talks* about resurrection, virgin births, sin and salvation. But deep down inside it's a way of expressing and fostering some real, very human needs and feelings. And the way it does leads people to stretch beyond themselves, to sense "something more," to touch the transcendent. And to pull each other into their rowboats.

Just after I had this second "ah ha" moment—that how they think about things has emotional and interpersonal effects—we, the congregation, began to sing John Becker's "Litany of the Saints."[5] The piece is call and response. The female "cantor" with a particularly beautiful soprano voice sang a few lines. In response, we chanted "Pray with us." Soon we began stretching out our last note—uuuus—and holding it awhile. Then she sang her lines over our drone. She chanted "Mary and Joseph" and we again chanted "Pray with uuuus." I soon realized that she was naming biblical and other religious figures. As she sang "Isaac, Sarah and Abraham," or "Ruth, David and Solomon," we'd chant, "Pray with uuuus."[6]

Because our part was simple and repetitive, we, the congregation, spontaneously harmonized more and more. With just enough vibrato to give her lines character, she'd sing "Peter, Paul and Andrew," or "James, John and the apostles" and each time our "Pray with uuuus" became richer. While an organ provided the rhythm and underlying chords, she'd again sing names— "Joseph, Samuel and Sarah" or "Isaac, Mary and Abraham"—and we'd respond, with more and more harmony, "Pray with uuuus." Finally, after about eight of these calls and responses, we'd sing a coda, "All you holy men and women pray with us."

As I thought about my leaving my wife and having no job and asking all those figures to "pray with uuuus," I found myself thinking, "Lord knows I can use *somebody's* help!"

And much to my surprise, with that thought and with the celestial soprano soloist and with our two hundred voices harmonizing beneath her, I began to *weep*. Not just a few tears, mind you, not just a decent cry. I was sobbing and sobbing in can't-catch-breath shudders. I just wept and wept, feeling about as vulnerable as I ever have.

The voice of that female cantor was truly angelic. But it wasn't only her. It was *all* of us, singing with each other in harmony, together. *That's* what was so beautiful, all of us helping one another reach beyond ourselves. *We* were the magic!

I've sung in choral groups. I've sung in madrigals and in operas. But in those moments of harmony and weeping that morning I felt, perhaps for the first time in my life, *accompanied*. All those people were singing *with* me. Feeling held and cradled by that rich "Pray with uuuus," hearing that woman's voice floating above and asking all the "saints" to pray, I felt part of an "uuuus." I was standing with, crying with, singing with, all those others. After all the rocks I had pushed up my hills by myself, after all my anxious efforts to achieve on my own, I thought, it doesn't have to all fall on my shoulders. "There is an us here. I'm not so bloody alone."

The phrase "lay my burdens down" came to mind. There's a community here, lots of people...and maybe, just maybe, I can lay a few of my burdens down. Maybe I don't have to carry them all by myself."

For how long, I thought, have I been pushing my rock up my mountain on my own? This simple thought—that others might actually help, that I might help others—was new. "Perhaps there *is* spiritual way other than doing it all alone," I said to myself. "There is an *us* here." And we sang together, beautifully.

I just wept and wept.

THE ENIGMA

When the service came to a close, I felt that spent, cleansed feeling that comes after a good cry. I could sense that some deep and ancient wound had been cleansed, some ancient weight had lifted. And I hadn't even known it had been weighing on me.

When it was over, I looked around, embarrassed that Lauren or someone else might have been staring at my shuddering shoulders. No one was.

I wouldn't say I was happy as I walked out. I felt more spent, cleansed and stunned. For reasons I could not say, this seemed huge. Probably for the first time in my life, I no longer felt alone.

As you can imagine, I wanted to return to a church again, and soon. I went the following week. And the next. And the next. By now, I've gone to a church every Sunday for eight and a half years. And every single Sunday I have wept![7] Wept with loneliness, wept with joy, wept over the beauty of the music or the power of the ritual, wept for reasons I did not know: I just wept.

But here's the mind-boggling thing: I have never believed a word. Not the creeds, not the confessions, none of it. I didn't believe it that morning in Mahwah and I still don't believe in some cosmic world-maker or in an only Son of that magical fellow. I have never accepted Jesus as my personal savior (a phrase that still makes my skin crawl!). No cosmic figure has appeared to me, no angel hath spoken words of comfort, nothing. In other words, I didn't suddenly start buying anything they were selling![8] And yet I have continued to weep.[9]

The church's words and metaphors are remnants of the worldview and ethos of some other people's world, one that thrived long, long ago and far, far away: in the Middle East during the so-called Iron Age. To folks back then, the only controllable energy came from people or perhaps animals. It probably made sense to them to think that the world was made and controlled by some person-like deity whose "mouth hath spoken" and whose "breath blows upon the grass" (Isa. 40:5, 7).

But it no longer makes sense to me. My worldview includes Einstein and Darwin and Pasteur and electromagnetic fields and cosmological time and quantum physics and Freud and sociology and the study of comparative religions. The worldview of the Bible or the pope or even the evangelicals is not mine. In fact, it seems painfully outdated and obsolete. To nearly every line of the creed that we recite or to the baptismal vows, I still think to myself, "Nah, I don't believe that." I just can't say "I believe in God, the Father almighty, creator of heaven and earth" without blanching. For my sense of a spiritual reality is nothing like traditional Christianity's anthropomorphic "Father," and even less like a potter who "*made* heaven and earth." Nor does it make sense to me that the vast spiritual reality could have "only one

Son." Either we're all "sons and daughters" of such a reality or none of us are! Nearly every line in the creed seems to me either *off* or *waaaay* off! The only line of the Creed that I can say in good conscience is "I believe in the Holy Spirit." Though the rest of those creedal lines seem to be pointing in some vague way to a spiritual reality to which I can relate, they come across as remnants of a very, very old view of the world.

And still, week after week, I am inspired. I laugh. I cry. I feel.

Something here has some powerful ju-ju! In my head it all seems like poppycock. In my guts, it's magic!

Though it took me awhile to be able to formulate it, in my ambivalence in that Mahwah Cathedral were the two sides of the enigma that has haunted my church life: how can an institution that we find dangerous and that teaches models and ideas we find utterly beyond belief move someone like me again and again to such joy and deep satisfaction?

LETTING DOWN THE HAND

Every week since, now eight-and-a-half-years' worth, those teary episodes have kept happening. At first, I was utterly baffled about why. After some months, I began noticing patterns in whatever was moving me. One Sunday it was kneeling with others that set me off (see Chapter 2). Another week, it was the simple elegance of people processing down the center aisle two by two (see Chapter 4). Another Sunday the sweet sounds of the chorus got to me. My tears seemed to be about being with others or seeing people being together. It was like inside, at some deep psychological level, I had always been as if holding up my hand in some sort of an inner stop sign. I used to kid around, tell stories, share ideas, be funny, or even seduce someone or show care to them. I could be friendly, loving. But never could I quite allow others "in," never quite welcome anyone.

Yet during that church service, and ever since, I have found myself letting down that defensive hand a little. I didn't know why or how, but in church I'm often just overcome with tears. Something there grabs my heart and wrings it out. For some reason I've become less afraid. It's not just that there are people around me in the church. It's a deeper allowing-in. That thought—that maybe others can help pull me into their rowboat—was really, I realized, a way to say to myself, maybe I can let them in. Maybe I can trust.

For fifty-five years I have been meditating and reflecting and workshopping and being psychotherapized. For half a century I'd been hot on the trail of spiritual openness, self-awareness and freedom. I'd been lucky enough to experience a good bit of what I was seeking: the openness of enlightenment percolating through my chest, shoulders and out to the world.[10] I had found a more open mind and greater awareness of my emotions. Considering how long and how seriously I'd been on this spiritual path, I'm embarrassed to say that I was, at this ripe old age, just learning to trust.

It was that afternoon, surrounded by other people—indeed with all of humanity—that I realized how profoundly I've been in a vast hermetically-sealed bubble of solitude. I've conducted my life, enjoyed friends, had lovers. But subtly I've held them all at a distance. Even my blessed wife. Oh, when I am walking in the woods, driving or sitting alone in my study, I often sense a vast spaciousness stretching out beyond my shoulders and belly. But with other people I've remained wary, scared that they will invade my space, scared that they will demand something that I cannot give. I've become wide open but, when someone got too close, not open at all. Something!

Whether it was a flaw in my upbringing or some dysfunctional genetic twist, I never felt accepted, never quite safe. Of course, I have no direct memories from that age, but even though my mother and father, grandparents, nannies and other caregivers had fed, housed and clothed me, at some level I felt I couldn't trust them. *Something* taught me to not trust, not really, really. *Something* taught me that others—and the whole world—were dangerous.

I was struggling with what Eric Erikson describes as the first and most fundamental human challenge: "basic trust versus mistrust."

> *During the first year or so of life the infant is uncertain about the world in which they live. To resolve these feelings of uncertainty the infant looks towards their primary caregiver for stability and consistency of care.*
>
> *If the care the infant receives is consistent, predictable and reliable, they will develop a sense of trust which will carry with them to other relationships, and they will be able to feel secure even when threatened...*
>
> *If the care has been harsh or inconsistent, unpredictable and unreliable, then the infant will develop a sense of mistrust and will not have confidence in the world around them. This infant will carry the basic sense of mistrust with them and...into the world around them (McLeod, 2024).*

At the depths, I was indeed wary of the world, never feeling really, truly safe. Maybe it had something to do with my mother, who was moody and could fly off into rages unpredictably and often needed to be placated. She could become a threat, a monster when I most needed her. And my father just wasn't there. Maybe that was why I grew up with constant anxiety, a kid on the margins. I never felt really protected nor seen.

So, when that hand began to come down, I seemed to be addressing something deep and ancient! This whole complex of anxieties and fear of others is what I was confronting during those early months of weeping. Slowly, tentatively, I was allowing in that maybe, just maybe, in the depths of my soul I could regard other people as not all that dangerous. Maybe others would neither smother nor abandon me. Maybe, just maybe, I could let go and let others—just a little—*in*.

Now this deep fear was (and still is, alas) one of *my* fundamental problems. Others of course have *other* issues, which are as varied as the families that birthed them. And yet, in our deep soul-longings to feel truly welcomed and loved, I believe we are all the same.

---

1. Frankly I'm not sure quite what I believe at this point about creation or the cosmos. But my sense of things is that the process of creation was closer to the cosmology I learned in 10th grade physics. My guess is that beneath or within the world is probably some sort of impersonal ground beneath things, a silent and unexpressed "energy." Physicists talk about a kind of unmanifest energy that's everywhere, the so-called Quantum Vacuum State. That idea still makes some sense to me. They say that ground state was there at the start, behind or within the Big Bang. And it's still there. All of light and electricity and gravity are interconnected through this Quantum Vacuum State. I can't say I understand it in detail. But it makes far more sense to me at this point that the iron age tale of a Father-Maker-Dude creating the cosmos in a "let there be light" moment.
2. Association of Religion Data Archives. "US Charity Work? Belief Statistics Topic." https://www.thearda.com/us-religion/statistics/beliefs?qsid=44
3. That was what I thought that day. In retrospect, I've come to think that it was probably true about medieval churches, but less so about modern ones, which are more likely to have hired workmen of any stripe.
4. Office of Planning, Research and Evaluation
5. If you've never heard it, here's a version that's close: https://www.youtube.com/watch?v=kIdoNBvNiCk.
6. I've since learned that these words were slightly modified from Becker's original, which has "Lord have Mercy" as opposed to "pray with us."
7. To be fully transparent, during the Covid period our church met by zoom. I found those services less moving and I was not always moved to tears.
8. And just for the record, I've never believed that the Bible is Divinely inspired or without error, that the only way to salvation is belief in Jesus, that women shouldn't be priests or head pastors, or that marriage can only be between one man and one woman. But, then again, I'm not a Southern Baptist.

9. Long after these tears began, I read about what some Christians called "The gift of tears" or "tears as a grace." In St. Ignatius' spiritual diary he describes tears from an overwhelming sense of the consolation of God. Overcome by the beauty of the worship and the profundity of God's love, Ignatius often became tearful. The medieval nun-like group, the Beguines, regarded the "gift of tears" as not only a gift from God but as a possible intercession, a way to access Divine contact. According to *Marge Fenelon, OSV Newsweekly, Aug 10, 2016,* Pope Frances said in a homily in 2013, "All of us have felt joy, sadness and sorrow in our lives, [but] have we wept during the darkest moment? Have we had that gift of tears that prepare the eyes to look, to see the Lord?" he asked. "We, too, can ask the Lord for the gift of tears. It is a beautiful grace...to weep praying for everything: for what is good, for our sins, for graces, for joy itself."
10. I tell the story in detail in Forman (2011).

CHAPTER 2
DISCOVERING PATH MATES

How to make sense of all this? To me, the tradition's claims of raising the dead and a flood-ark seemed, at best, dubious. So how on earth can a religion in which I don't believe move me so profoundly? This is the puzzle that I found myself pondering, and have continued to ponder all the years since.

Being a retired professor of religion, about a year after I started crying in the churches, I got to wondering if there were other people in a similar boat. Though probably few were weeping and sobbing like I was, were there others who also disbelieved in a "Father in Heaven" yet were themselves having *some* sort of emotional responses or sensing "something more" in church? And if there were such folks, how did they solve this puzzle?

I began asking ministers and other contacts if they knew of any such folks. I soon discovered that almost everyone I asked knew at least a few. So, I began conducting long (90 minutes or more) interviews with the thoughtful, open-hearted souls to whom I was pointed. At the end of those interviews, by now more than 60, I asked if they knew of any others in a similar boat? Most did. This is known as the "snowball technique" and in no time I found myself with a large rolodex of such people.

About the "snowball procedure." I used it to good effect when I was researching the experience of mysticism and doing research for *Grassroots Spirituality*. The technique is designed to ferret out people who have similar experiences or are confronting a similar paradox. Here I was looking to understand how people like me, who don't accept the church's language but had spiritual experiences, made sense of God, Jesus, the ritual, sin, the eucharist and the rest. The snowball technique was a great tool for this.

However, the downside of the snowball technique is that it doesn't tend to generate diversity or identify demographics. As we spoke, I asked my interviewees about their feelings or beliefs about their religion, and about how they solved the riddle. But I never asked about their race, their sexual orientation, their wealth, etc., as it wasn't germane. In the course of our conversations, several told me that because their experience of Christianity was shaped by other peoples' responses to it, I heard they were gay. But if someone didn't bring such matters up, I didn't either.

Nonetheless, since I began each interview by asking about their spiritual background, certain facts became obvious. Most were college educated or above. Most were politically more or less liberal. Many indicated that they were comfortable with people who are gay, trans or straight, etc. Many implied that they had lived in other countries, and were thus fairly comfortable with alternative ways of thinking. Many had been part of the spirituality movement and had explored a range of spiritual traditions.

My work as a hospital chaplain turned out to be something of an antidote to the "snowball technique's" lack of diversity. I spoke with people who were white, black, Hispanic, rich and poor, educated and not, as well as both evangelical and liberal Christians, Jews, Muslims and "spiritual but not religious," all in proportions that matched my New England hospitals' constituencies.

So, after conducting some 60 interviews and countless conversations as a chaplain, the answer to my first question was clearly yes: there are many, many others who have had important spiritual experiences in church while disbelieving in the traditional models!

Given that discovery, my second question became: how did they make sense of their religious lives?

The more I talked with them, the more I realized that we had all been developing a similar approach to Christianity. Their Christianity and mine, I discovered, was not centered on beliefs in some world-creating Divine being or in a figure who watches over our fate or in the claim of resurrection. None based their religious understanding in any straightforward way on the Nicene Creed, on the Baptismal Vows or on some theological theory. Instead, what brought us all back week after week was the felt-power of our communities, the opportunity to join with others in service work, and some important experiences of "something more" that we sometimes encountered in our churches.

I came to see that at the beating heart of each of our religious lives were spiritual and emotional *experiences*. We've each been reorienting our religious lives around them, trying to make sense of them in the context of what we were hearing in church. No one interviewee described the whole of this new approach. But as I listened, a fairly complete vision began to emerge. This book is my attempt to collate it.

Now, neither I nor the thoughtful churchgoers with whom I spoke focus solely on the words of the Bible. I never heard about a supposed "ontological" reality of "Jehovah," "Christ" or "holy spirit." No one focuses on the supposedly right *beliefs* but rather on something more fundamental, more raw. It's the visceral, the immediate, the intense bodily feelings that bubble up out of the music, the connections, the kneeling and the experience of coming together with others in their churches that matter to us. It's direct experience from which we speak. Our understanding and approach begins with our sense of deep presence and connection, our service commitments and our rich feelings about being in community. We speak out of the magic of aligning—like a tuning fork—with our community or with the larger Flow, that seems to accompany our sense of aligning ourselves with what is ultimately right. Thus, our language is a language of belly-dropping feelings, of tears, of mystical openings and of the felt impact of the ritual.

BROADENING THE QUESTION

When I have given talks about this material, I often begin by asking the audience to reflect on the two questions I posed to you in the Introduction: What was your deepest, most important spiritual experience? What has been your experience of spiritual growth? Virtually every person has had experiences of both. Also, as a scholar of religious experiences, I have argued that human beings in every tradition have had such experiences (Forman, 1998). And scientific evidence suggests that physiological patterns that correlate with such spiritual experiences—the deactivation of the prefrontal cortex, the increase in serotonin and oxytocin, the slowing down of brain waves into alpha and theta—happen in the skulls of people from any tradition (Newberg, 2010). I see no reason to think that these experiences are confined to people in only one particular group, belief system or era. Rather, these experiences and their correlated biological patterns are panhuman and transcultural. They're built into the "architecture" of being a conscious human being.

It is my sense that Buddha, Lao Tzu and others were all pointing in their way to similar "non-ordinary experiences": what the Buddhists call satori, "stillness joined with insight"; what the Upanishadic Hindus described as moments when knowing, known and knower are all one; and what the fourteenth-century Christian, Meister Eckhart, described as moments when the "eye with which I see God is the same eye as the eye with which God sees me" (Eckhart, 1981). Modern Christians might call these extraordinary encounters "moments of contemplation" or "Christ consciousness." When people are taken over by a wave of ecstasy, naturally they will use their respective languages and models to point to and offer paths to such life-changing encounters. Though we cannot confirm this, Jesus of Nazareth probably had such experiences, and spoke of the object of such ego-free openness with his culture's terms: "Abba," "Father," and in Luke 6:35, "Most High." If this is correct, then *your* and *my* non-ordinary experiences are probably not too dissimilar from those of Buddha, Eckhart and Jesus.

When I began my interviews, I was simply trying to understand how the group of people who enjoy church but are disenchanted with the traditional models made sense of things. I assumed that what I was hearing about over and over—particularly the emphasis on direct spiritual experience—was unusual among Christians. But as I continued to research the phenomena, I came to realize that my interviewees may not have been as anomalous as I had thought. A recent Barna poll found that only 9% of Christians live in what they called a "biblical worldview." That is, less than 1 out of 10 Christians believe in God, Jesus, salvation, prayer or sin in the way that the tradition presents them. Large majorities of Americans report feeling a deep sense of wonder (71%) and/or a deep spiritual peace (66%) several times a year or more. Nearly half (45%) report a sudden feeling of connection with something from beyond this world (Pew Research Report, 2023). Though further polling would be necessary, perhaps the people I was interviewing—with their emphasis on community and direct spiritual experience—were not the aberration I had thought but rather are the point of the spear that's Reimagining Christianity.

In this light, Jesus of Nazareth was probably pointing in his way to similar experiences and processes of spiritual growth. I make no pretense of being a Biblical scholar, but I am convinced that the traditional stories, terms and imagery are evocative of processes and experiences that are similar to our own. Biblical authors were likely using their models and language to point to similar experiential shifts. But their models are long out of date and archaic. One of my interviewees, JoAnne Kraus, who attends the episcopal Cathedral of the Incarnation in Baltimore, put this well:

> I continue to struggle with the archaic language of the church. I can say the creed or not because it doesn't mean that much to me. But as a wise priest once told me, in reciting the creed over and over, it becomes part of who you are. It's there, a patterning inside of you, to be called on in life. And some of the lines do come to me at times. They point often obscurely to some truth, some reality.

Given this, part of my task and that of my interviewees has been something like translating. Well, what happens when we translate? Let's say you're in New York City and a foreign woman comes up to you. In very halting English, she says something you don't understand. She asks and gestures "way... eat...?" and makes little hand motions of eating something like a cylinder. Your task then is to listen through or beneath her grammar to try to sense what she is trying to ask. "Way?" you think to yourself, "she seems to want to know where to find something." "Eat?" Is she looking for a grocery store? For food?" So, you might ask her, "Are you looking for food?" When she nods, you probably would wonder if she's looking for a hot dog? A Burrito? A spring roll? Rather than taking her words literally, you'll listen to her words seriously but with what we might call a "soft focus." That is, you'll listen through or beneath her words to try to intuit what she wants. It's an intuitive process; unconsciously you'll use your background life experience to guess what she is likely to be saying. In doing so, you'll implicitly assume that she's somewhat like you: a human being needing something. So, she's probably asking about something that you know or can guess. You will probably empathize with her enough to sense, based on your life experiences, what she might be needing. If you do this well, you'll send her off happy.

Similarly, many of my interviewees don't take the antique words of Jesus or the Bible literally, but listen to them with a similar "*soft focus.*" That means that, knowing what we know and having experienced what we've experienced, we try to sense what the words *seem* to be getting at. Most of us have been on a psychological and/or spiritual path for many years and have had our share of what we call extraordinary experiences: a vulnerable heart, an opening into deep human contact, a sensing of a vast mystical reality. Most of us have known firsthand the general outlines of psychological or spiritual growth.

Given our background, we listen for the human spiritual experiences that seem to shimmer behind the texts. We ask ourselves, what sorts of experiences might they be pointing to that we've heard of or had? We do so keeping keep in mind that Christianity speaks of solitary mystical experiences and emphasizes community, relationships, interpersonal processes and the words of Jesus of Nazareth. Listening with a "soft focus" means we listen *beneath* or *through* the text, intuiting the kind of process or growth to which some text *seems* to be pointing. This requires a leap of empathy and imagination. With this "soft focus" we can allow the antique language to speak to us in our language about being with one another, about the ground beneath reality and about life.

Understanding the Christian worldview and lexicon in this way has taken me years, but I hope that my efforts and those of my interviewees can help others understand the tradition in this way with less confusion than I had.

Now, what shall we call the group of churchgoers that I interviewed?

"Mystics on the Margins." My interviewees are all "mystics" in that they have had some spiritual experiences and think they offer a way to understand. As they don't accept the traditional doctrines at face value, they don't tend to talk about their beliefs with their churchmates, so are often on the "margins" of their churches. Thus, I will call them "Mystics on the Margins."

"Christians Who Doubt" or *"Doubting Christians."* Traditionally, church members are taught that they are required or expected to *believe* certain things. They are to believe in God, believe that Jesus died for our sins, believe in heaven and hell, or whatnot. Nonetheless I, and the people with whom I spoke, are feeling or sensing something powerful and important, even though we often don't believe such things.

As most of us don't believe the traditional creeds or doctrines, we have our doubts about their meaning. We are "doubters." But as we are all active members of our respective churches, we are "Christians." Thus, I will sometimes refer to this group as "Christians Who Doubt" or "Doubting Christians."

"Mystics on the Margins," "Christians Who Doubt," and "Doubting Christians" all refer to the same group and I will use them interchangeably.

It seems to me that our intuitive and sensate way of engaging the religion fits comfortably with today's educated, questioning, scientific and experientially oriented approach to life. To turn a technical phrase, we are developing a new *phenomenological theology* (see Chapter 7).

Nonetheless I believe that Mystics on the Margins are reviving something that is actually not new. Throughout history, reflective people, contemplative people, and even countless ordinary people have been encountering, feeling, sensing, and experiencing something beyond their five senses.[1] As Fred Plumer, the former president of Progressive Christianity, wrote,

> People throughout history have been able to have experiences of infinite mystery and describe much about it. It is something in all things (Plumer, 2014).

"People throughout history" have enjoyed experiences of the infinite mystery, he claims. In fact, as I argued in *The Innate Capacity*, I believe the capacity to have these experiences is innate in human beings.[2]

The Mystics on the Margins that you will meet are re-enlivening and speaking in a modern idiom about clearly similar mysterious encounters with the sacred that have been enjoyed by people throughout the ages.

---

1. See, for example, examples of mysticism throughout the world in the essays in Forman 1990. For examples from the ages and continents, see Underhill, and Forman 1999.
2. See Forman 1998b, pp. 3-44.

PART TWO
THE HORIZONTAL SPIRITUAL POWER REIMAGINED

CHAPTER 3
THE CRACK WIDENS

Whatever had happened to me in that sanctuary of oak and stone, it had happened 200 miles from my home. I wondered if it would happen again, hopefully not so far away. The next week I attended another church, closer to home, and much to my surprise and perplexity, I found myself in tears again.

So, I began "church shopping," as it's called. I tried out the local United Church of Christ, Catholic and Unitarian churches as well as a local synagogue. Eventually, I found that the somewhat ritualized, Episcopal churches were moving me the most. Eventually I settled on the Trinity Church in Concord, Massachusetts.[1]

Trinity is a striking modern building, all stone, dark wood and broad A-frame roof. A simple yet elegant wooden cross stands on the landing above the steps to the building. It is a tall yet welcoming sentry, high, straight and wide. Behind it, the lee of the roof creates a wide, wide porch, which is framed by a pair of stylized teak benches. A heavy door of wood and brass leads into the sanctuary. Trinity's exterior is stark, Zen and beautiful.

The space inside is Zen as well. The high and cavernous ceiling is supported by arches of exposed wooden beams. Angling sharply across the ceiling and the white walls are obtuse blue and green patterns projected from its triangular stained-glass window. Rows of comfortable wooden pews arc gently across the nave. A high altar, quiet, elegant and Scandinavian, stands nobly in front. Trinity is tasteful, sumptuous without being ostentatious, and intimate. Its members are obviously wealthy, and they have spent their money well.

The first time I walked through those brass and wood doors, a white-haired lady handed me a bulletin and said with a smile, "Welcome!" It struck me that she had no idea who I was. She had no idea that I'd written a few books or how much money I had or didn't have. She didn't seem to care. She just said, "Welcome!" like she meant it. Frankly, it's the kind of thing any decent organization should do and I'd heard it in other churches. But there was something about her "Welcome" that meant something to me.

And it matched what happened when I walked inside. The nave felt settled, cool and inviting. Surrounded by the handsome architecture and the hundred or so people who were there, as I watched all the handshakes and warm smiles I felt a sweet, almost palpable sense of togetherness. Sitting down in the back of that church, I seemed to have a place.

BREAKTHROUGH ON MY KNEES

About three weeks after I'd started attending Trinity Church, it finally registered when Tony, the teddy-bear of a priest, announced that "all are welcome at our table." He no doubt had said that every Sunday, but only that morning did I hear it. I decided to try taking communion.

When the usher nodded to our row, I stood up, a bit

anxious, shuffled across the pew and joined the line snaking slowly down the center aisle. I felt a little like a traitor to my natal Judaism, and I was slightly afraid that some usher would kick me out of the line. But no one asked about my background or whether I'd been baptized. As I got to the front, again without asking me about my beliefs or status, another usher pointed me to a padded kneeling pad on the right.

Following what the people on either side were doing, I knelt. Down on the left knee, down on the right. I cupped my hands and held them out like a beggar.

Other than the romantic moment that I'd asked Yvonne to marry me, I don't think I had ever kneeled down to anyone. To kneel and to beg with my hands like that felt weird, like I was breaking some sort of law! I was showing my weakness, being needy in front of everyone. Bowing my head, exposing my neck and cupping my hands, I felt powerless.

Kneeling and begging like that was utterly new. I was expressing, and feeling, defenseless, weak. Though I wasn't clear just what I was begging for or from whom, I felt *below* something, vulnerable. It was intense! Never had I acknowledged, certainly not publicly, that I am beneath something. Acknowledging that I need, in a posture of begging no less, ran utterly counter to everything I had been taught. "Never, never put yourself down" was a family dictum. "Never, never beg," not for money, not for safety, not for mercy. "If you have a problem, fix it... If you want something, earn enough to buy it." The point was unmistakable: Never, never be in a position where you need to bow down and ask anyone for anything important. Yet there I was, saying with my hands, knees and back, that I actually needed help.

I used to think this emphasis on self-reliance was only a quirk of my own family. But since that morning, I've discovered how common it is to resist asking for help. Middle and upper middle-class men especially, studies show, often feel that they're expected to be self-reliant and never to ask for help or gifts (Emmons, 2007). It's like we all took our marching orders from Ralph Waldo Emerson that "it is not the office of a man to receive gifts. How dare you give them? We wish to be self-sustaining. We do not quite forgive a giver." (Quoted in Bass, 2019). We are a capitalistic, self-reliant civilization and "if you want something, go earn it" runs deep. Especially in the males of the species.

But there I was, on my knees, in the exact reverse of my life-long efforts to stand up on my own. To put myself in this posture of subservience, to acknowledge publicly that I actually needed help—from the community, from the minister, from the greater energy—honestly, I felt like I was breaking a rule, a very old one. It was a huge letting go.

Yet what I felt on that cushioned kneeler wasn't guilt or terror. What I felt, frankly, was *trust*. Trusting what? I had no idea. Trusting the community? Hardly, since I didn't know anyone there. Trusting the kindly minister, Tony, whom I barely knew? Trusting the "something more" in the space? To this day I still don't know. But whatever it was, something here felt, and still feels, trustworthy. Kneeling, bowing my head felt...well...deeply right.

I felt safe.

In those brief moments, I was also recognizing how little I've ever been able to trust. Oh, as a kid I'd been safe in thunderstorms and there was always food on the table. But *something* back then taught me to be wary. Of course, I have no direct memories from that early age, but when I was very, very little, maybe two or three, *something* taught not to trust. In the way that a two-year-old knows these things, at some level I knew that I couldn't really count on my mother or father, or my grandparents, nannies, or other caregivers. Not really, really. I grew up anxious in a world that seemed dangerous.

Whatever the causes, that anxiety made me something of a kid on the margins. Wary of people, wary of life, wary of the world, I hung back. Was this the reason that I felt I was pushing that rock up the hill, always on my own?

When we don't learn it as infants, how can we build a fundamental sense of trust? How do we counter a lifelong wariness about people, about life, about the world? Perhaps those padded kneelers were the beginning of an answer. Here was a smiling teddy bear of a man, dressed in a purple robe, offering a simple gift. He seemed trustworthy. Whatever small gift he was offering, I felt I *could* trust him. And here was a community that I could perhaps trust.

And whatever mysterious energy I was sensing in that cavernous space, maybe I could entrust myself to it a little. Maybe, just maybe, I could let go some of the fear that still hid in my long-defended and scared soul. Maybe I could begin to trust here.

"I *want*—no, I *need,* help," I thought to whatever unseen forces were there. "Please help!"

What I didn't realize that day was that, in retrospect, on my knees with my hands extended, I was indeed beginning to let go of my endless craving for safety, for recognition, for love. It was the beginning of giving up some of my pursuit of fame or wealth or sex that I had always thought would make me feel deserving. With my outstretched hands and my bowed head, I was saying to myself that it's not only me I can count on, that I don't have to count only on *my* power, *my* efforts, or *my* energy. I was acknowledging, without saying it aloud, that I have *never* been able to do it all on my own.

Such trust seems to have been a first step in relinquishing that hard-earned wariness, that lifetime of isolation. I was beginning to recognize that I *do* need, that there actually is "something more" that I can trust. We *can* let go and allow the forces of the cosmos to support us.

And I knew, as I waited for Tony to come over, how overdue this was. I have *always* needed help. Months earlier in Mahwah I had blurted out, "Lord knows I can use *somebody's* help!" And here I was on my knees, seeing how I *do* need help and always have! How I am *not* alone. Beneath the soaring heights of Trinity's A-frame ceiling, I knew I was part of that community, that church. And part of this grand and starry cosmos. I was seeing that I *am* part of.

Then it hit me: what I am really doing here is *surrendering*. I am offering myself up to this man, this community, this vague sense of something transcendent around me. I was surrendering my ego, or starting to, and taking the risk of trusting. I was acknowledging that it's not only me here, not only *my* efforts, and that I *am* lesser than this community and this whatever-it-is. It was freeing, for to kneel on that kneeler was to let go of some of my damnable ego.

No wonder that on my knees that morning I again began to weep, my whole body quaking. The simple phrase kept repeating in my head: "Help! Please help!" I sobbed with the release and the letting go and the not-being-in-charge. I sobbed with the stunning realization that I actually *can* trust. "Help, please help!" I wept for all the years of pushing and struggling and wanting and being on my own. I wept for all the energy it took to do it all on my own and for all the tears I couldn't allow myself to weep as a kid or as a grown-up. I wept for the damnable feeling that I must always, always stand on my own. "Help! Please help!"

The tears that rolled down my cheek that morning and every Sunday since are telling me how long I've been longing for this. I have been bereft for so long of real trust! Those tears were saying that there *is* love, that there *is* trust, and that there

THE CRACK WIDENS

are other people, some of whom may already be there for me. Those tears were the beginning of a recognition that I *have been* loved, *am* loveable, and that I *can* love. They were tears of this astonishing possibility.

I want to be clear here. I've never been a cold fish. I have felt and offered conventional love, if you will, as a husband, a father, a friend, a teacher and more. I have shown and received love in all these contexts. But in the deep place where we unhesitatingly open our arms wide to others and breathe them in, I have not.

I am crying as I write this. To accept that there is someone or something deeply there for me, that I too can feel truly welcome—this is terribly difficult for a self-reliant striver like me. Since I have grown up feeling none of these things, it has been stunning to realize that I too can be loved unhesitatingly. I've been looking for this constantly, if unconsciously. I've been longing for it, in ways sane and not. I've even tried seducing others to get it. All my life I have been longing for the love I have never been able to give or to receive. No wonder I wept!

In the weeks, months and years since that Sunday morning, I have come to recognize that the world may just be different than what I had feared. Somehow, I have been able to allow in some of the affirmations and the love I have craved. Little by little I am coming to sense just a smidgeon of that love. Little by little, I have been healing. I hope it continues.

I can't tell you how *new* this has all been. In kneeling like that, week after week, all my years of work and ego-striving and longings have begun to lift. I have bowed my head not because I have felt vanquished, not because I have felt pain—but because I am acknowledging my weakness. "Help, I need help." After all the years of pushing and struggling and wanting and trying to do it all on my own, I weep. Because I felt so damned alone as a child, as a teenager and as a grownup, I weep. Because I have been pushing that rock up one hill after another as a lonely conqueror, always on my own, I continue to kneel, hold out my hands and bow my head: "Help, please help!"

I like the way my Swedish friend and wise therapist Anna Christena Sundgren described this process: we are "re-mothering" ourselves. And indeed, for many of us, taking communion often feels like a deep "re-mothering." This work is quiet and slow, but it's important. It's quite similar to good therapy in that it heals old wounds. With our hands out and our heads bowed, we are acknowledging to ourselves and to the world that we *don't* have it all together, that we *don't* have to prove ourselves to earn love, that we *don't* have to do it on our own and that it'll be OK. With our hands, knees, neck and bowed head, we are saying "there *is* something greater than us." "Whatever is beyond, help, please help!"

After I got up from that kneeler, still teary, I walked back to my pew, wondering what on earth had just happened. I certainly didn't believe that I had eaten somebody's body. But why was I feeling such deep trust? What was there about that community, about Tony? And what was it about this "something more" that was leading me to feel so welcome?

Over the years since, talking with countless patients, Mystics on the Margins and fellow church members, I've come to see that nearly everyone in the church has, like me, struggled with feeling, receiving and offering love. At some level, all of us sometimes feel alone or separate. We all long to be seen, to be valued, to be loved. Each of us talks about it differently, tells a different story about it. But all of us have struggled, are still struggling or will struggle to feel welcome, worthwhile or deeply supported. My realizations that day weren't just for me.

This is no doubt why Christianity talks about love as endlessly as it does. But for people like me, who cannot really accept the ancient ways to put it, it's been wonderful to recognize that through our bodies, postures and gestures, the Christian ritual offers practice-sessions in trust. And you don't need any beliefs, any father-like figures or any doctrines for it to do so. These simple movements and postures offer lessons in surrendering.

I am fully aware how deeply uncomfortable and counterintuitive all of this talk about kneeling and surrendering will seem to many, especially many of us men. Before all this began, I would have been very uncomfortable with it too! It seemed anathema to my and to our whole culture's obsession with self-reliance, with the solitary hero, with going-it-alone. James Bond or Indiana Jones just don't surrender!

But that's why a ritual like this can be so valuable! For recognizing that we are not alone, that we can and must trust, can be the beginning of an answer to the epidemic of wary loneliness that is the dark shadow of our culture of self-reliance. "There is safety here," "I can trust here," "I can love" are only partial answers. But they're a beginning.

One caveat: I have responded happily to Christian rituals. But I need to acknowledge that it works best for people who try to be present in the church or to connect with their deepest experiences as opposed to approaching the ritual out of habit or just following what others tell you to do. A healthy ritual is most alive when it brings you back to your spiritual experiences or stimulates them in the here and now. Christianity may be unusual in that it seeks to help you connect through those experiences with others.

---

1. I enjoyed Trinity Church for many years, but a few years later I moved to Great Barrington, in the Berkshires in Western Massachusetts. I "church shopped" there for a while, eventually settling on the delightful Episcopal Grace Church in Great Barrington. Unlike Trinity, Grace has chosen to own no church building, meeting in a community center auditorium. It

comes across as much less formal than Trinity. But the feeling of welcoming, the structure of the service, and the general warm tone are all virtually identical. It's not the building that makes the church but the people, the ritual and the spirit.

For simplicity's sake, I've collapsed all of these churches and experiences into a single, somewhat fictionalized, minister and church.

CHAPTER 4
THEY ARE MY FAMILY NOW

PROCESSION

About nine months after that time in Mahwah I went to New York's beautiful Cathedral of St. John the Divine. I watched the long procession stream slowly up the center aisle. It was led by a young man in a white robe carrying a cross on a stick. Then came a tall fellow in a white robe swinging an incense burner, offering clouds of frankincense to each side. After them a couple of older guys led the choir of about 20, all dressed in their matching white robes and black collars. Several priests brought up the rear. They all walked slowly two by two towards the altar. It was a graceful column.

As I watched, I again began to weep.

They seemed so unpretentious, those two white-haired guys in the front of the choir. Just a couple of balding dudes, holding their music out from their chests, singing. I couldn't pick out their voices from the rest of the congregation's, which was probably the point. It wasn't about *them* as individuals. They were offering their modest sound into the whole.

Their voices were part of "us." And that, I think, is what

made me cry. I've sung all my life: opera, rock and roll, blues and in several church choirs. I sang in several high school musicals. I've sung madrigals in medieval music groups. I like to think I've been a decent choral member. But in all these settings I never really felt part of the assemblage, not really. When I sang I always half-thought it was my voice people heard and me they were applauding. I sang as my voice teacher trained me: "Here's how to breathe, here's how to support your voice, here are exercises to sing at home." I was always encouraged to sing strong and clear, so I did, singing heartily. So even in a choral group I felt pretty much on my own, felt that I was carrying it.

But here they were, two by two, their voices disappearing into the whole, part of the sea of white surplices and black collars. They were part of the whole.

How freeing it must be to sing in a choir so that you're not a solo! How freeing, to be consciously and intentionally part of an "us," and to sing not as an *individual* but as a *member*. And to walk in such a simple order, two by two…Talk about not pushing the rock up the hill by yourself!

Oh, don't get me wrong. I have taken direction from lots of choir directors and have lined up in countless columns. But watching that procession that day, with my spirits attuned to the newness—it hit home. These people chose to become part of a group and *not* to be the boss. And no one in that choir seemed to be chomping at the bit! They each seemed so easy with being part of an "us."

Seeing them be together so easily is why I wept. I wept for my years of pushing that rock alone, of striving always to be the star. I wept for my loneliness. I wept for the wariness that had led me to cut myself off for so long. I wept for the energy it took to always have to do *something* to be noticed. I wept because I so longed to be loved.

COMMUNAL SPIRITUALITY

When I began interviewing Christians Who Doubt about why they attended church, one word was emphasized again and again: "community, community, community." Sometimes it was the only thing they mentioned! One of the first people I interviewed was Kathy Clausen, who was the "senior warden" (chair of the board) of my church. Kathy is a thoughtful, energetic and charming grandmother of two. She grew up Lutheran but became suspicious of religion when she was in college. After she became a mother she started attending Episcopal churches. Kathy said,

> For me, the church is community... Even if there were no Divine at all, even if that was never mentioned, I'd still go to church. I sit next to someone I don't choose. I keep rubbing up against a variety of people I would probably never have had conversations with. Yet we're doing something important together. It's a beautiful journey we're doing. They, my church friends, are my family now.

"They are my family now" captures what she feels about her church mates. She counts on them to be there, as if a new family. She speaks her mind to them (within limits). She struggles with certain members, as she might in her own family. The crux is the sense of trust and intimacy that she feels with them.

Again and again in my interviews and hospital conversations, I heard about family, community, fellowship and the like. More often than any other aspect of Christianity, people told me how close they felt to their communities, how they could count on them.

Several told me that in addition to connecting with their churchmates, they sometimes feel themselves part of the long litany of souls who have been part of the church. "I think about all those people before me and after me and it's the same story," said Christine Anders. "It's a centuries-old tradition that has always gotten people through tough times. I feel part of a long line."

Some of my fundamentalist interviewees stressed this as well. Chelsey, thirty something, attends an evangelical church in Texas. She told me,

> When I come into church when I'm sick and tired or emotionally just wrecked, I can walk into it and know that I'll just feel safe there. It feels like home. And I know that if I reach out there's going to be someone that's going to help me get through whatever it is. Or know someone who can. It's like a portable emergency room.

All these responses reinforced my original insight at Mahwah, that if you are drowning in pain or trouble, people in a church may very well pull you into their rowboats.

To understand why these connections are so important, I turn to David Brooks. In a masterful historical sweep in *The Atlantic*, "The Nuclear Family Was a Mistake," Brooks summarizes the changes in our nation's family structures, and in those of the whole developed world. Brooks traces how society's growing wealth led to both greater personal autonomy and to greater distance between us. Whereas a hundred fifty years ago most people lived "within a dense cluster" of parents, siblings and extended kin, as Americans moved into the middle class, they tended to purchase or rent single family homes and apartments, thus moving away from their extended families. As people's wealth grew, their families and homes fragmented into "ever smaller and more fragile forms." America and the developed world became a society of smaller and more constricted "nuclear families" of mom, dad, kids and the dog. And with divorces, increasingly autonomous children who moved away, and our ever more solitary lives, even those nuclear family units tended to fragment even more. TV and the internet have only exacerbated this fragmentation and locked us even more into our respective silos. We have become isolated, wrapped up in our lives (Brooks, 2020).

A 2024 survey of more than 20,000 U.S. adults ages 18 years and older revealed some alarming findings:

- *Nearly half* of Americans report sometimes or always feeling alone (46 percent) or left out (47 percent).
- *One in four* Americans (27 percent) rarely or never feel as though there are people who really understand them.
- *Two in five* Americans sometimes or always feel that their relationships are not meaningful (43 percent) and that they are isolated from others (43 percent).
- *One in five* people report they rarely or never feel close to people (20 percent) or feel like there are people they can talk to (18 percent).
- Americans who live with others are less likely to be lonely (average loneliness score of 43.5) compared to those who live alone (46.4). However, this does not apply to single parents/guardians (average loneliness score of 48.2)—even though they live with children, they are more likely to be lonely.
- Many young people feel a kind of emptiness and directionlessness. This leads to a superficiality of life, but they find religion out of date and meaningless.[1]

No wonder the surgeon general said there's an "epidemic of loneliness!" (U.S. Surgeon General's Advisory on the Healing Effects of Social Connection and Community, 2023). No wonder that *at least* 25% of Americans report being "often lonely. No wonder that 12% of Americans "have no friends," and that nearly 4 in 10 "have only one person they can talk to" (Witters,

2023). No wonder that even fewer have someone with whom they can discuss their pain or a problem in their marriage!

And no wonder there's such an explosion of psychosocial ills like depression, anxiety, addiction, overdoses, suicide and other illnesses of despair. No wonder that our modern, secular society is struggling with an "anomie epidemic," with the lack of a sense of shared meaning or purpose. And no wonder that beneath these symptoms of loneliness and alienation, many people—especially men—further struggle to allow in or feel love, even when it's offered (Real, 1998). Too many of us, especially men, are not sure that we're loved or even worthy of being loved. Too many of my fellows feel, as I did, unloved and unworthy, starved for connection and somewhat adrift.

In their church connections, Kathy, Stacy and other Doubting Christians are forging what Brooks calls "fictive families." They're finding readymade webs of people that might be there for them, communities of people who might help them in hard times or to whom they might turn. They're developing new connections, finding new people, building new relationships. As Atlantic writer Derek Thompson put it, religions work like "a retaining wall to hold back the destabilizing pressure of [our culture's] hyper-individualism" (Thompson, 2024).

Participating in a church community can actually help. In a survey of 300,000 people, people who attend church are generally happier and have more positive emotions than people who don't (as measured by the amount of laughter, enjoyment, happiness and the like which they exhibit) (Thornhill, 2012). And strikingly, middle-aged men and women who attend church (or other houses of worship) have a 55% lower risk for mortality (Bruce, 2017). Going to church, creating a so-called "body of Christ," may turn out to be an antidote to our civilization's loneliness epidemic!

Brooks was right. When we moved away from our extended families, we lost the sense of being part of an intact community.

A spiritual community that offers real connection, a place for sincere growth and for taking responsibility may be the best way to recover some of that delicious sense of being held, nurtured by a greater whole, and loved.

I want to note here that several interviewees mentioned that their churches have this effect especially when people in them are *active*. Jack Brown, an avuncular, freethinking and openhearted choral director from Stockbridge, Massachusetts, extolled the importance of being actively involved:

> *Some new folks come to experience the church life. They might stay for a while and then disappear. It's like they dig a two-foot hole. But this stuff really affects us when we begin to play a more serious role. It's when we sing in the choir, sit on the vestry committee, feed the poor with others, arrange sanctuary flowers or do whatever in a more committed way that communal life actually feeds us. When we do this, we're digging a 30-foot hole. What you invest in it you get back.*

As individuals we get more out of our churches and our church communities thrive when people make them thrive. The more involved the better. Making real contributions to the group seems to be, paradoxically, part of an answer to our society's divisions and to our own loneliness (Khullar, 2016).

Now, "fictive families" in churches or synagogues like Kathy's certainly aren't as intimate or permanent as our natal families. Blood, as they say, is thicker than water. Nonetheless these church families can be quite important. And they have the advantage of including a broader range of members. One of the facts of church life is that in them we may, as Kathy put it, find ourselves "rubbing up against a variety of people I would probably never have had conversations with." The churches that the Mystics on the Margins tend to choose often include such variety. They're generally comprised of members who are both like and unlike themselves: abled and disabled, addicted and sober, seeing and blind, etc. Churches that are mostly Caucasian may include African-Americans, Chinese, Caribbean Islanders, and vice versa. There may be wealthy couples in suits and pearls as well as people who struggle to pay the rent. It's in part this polyglot, polycultural, polymorphous, messy nature of these religious communities—with their various backgrounds, differences, cultures and levels of brokenness—that makes it all work.

The churches that we Mystics on the Margins choose tend to be welcoming, open-minded and less exclusivist than some other churches. None require, for example, that members believe or espouse any particular doctrines. None ask anyone to "accept Jesus as their personal savior" or to espouse any political view.

Such openness is very important, considering why so many educated souls bolted from the churches. The communities with which they're comfortable don't demand conformity in background, dress, thought, belief or behavior. They welcome questions of almost any sort. Most have only one criterion for membership: do you show up? Do you participate?

SOLITARY PATH, COMMUNAL PATH

It has struck me again and again how different these churches are from my Transcendental Meditation practice and other pathways in the so-called spirituality movement like Buddhism and Mindfulness Meditation, Tai Chi, Advaita Vedanta and the others.

I learned TM in 1969, early in the burgeoning spirituality movement. I became a certified teacher of it (a so-called "initiator") in 1972 and have taught perhaps 500 souls. When we meditate, we sit alone on a bed or a comfortable chair and close our eyes. (In other practices one is to keep the eyes unfocused and/or downcast.) We think a mantra, a meaningless sound, effortlessly and don't get caught up in the sounds of a car going by, in our thoughts, in the sensation of the breeze or the like. We pay little attention to other people, to our emotions or to any contact with the world. We allow the mind to go where it will, hopefully leading us into deeper and deeper levels of the Vastness that is within. These practices are solitary. The attention is directed not to other people but within.

Such meditation practices are not interpersonal but intrapersonal: within the mind, not consciously between people. Whether intentional or not, when we meditate, we remove ourselves from the outside world and from others. Its spiritual effect—enlightenment, the sense of the Divine energy—is something that may dawn, but only within an individual. We like to think that the peace we gain by meditating helps our relationships, but if that comes it comes only indirectly as a side effect of the individual's growth.

Most meditative paths offer group meditations, for people often report richer and stronger experiences of depth and joy in groups. Even so, in group meditations we don't interact *per se*. We're meditating alone side by side, if you will, more parallel play than interactive. And since different people might come to a group each week, we don't tend to build up regular communities.[2] As Rev. John Rowe Adams puts it,

> the primary focus of Christianity may not be about believing but about living in a community—a community in which you find companions in the search for meaning, a community where you can celebrate your triumphs and joys and can find support in failure and in sorrow, a community that provides rituals for the transitions of your life, a community that tells a story in which you can find a place for yourself (Adams, 2024).

Buddhism stresses its *sangha*, the community of monks,

more than does TM. Tai Chi also stresses its *kata* (form) group. But in my experience, the communal aspects of these pathways are secondary to the inward processes. Group meditations in a *sangha* employ the same meditation practices as solitary practices; again, parallel play, not interactive.

On the other hand, Christianity is self-consciously and intentionally *communal*. The community, the fellowship, the so-called "Body of Christ," are so central to the religion as to be implied in the very word "church." The core ritual practices—the "Prayers of the People," the recitation of the creed, the Eucharist and the singing—are all performed by the community *en masse*. Based in part on Jesus's thought that "where two or three are gathered together in my name, I am there among them" (Matt. 18:20), the religion has stressed its congregational nature for 2000 years. Christianity's focus is on "being there" with others, being for one another, serving each other and on using the interactions as part of one's spiritual journey.

Another element that distinguishes the Christian orientation from my TM path has been *emotionality*. In TM, emotions and thoughts are devalued. We used to teach that both thoughts and emotions are the products of some sort of stress which is stored in the body's nervous system. If I was deeply unhappy some few years ago, for example, I might have stored the tension or stress of that unhappiness somewhere in my nervous system as an inner "knot." If I then experience some unhappiness during meditation, we taught that such a feeling was the effect of that knot of stress unwinding itself. One should let that feeling go and *not* pay attention to its content. "It's just the product of some unstressing," we'd say. Thoughts too are the result of some "unstressing" to which our minds have probably added some mental content. The upshot: in TM we don't take thoughts or other responses at face value. In effect, we ignore any emotions, any feelings that come up. All of them.

Other spiritual traditions teach a similar approach to emotion. If a student of the Buddhist Vipassana meditation technique, for example, feels some emotion in meditation, they are to label it "feeling, feeling, feeling," and then let it float away. For them too, the content is largely irrelevant. One is simply to label it an emotion and then let it go. These practices certainly can help people evolve to greater depths and find peace. But they are not designed to directly understand or develop a practitioner's emotional life or their connections with others.

Meditation practices like Advaita Vedanta that have a "nondual" orientation, suggest that all things and all people are part of the same underlying unity. But emotions, whether about other things or other people, require, well, an "other." Thus, such practices tend to discount the emotions.

As I reflect on it, meditation is more than just unemotional. Sitting on my meditation cushion with my eyes closed, doing a slow Tai Chi form with my eyes downcast, or even free-associating on the therapist's couch, were all wonderfully valuable forms of self-help. At the same time, however, they unintentionally exacerbated my tendency to keep others at a distance. When I shut my eyes to do TM, I talk with no one. When I tell a secret to my therapist, I'm not necessarily sharing it with my wife or anyone else. Without realizing it, these practices may be exacerbating *narcissism: my* path, *my* cushion, *my* meditation and *my* loneliness. All to help *my* self.

On the other hand, feelings *are* stressed and valued in Christianity. They are regarded as significant, and sometimes as signs of our relationship with the Divine. Tears, laughter, feelings of love are often mentioned. This may be related to Christianity's emphasis on community, for inevitably, interpersonal interactions in churches tend to foster laughter, sorrows, celebrations and griefs. Often the church interactions *generate* and *include* emotional highs and lows. I heard about tears, being moved and being "transported somewhere." A Swedish informant, Bengt Johansen, described one such:

> I was in a church in Holland. When I took the eucharist I felt "this is close. This is a part of me, a serious part. We're standing here together, showing that we're all here together. And I'm showing that I'm here too." I had my eyes closed, feeling the community and feeling that this is me here in it. It was so moving, I cried.

Trisha Frey, a new member of an Episcopalian church, also had a powerful emotional response:

> I look around the church and see everybody show up to church week after week. Sometimes it's full and sometimes it's not so full, but it always _feels_ full. There are a lot of big hearts there all here with a sense of the Divine. There's a feeling of abundance in the room. I know what it takes to make something like this go, and seeing them do this week after week, I find it very emotional, very moving.

Note how Bengt cried over the sense of being held by his community and Trisha over the cooperation she sees there. Like other Mystics on the Margins, they found the service moving, powerful. And they connect through those feelings with others. The kind of churches that Mystics on the Margins tend to choose seem to value such feelings and vulnerability. And often, when they hear of their neighbors' sorrows and joys, they empathize.

I've felt a lot of things in my meditation life. I've enjoyed my meditations, loved my group meditations, enjoyed learning Yoga and more. I've been pleased to grow and to come to perceive differently. It's been exciting to sense my consciousness expanding.

But never have I been so emotionally moved as to weep. Not once.

But many Mystics on the Margins told me about their feelings of love, of rage about some injustice, of gratitude and more. Some described being moved to tears during a prayer request time, when a church mate told of a tragedy, or as Elizabeth poetically put it, hearing of their needs "sometimes grabs my heart and wrings it out." Many laughed in a church ceremony at some funny thing a child said. Many told me that, like me, they feel such things in church more intensely than usual.

This emphasis on community, group action and emotionality, which is so different from our wonderful but drier meditation life, may be one of the reasons that many from the spirituality pathways have been drawn to the churches. I know it was part of my choice.

Being part of a church community has had another surprising effect on me. In a way I did not anticipate, it has been profoundly *humbling*. Meditating, doing Tai Chi forms and even doing psychotherapy are lone wolf pathways. But Christianity is the path of the group.

There's lots of ego in church communities, of course. But Christianity's whole orientation is towards helping people grow in humility. Its rituals challenge us (not always effectively) to let go of our damn narcissism. But at the same time, they also work to help us dissolve the social hierarchies that so divide us.

To invite a community into my life, to relax into what the group is doing in the ritual, is to remind myself—or rather to feel—that I am not the only one on this path. It is to recognize —with however much grace and awe that I can muster—that we're all in this church-thing and this life-thing together. Even though others in the room may think with a different set of models or speak with words that I don't use, we're all engaged in the same search.

Though she was writing about a ritual of the !Kung, anthropologist Lorna Marshall wrote that collective rituals help...

draw everyone together...whatever their relationship, whatever the state of their feelings, whether they like or dislike each other, whether they are on good terms or bad terms with each other, they become a unit...moving together in an extraordinary unison... No words divide them; they act in concert for their spiritual and physical good and do something together that enlivens them and gives them pleasure (Marshall, 1999).[3]

She's saying that rituals can help people let go of their self-protective shields while binding people together into a larger whole. As we sit, kneel, stand and sing together in a Christian Mass, for example, we're becoming what's called "the body of Christ." Creating special events together, like a Christmas or Easter pageant, can also help people overcome the hierarchies of everyday life: when becoming Mary, Joseph, the sheep and the other traditional figures, we're all equal.

COMMUNITY AS HYPERBRAIN

I want to tell you about a new type of science that has begun to look at what happens in us when we do something together.[4] In these "Hyperscanning" studies, neuroscientists place EEG leads or other devices on the heads of two, three or up to a dozen people at the same time, and record the brain waves of all of them.

What these scientists have found is that when people interact or do something with one another, their brain waves tend to become *synchronized*. That is, the peaks and valleys of their brain waves begin to go up and down in alignment. When people interact in a positive way (i.e., not arguing or fighting), shake hands, listen to a speaker (Pérez, 2017), make eye contact (Hirsch, 2017), play a duet (Lindenberger, Sänger 2012, Müller 2013, Müller 2019), or recite something together, the coherence between their brains gets measurably stronger.

They've also found that when we *feel* emotionally connected to one another, our brains become even more deeply synchronized. In one study scientists asked partners to kiss, for example. When the pair reported a kiss during which they *felt* particularly connected, hyperscanning showed their brains became more deeply synchronized (Müller & Lindenberger, 2014). This suggests that when we *feel* connected with one another, our brains are becoming measurably more coherent.

Another study looked at a relatively large group like a chorus singing together. They saw an astonishing number of their bodily processes becoming coherent or synchronized. Not only did their brains become coherent with one another, but also their breathing, heart rates, other functions and of course their voices all became more synchronized Müller et al., 2018). Without knowing it, a group like that is creating a complex and dynamic set of interconnections between our various systems. They're becoming part of a single physiological network, something like an individual-transcending organism. Neuroscientists call it creating a "HyperBrain."[5]

Now, some Christians have said that a church community is "the body of Christ." Though there are no hyperscanning studies of a church community (though I'd like to conduct one), we might now say that the "body of Christ" is likely to have a correlate, creating a "HyperBrain." In both these frames, we're joining or creating a larger organism. These studies reinforce and amplify the common experience that when we feel connected in a church (or a synagogue or mosque) our physiologies are likely becoming *measurably* interconnected. As we sing, kneel, eat, drink, listen to a sacred story or a sermon, our brain-to-brain synchrony is no doubt rising with it.

While no Mystics on the Margins I spoke with knew of these studies, every single interviewee to whom I described "hyperscanning" and "HyperBrains" said they were "not at all surprised." Since the community feeling in a church is often so palpable, they were not surprised that such feelings would have physical correlates, that they are more than merely subjective chimeras.

It is always reassuring when science confirms what we have known through personal experience. These studies match what our experiences have suggested all along—that deep spiritual experiences and relationships are a nonlocal, interdependent field phenomenon. Rather than being like children in opposite corners of the sand box doing parallel play, in collective worship we are entering into a shared reality that spreads throughout the sandbox and perhaps beyond.

Over thousands of years, highly intuitive people like St. Paul, Athanasius of Alexandria, St. Benedict, the Popes, Martin Luther and several Archbishops of Canterbury have refined these practices, mutterings, songs and ritual scripts in part to help foster such interconnections among Christians. Reciting words, singing, eating, and deep conversations, all done together and with intentionality, are a kind of spiritual biotechnology that is designed to help us connect with one another and foster collective participation in a great and mysterious flow.

Of course, we Christians Who Doubt don't need a neuroscientist to tell us that we feel connected to others or to something larger. Hyperscanning studies don't *prove* that we feel these things. Only *we* can prove it, and only for ourselves. But I for one find it reassuring that what I sense subjectively is being confirmed objectively.

In the next chapter we'll ponder how church groups can deepen our sense of connection and extend the "HyperBrain" effect towards the experience of the transcendent.

---

1. MultiVu: Multimedia Production & Strategic Distribution, 2024.

THEY ARE MY FAMILY NOW

2. In the late seventies, TM began to encourage large group meditations, which was explained as a way to bring more of the benefits of meditation into the wider society.
3. Marshall, 1999, pp. 63-90, quoted in Haidt, p. 305.
4. I have found these studies both exciting and helpful. For those who are interested, please see my article, written with Melanie Wald-Fuhrman, "The Body of 'the Body of Christ': An Introduction to Hyperscanning Research and a Discussion of Its Possible Implications for Understanding Social Experiences During Religious Gatherings." *Pastoral Psychology* (2024) 73:379–394.
5. Viktor Müller (2022) recently argued that we may think of interacting brains becoming a hyperBrain when certain groups of cells form an "interbrain community" through synchronized oscillations.

CHAPTER 5
"MORE WILLING TO BE VULNERABLE THERE"

We Americans have countless ways to form Brook's "fictive families." We play instruments in marching bands, join rowing teams (Brown, 2014),[1] enroll in support groups, play in neighborhood Garage Bands or go to square dances on the first Saturday of the month. Recently local political clubs have become fictive families (Sullivan, 2018). Such opportunities are endless. They all answer the secret longings for connection and can supply "fictive kin."

In addition, we've seen that there is an emotional and a spiritual power in gathering. Especially in a religious context, a community generates what Durkheim called an "effervescence," a spiritual energy, which often leads to a sense of "something more." We could also say that creating a "Hyper-Brain" with one another can foster such a sense.

Yet church communion does not stop with that. Christianity offers a "deeper" or "higher" spiritual flame to which the "horizontal" energy of a community points—and which it can sometimes help ignite.

"MORE WILLING TO BE VULNERABLE THERE"

SACRAMENTAL CONVERSATIONS

About a year and a half after I started weeping in churches, I shared my experiences with my friend Christopher Schaefer, a highly regarded student of Rudolf Steiner's work. I told him about weeping week after week, about being touched by some inexplicable tenderness. I shared how important those emotional moments were for me, and how they were helping me pull down somewhat that defensive hand I've been holding up.

Chris was clearly moved. "You know," he responded tentatively, "sometimes I've felt I could count on my men's group in that way. I've let down my guard a little with them. I think I can count on them to be there when I'm confused or down. Now that I think of it, I have often felt that in my conversations with you." As did I, I told him.

Soon we were sharing about our feelings of loneliness and about some of our relationship struggles. I often feel a little at risk, a little anxious, when I tell a deep truth to someone and I was feeling that way with Chris. As we both continued sharing in that way, the space around and between us seemed to open out; I could have sworn that the walls of the lunch booth had fallen away and we were all alone in that diner. We both found ourselves speaking honest, real truths. I, we both, felt more alive.

Chris has an evocative name for encounters like these. He calls them *"sacramental conversations."*[2] "Sacrament" is of course a religious word. It comes from the Latin *sacrare*, the same root as "sacred," i.e., to "set something aside," "to hallow" or to "consecrate" something for a special purpose. Our "sacramental conversation" was not explicitly religious, but it was indeed "set aside" from our normal everyday chatter about children, sports, health or house repairs. It's his name for a deep and vulnerable conversation like ours, whatever its content, wherever it happens.

Many of my conversations as a chaplain were "sacramental" in this sense, especially when I was with patients who were facing death. A peace sometimes come, a spirit bubbling up between and around us.

Though such "sacramental conversations" can happen wherever people share deep insights, in my interviews, many Doubting Christians told me of times that they had dropped into unexpected vulnerability with someone in their church. They told me of articulating new ways of thinking about who they each were, what it was to live in our times, what the church meant to them or what they were actually grateful for. Few connections glow as brightly, I think, as those that reveal to us new perspectives on who we are.

Every person's experience of depth is, no doubt, different. But for all of us, those "sacramental conversations" seem to bring to awareness a vague but palpable sense of "something larger." These deep and vulnerable connections always feel downright "holy."

I love the feeling in my belly that comes when I am sharing real truths, either as a chaplain, a spiritual counselor or a friend. I love emerging from a conversation with some new insights about someone or about myself, about the world or about the sacred. I love the sense that I've been helping someone drop into their heart's truths and that they've helped me drop into mine. I love the sense of touching another and touching what is more.

Swedish psychotherapist Anna Christina Sundgren has always centered her life on depths like these. As I mentioned earlier, growing up on an island in the Swedish archipelago, her spiritual life came to life in experiences of deep connection with nature. Though she fell away from religion as an adolescent, when she became a therapist, she discovered the value of

"MORE WILLING TO BE VULNERABLE THERE"

its deep relational bonds. That led her to rediscover her faith and led her to a lay Franciscan community, in which members often open up in a heartfelt way with one another. When that happens, Anna Christina feels "part of something bigger" with them:

> Most of us have friends, but few of us are able to share our deepest feelings. Most feel that there is no one like me, that I think differently than others. But it's different when we are together in a deep way. Singing together in harmony with others, being with others in this kind of quiet way, creates an openness... When I'm with people at these depths, I feel part of something bigger than me.

She describes such connectedness as a kind of "faith." She doesn't mean "faith" in the traditional sense of believing in some Biblical sentence or some loaves-and-fishes miracle. Rather her "faith" means becoming wide open and "in a kind of quiet way" leaning in, undefended and curious, to own's own and the other's hidden impulses. She finds in these moments of person-to-person presence a gateway into the wider mystery that is all around us.

Elizabeth Young, a vivacious woman who attends a United Church of Christ in Stockbridge, Massachusetts, took a different route to arrive at a similar place. Elizabeth grew up in a fairly radical American Baptist Church, but fell away at 32, when a pair of ministers laid some "shockingly paternalistic advice" on her. But like Anna Christina, after becoming a therapist, at 55 she found herself drawn to a church again. She soon came to value her church relationships over the everyday relationships in which she keeps herself somewhat guarded...

> But in some relationships, especially in my church, I can be more revealing. If I can allow myself to be vulnerable, show my own

human fears and mistakes, there is such a connection! It carries me out of myself!

In such relationships, observed American poet Adrienne Rich, we create "a process of deepening the truths [that two or more] can tell each other. It is important to do this because it breaks down human self-delusion and isolation" (Garrison Institute, 2018).

Interestingly, when someone shares at such a level in a group, be it a church or therapy group, everyone there can feel it. When one person risks "dropping down," the whole group soon risks dropping down even more. It's quite noticeable.

To have such a "sacramental conversation," we don't need to be in a religious setting or talking explicitly about the Divine, though a church setting may help. Getting together with a group of friends or talking with a date over drinks, sometimes things just click in a way that you think, "Ah, this is bigger than me." Any conversation can become a sacrament when everyone involved stretches with and through each other towards deeper and deeper truths and more vulnerable connections. It is not the content, not words like "God" or "Jesus" that make a moment a "sacrament." It is the sense of *wide openness* that results from honest and deep truth-telling. The sense of sacrament comes with being wide open together, towards whatever-it-is that's beyond us. No wonder these conversations seem so holy.

In this context, I've recently had an experience that taught me why I'm sometimes moved so by beauty. A little while ago, I was having one of those "sacramental" conversations over zoom with two dear friends. We were each sharing vulnerably. My heart had become wide-open and undefended. While we were talking, I happened to glance outside my study window. The setting sun, barely visible through the clouds, was peeking through the trees. Snow was coming down in large flakes and the branches were mottled in browns and whites. The openness that I was feeling with my two friends seemed to slip into an openness towards the scene. And immediately I was stunned with its beauty. On a normal day, I probably wouldn't even have noticed the scene. It was the vulnerability of the moment, the openness of heart, that led me to recognize its grandeur. Usually, I realized at that moment, when I see a scene or listen to some music, I am, in some dim and unconscious way, shielded. Much as I am with other people, my inner hand is raised up. But not that day. Because I had opened my heart to my two friends, I was just as open to that snowy scene. Had I not been struck with it that day, I would never have realized how little I typically allow such sights *in*. It was *because* I had let the scene in like that, *because* I was as vulnerably open to it as I was to my friends, that the scene had been transformed into one of almost unbearable harmony.

Now, I may be unusual in connecting beauty with an inner attitude. But I don't think so. I believe that it's when most of us see or hear something with our usual defenses down that we find ourselves ecstatic over a painting or a pastoral view. Loving a dear friend and loving a snowy scene are both loves.

As I write this, I find myself again looking outside my study window. It's coming towards spring; the branches are just beginning to sprout. A light-green fuzz is barely visible around the branches as on a newborn's cheek. I've seen scenes like this countless times, of course. But today I'm really welcoming it. My inner protective hand is largely down. The faintest of faint green, the sharp yellow of the sun, the light-blue of the sky all make my chest swell out. It's so beautiful I almost can't contain it!

To be present to a panorama like this, I now see, is an expression of the very same openness that I, like many, feel in the churches. In this sense, this snowy scene is what Borg calls a "thin place." Right now, I don't feel separate from what I'm seeing. Indeed, I'm in love with it. I've come to think that whether I open my heart to an "it," a "who" or a scene like this is...well...irrelevant. What matters is that I'm allowing my chest to open out, as if I'm stretching out and out, towards the sky. The beauty that I feel burbling in my chest and belly is the same burbling I feel with a friend or a lover. To see, to really welcome without my usual inner defenses, is what allows me to be struck today with this beauty. To allow in beauty like this is to be *with* it. And to be with it is to love it!

THE SPIRITUALITY OF PRESENCE

The Rev. Stephanie Bradbury, a sixtyish Episcopal Priest from Lowell, Massachusetts, grew up in the Episcopal Church. Like many Mystics on the Margins, she rejected Christianity in her teens as hypocritical, but after a series of transcendent experiences found herself exploring church again in her mid-20s, and eventually felt herself called to ordination. She has come to read the scriptures through a mystical lens, taking the transcendent realm seriously that she feels offers a richer and more nuanced spiritual path than is understood by most Western Christians. She writes a newsletter in Substack called "Jesus and the Enchanted Cosmos" and is currently working on a book. In order to create "sacramental" connections, she told me, one must...

> become really present, fully there with oneself and with the other. To be present, to be in the moment here and now, not thinking about other things, just being with the other person without judging, feeling the other, taking in the other person—when we do this, we let go of all that preoccupies us.

Most important, she went on, in those moments of connecting, of being really present,

> we get projected into "something more," the transcendent. In a meeting with the other like this, we stretch beyond our usual concerns and the transcendent happens. This is how I understand, "where two or three are gathered in my name..." The Divine is in their (or our) midst.

Brother Michael Gallagher wrote,

> *In the experience of human presence and relationship we glimpse the gateway into the mystery that surrounds us—that we live and move within another Presence.*[3]

In saying that they're "projected into something more" when they're with someone like this, Stephanie, Anna Christina and Brother Michael are all suggesting that when they're fully present to the other, when they're paying full attention to what they're saying or hearing, when they're feeling the feelings beneath the words, they all find themselves sensing something beyond themselves, as if seeing a hidden figure emerge behind a scrim. They're each sensing a wide-open spaciousness beneath or beyond themselves and their conversation-mates. The experience is one of opening out towards the transcendent.

I want to be clear about what being "fully present" means. I was confused when I first heard Stephanie say it, for she seemed to be using the phrase differently than I might have. It doesn't mean merely focusing on one thing to the exclusion of everything else, as so many of our high school teachers and supervisors endlessly remind us.

In addition to not being distracted, she's also pointing to our being open to more subtle levels than usual. To be present in this way is to pay attention with our feelings, our senses, the sensations in our chests and shoulders, as well as with our minds—with all of us. When we're present like this, we're open to subtle hints and feelings about ourselves and our conversation partners. We listen to what is said and what is unsaid. We're present with something like a wide-angle lens to everything that is going on inside ourselves, inside the folks we're with, and perhaps in the space around us.

Again and again, my interviewees and my patients stressed being present like this. To be present, "really here" and open is more central to the Christian spiritual life than are any words, beliefs or doctrines. Being present, especially with others, is something that makes possible our sense of being supported, of being loved, of feeling trust and even of sensing the mystical reality.

When we listen for the subtle, unspoken and mysterious layers of another person or the world like this, or when we listen to a piece of music with our hearts wide open, we become more fully "present" in this spiritual sense. It's not exactly cognitive. It's a feature of how we're paying attention. To be wide open and present like this is a gift to whomever we're with and a gift to us. And a dose of the transcendent.

Elizabeth Young, whom we met before, described this connection:

> *In a really good conversation, I feel I'm launched into the transcendent through relationship. It's a sacred conversation. In the exchange I'm projected into the transcendent, I touch the transcendent.*

In a wonderfully insightful conversation, my Swedish friend Anna Christina observed that it's easier to be fully present when we are with someone who is as or more present than we ourselves are. We may not be able to name it, but when someone is truly present, we can feel it. To be with someone who is not afraid of their own pain, to be with someone who doesn't avoid what is deeply or scarily true about themselves, it is easier to be wide open to our own pain and deeper truths. Sometimes, I think, even merely being in a room with such a person can help.

I came to see that being present, opening ourselves without our usual defensive shielding, is connected with sensing the spiritual reality. I heard phrases like "I was just there, fully present" or "I was projected into the transcendent" countless times and these are *precisely* how many people describe their mystical experiences of being "with God," sensing "The Ground of Being" or "being in the flow." For many, the experience of the transcendent is *none other than* the experience of being fully present, nothing added. When I am unconflicted, when I have no inner distractions that stop me from being fully and unconflictedly "here," I am immersed in the transcendent Divine.

Several of my interlocutors went further and asserted that Jesus's ability to be present was the source of his teachings. It was only because he knew it firsthand that he could speak of it so elegantly. Margareta, another Swedish contact, suggested the story about the road to Emmaus (Luke 24:32) points to just this kind of deep person-to-person contact. On the day after the Easter events, she relayed, several folks met a man on the road. As they talked with him, they were...

> filled with a feeling of wonder, of holiness. Their "hearts were burning within them while he talked with them on the road."

This, she went on, is just what happens when we come together vulnerably, honestly with other people, either in church or outside of it. With such undefended contact, our hearts "burn within us."

1. Brown depicts the emotional valence of a coherent forged family in a stunningly successful rowing team.
2. See Christopher Schaefer's forthcoming book on the subject, tentatively called *Sacramental Conversations.*
3. Gallagher, p. 15.

RUMINATIONS ON THE HORIZONTAL

At this moment I find myself visualizing people on their knees at the altar, shoulder to shoulder with others, waiting for the priest who's coming slowly down the way. Their arms are draped over the railing, their hands are outstretched. A moment like this is, at heart, a community experience, and it is very moving. If someone takes communion separately, as people sometimes do in a hospital room, it can be powerful in its way, but it loses some of the humility that comes with gathering.

For on that kneeler, I and others are sharing this very meaningful moment. It is deeply meaningful, yes. Some of us believe in Jesus *per se,* some of us don't. But we're all affected by a sensibility or a feeling, which is what makes this posture work so well. On our knees shoulder to shoulder, our arms and hands reaching out as a child might, we're all stating our weakness, our needs, to ourselves: "Help, please help!" It's an ego-challenging act of humility, and a communal one, an act of self-transcendence.

There's an energy that arises when we come together in church. It's different than the kind of energy that rises when people come together to cheer in a football stadium. Becoming roused up in a sports event is highly spirited—of course, there's certainly energy there! But it's shot through with us-against-them.

But coming together in a church, especially when we bring our presence, brings a different kind of spirit: the deep and self-transcending energy of openness. It's quite palpable. Our hearts just open in a way they don't anywhere else.

I can also understand why a "sacramental conversation"—being interpersonally connected or opening our hearts to one another—can be especially helpful on our pilgrimage towards self-transcendence. For being profoundly present to someone in a conversation is *none other than* being profoundly present to the wide openness that comes with the experience of the Ground of Being. Being present to someone, as Anna Christina reminds us, is a whiff of the infinite. Thus, the horizontal feeds into the vertical. And we don't need the word "God" or "sacred" to make such energy rise.

Such self-transcendence can also be part of resolving our conflicts and differences. I can't tell you how many times I've heard of couples and groups that love one another but end up squabbling about money or decisions or next steps. This is especially heartbreaking in a church, which speaks of and teaches love. But if we can keep in mind the path of self-transcendence, we may be able to let go of our individual positions, hopes or demands enough to really hear one another. Grounding ourselves in the depths, we may be able to flush out each other's deeper longings and discern the *real* issues that drive us, and move towards resolving things creatively and with heart. The challenge is to have a "sacramental conversation," even when we're under tension!

… PART THREE
THE VERTICAL SPIRITUAL POWER REIMAGINED

CHAPTER 6

"BEING AND AT-ONENESS"

About two and a half years after that breakthrough in the Mahwah church, I found my attention drawn to the tussle-haired teenager who was leading the procession down the center aisle, carrying a cross on a stick. (Since then, I've learned it's a "processional cross" and the gawky teenager a "crucifer.") It wasn't the fact that he was so adorably gawky, with his jeans, striped socks and orange sneakers sticking out of his calf-length surplice. Or that he looked so self-conscious and so proud, concentrating no doubt on walking slowly enough that the little parade behind him could keep up. Nor was it that particular cross that got to me, though with its shiny brass surface and cloverleaf spars it was lovely.

What struck me was how it wobbled three feet over his head as he walked, swaying back and forth with every step. The slow wagging was so...well...human! He was just a kid, I thought, trying to walk a straight line slowly enough, gripping his brass insignia with both hands. He was an ordinary kid, bearing a 2000-year-old emblem, in orange sneakers.

Which tied us all together. There we were, all in our pews,

two feet beneath that wobbling, shining symbol. Its two horizontal arms pointed outwards to us, the assembled community. The other arms were vertical, pointing "up" towards the infinite energy or "down" towards the Ground of Being. It was that teenager's very ordinariness, juxtaposed with the transcendent mystery towards which his shining symbol pointed, that got to me. He was at once so utterly human, bearing a symbol of that which is not.

That teenager in orange sneakers and the shining standard he held is why a church is different from a bowling group or a marching band. He was utterly commonplace. Yet he carried that which is anything but. The whole church service, like that teenage boy and his cross, is at once "fully human" and "fully Divine."

EXPERIENCING THE VERTICAL

Just to give you a sense for what I mean by "fully Divine," here are three experience reports. The first comes from a sermon by the Rev. Cristina Rathbone, the charismatic priest from an Episcopal church in Great Barrington, Massachusetts:

> I had been swimming. The stream tumbles down a little waterfall and opens out into a gorgeous, round swimming hole. That afternoon, the entire pool was bathed in a golden light and the water was flowing fast in places, winking and flashing. I was sitting on a sandbank, tired and happy from the swim.
>
> And suddenly the usual realities of separation and struggles simply melted away and I was left in a kind of being and at-oneness. Whatever it was, that oneness felt incontrovertible and utterly true. And I knew that what I was sensing really was true. It was a dipping into reality.

Cristina added that church pews are filled with people who

"BEING AND AT-ONENESS"

have experienced something similar. Most people in the church, she believes (as do I), probably have had "at least a fleeting experience of some deep reality" like hers, moments that are utterly unlike our everyday experiences.

Our second experience is Doug Kruschke's, a deeply thoughtful Los Angeles corporate facilitator. Doug grew up quite involved with a "nondenominational Christian church," especially with its youth group, but fell away in late high school and became an agnostic. After getting a degree in psychology and leading several weekend encounter groups, he found himself reconnecting with his spiritual life, exploring Buddhism, Native American, Non-dualistic Hinduism and other paths. These days he describes himself as a Christian but, like many Mystics on the Margins who are both spiritual and Christian, he does so as "in part a nod to my heritage and in part as a symbolic presence in my psyche." Whatever his tradition, his experiences of the mystical reality have remained front and center for him. To him it is...

> *an impersonal presence that is greater than me. It reaches beyond my shoulders, beyond the physical scene and beyond what I can know. Sometimes I experience it as more connected with me, a personal presence I feel up against me in a warm way. It's a caring, almost smiling sense that it's all ok. And yet it's impersonal, without a face or personality. Whatever it is, it is something holy.*

He describes the "impersonal presence" that he senses as "closer than my own skin..."

Our third experience comes from another Episcopal Priest, Rev. Stephanie Bradbury, from Lowell, Massachusetts. Years before she became a priest, she was riding in the back of a car looking out the window, when

> *all of a sudden reality shifted. I could see beyond reality. It was as if the cows and trees were transparent. I could see a deeper reality behind them, an energy that was moving. I could see everything was connected and unified and whole and beautiful. I was so struck by how gorgeous it was. It was a beautiful shift in consciousness. I didn't identify it as God. It was not about some personal being. Rather I was seeing the unity of reality behind physical reality... I was sensing objects as pervaded by some sense of shared inner subjectivity or consciousness...which binds all the elements. It was as if the multiplicity in the world somehow disclosed a normally hidden unity.*

Much like Doug and Cristina, Stephanie perceived some semi-palpable connection between things, a "shared inner consciousness" stretching out through the trees, hills and clouds. Whatever it was, it seemed to unify everything on some unseen plane of reality beneath what she could see, touch, hear or understand.

I'm struck by two commonalities in these accounts. First, all three of these transcendent experiences came while they were alone. They were caught up, unaccompanied if you will, into the "vertical" arm of that teenager's shining cross. No church community, no conversational partner, no obvious relationships.

Second, they all encountered an impersonal presence or a sense of "being and at-oneness." None saw a face, visualized a personage, heard a voice or the like. Fred Plumer, former president of ProgressiveChristianity.org, suggests that experiences like these are more common that we might think:

> People throughout history have been able to have an experience of the infinite mystery and describe much about it... It is something in all things... For all reality is one connected thing. Jesus [and others] taught us to see ourselves as part of this One (Plumer, 2012).

Indeed, over more than 60 interviews, only one person described to me an encounter with a human-like figure. Most were more like Mary Anne, a fifty-something former actress who attends a liberal Episcopal church, who told me,

> I now find the image of God sitting on a throne or the "Holy Ghost" just bizarre. Even the "holy spirit" is more of a fairy tale to me. I can put my faith in love and the communal energy of love. But I can't put my faith in that guy. Oh, come on, it's ridiculous! To me, God as a person seems a foreign concept.

Much more common were abstract experiences of presence, expansion, centeredness, or awareness itself. Not one mystic on the margins maintained that the ultimate watches over us or intervenes in our destiny.

One of my Stockholm contacts, wise woman and retreat leader Patricia Stendahl, describes something similar:

> In church I feel sometimes that the line between me and the world has become thin. I feel myself part of something bigger, a sense of some ultimate reality or level (this is my word for God) where I feel connected to the people around me and to everything. This ultimate reality is unformed but connective. I feel myself part of everything, including people. I sense our lives are intertwined like threads

woven into a single carpet. This, by the way, is a feeling, not a thought.

Like Doug, Patricia senses an ultimate level "below" ordinary reality, and even calls it "my word for God." This oneness interpenetrates her and connects her to everything and everyone. And it's more a *feeling* of connection than an idea or thought.

When I asked my hospital patients or interviewees what it was like to "find God" or to "feel the support of Jesus," they inevitably described their emotional or spiritual shifts. When people talked of "finding God" or "feeling the support of Jesus," what they were really extolling was the felt-sense, the emotion, of peace or love that they had "found."

Similarly, the common plea to "let go and let God" or "trust God's will" are at heart statements about their inner attitudes. They were telling me or themselves that they wanted to release their need for things to go the way they'd prefer and were attempting to relax about their fate. If they were scared of an operation, for example, when they said they wanted to "let go and let God," they were telling me or themselves that they wanted to release the hold of their fears and trust that they will be able to handle whatever comes. They wanted to be able to "go with the flow."

Not once in my hundreds of conversations and interviews with patients or Doubting Christians did anyone mention *homoousios* or recite, much less explain, the Nicene creed. No one ever mentioned the substitution theory, the payment theory or the great Catholic vs Protestant debates. Not once.

This is what counts for us and, I daresay, for most Christians: our *feelings* of trust, comfort or flowing. Experiences of the sacred, not beliefs about its nature, are primary.

In other words, most Mystics on the Margins—and indeed, most spiritual people—tend to orient our religious or spiritual

"BEING AND AT-ONENESS"

lives not around a thought of a creator or protector, not around a theory about it, but around our own (or someone else's) spiritual experiences.

An astonishing percentage of people are having such experiences *today*. According to Pew Research, about half of the U.S. public (49%) has had a "moment of sudden religious insight or awakening (Heimlich, 2009). This includes a roughly equal number of conservatives (55%), liberals (50%) and almost as many moderates (43%). Such experiences are also common among the "religiously unaffiliated" (51%). Two-thirds of U.S. adults say they feel a deep sense of spiritual peace and well-being at least several times a year, including 44% who have this feeling monthly or more (Pew Research, 2023).

The renowned and soft-spoken Benedictine Monk, Brother David Steindl-Rast, suggests that the mystical is "the birthright of every human being."

> *We all have this experience of belonging, once in a while. Out of the blue, this comes. Women often say that when they give birth to a child, they have it. When we fall in love, we have this sense of belonging. Or suddenly, without any particular reason, out in nature you feel one with everything. And every human being has this* (Tippett, 2016).

Brother David continued that history's truly "great" mystics were only great because they "let these experiences determine and shape every moment of their lives."

I can't agree with Br. David that the mystical is the "birthright of *every* human being." Though every human being may have the *capacity* for the mystical, it is my sense that, as in basketball or singing, some people have more innate talent than others. Among those who do encounter the mystical, many find that it just doesn't fit with the rest of their lives, so they shove the memory of it into the background as "weird" or "crazy." Many patients and interviewees remarked that I was the first person they had ever told about their experiences. And yet these extraordinary moments were always important for them, sometimes life-changing. For many they became a guiding light.

Sometimes these experiences come as an intense emotional response to music, poetry, literature, the visual arts or perhaps an intimate conversation. Experiences of silence can also arise during moments of quiet contemplation or prayer. The author Gunilla Norris beautifully captures this sense of a meaningful silence:

> Within each of us there is a silence—a silence as vast as the universe. We are afraid of it...and we long for it. When we experience that silence, we remember who we are: creatures of the stars, created from the birth of galaxies, created from the cooling of this plane, created from dust and gas, created from the elements, created from time and space...created from silence (Norris, 2004).

In all these experiences, as we become less anxious and worried, we become more ourselves, present and alive to the world.

Christian Theologian Marcus Borg describes such mystical or ecstatic experiences as "thin places." In such a "thin place" the veil momentarily lifts, our hearts break open and the boundary between ourselves and the world momentarily disappears. In a "thin place," he continues, we can experience a "nonmaterial layer or level of reality that's all around us, as well as within us."

In technical terms, what Cristina, Stephanie and many others around the world are experiencing is a spiritual reality

"BEING AND AT-ONENESS"

that they sense as *transcendent*. That is, they sense it as something that's beyond or above the range of everyday physical perceptions.

Such a reality also comes across typically as "connected with me": it seems to interpenetrate the things of the world as well as we ourselves. When something indwells or interpenetrates our bodies and minds, we scholars call it *immanent*.

The doctrine that a non-sensory reality is both immanent and transcendent, both *within* and *beyond*, is technically called *panentheism*. "Panentheism" is from the ancient Greek πᾶν ἐν θεῷ, pān en theó, literally *pan,* everything, *en,* in, and *theos* God. In a panentheistic ultimate, everything is within a non-sensory reality and that reality is both within everything and yet is more than the things in it. For example, the ocean is "panentheistic" to the fish in it. The ocean clearly reaches beyond all the fish. Yet inside a fish is mostly seawater (fish are 65%–95% water, to be exact); the ocean is within and at the heart of the fish.

Cristina's and Stephanie's experience was that the Divine energy is a non-sensory *panentheistic* level reality around and through us all. And that this nonmaterial, panentheistic layer of reality consistently carries a positive emotional tone. That is, it comes across as pure love.

Though few of my interviewees used (or even knew) this word, every one that told me of their experience of their sense of the Divine spoke of it in similarly *panentheistic* terms, and that it came across as warm and loving.

SENSING THE VERTICAL

For most Mystics on the Margins the vertical arm of the cross points to the "something more" or the "Ground of Being." It was Stephanie Bradbury who helped me understand this. Terms like "God" or the "Divine," she said, are connected with our experiences of what seems the panentheistic reality:

> *What we call "God" IS the ground of being. It permeates everything, including human beings. All of us are permeated by that, not only Jesus. In fact, what Jesus encountered was that same Ground that permeates us all. We're simultaneously physical and spiritual beings who are living into the Divine Flow. There is no separation. Just as Jesus modeled it, we're all permeated by this Divine life.*

To Stephanie, like most Mystics on the Margins, driving the word "God" is our (or someone's) impersonal experiences of the panentheistic Ground of Being, the Divine flow. Rather than being a mythical figure who intercedes in history, "God" points to such an impersonal reality which we can sometimes sense permeating us.

I say this fully aware that traditionally "God" implied far more than just a transcendent or panentheistic field. Even today, to many it implies an anthropomorphic creator of the universe, "he who sits above the circle of the earth...and stretches out the heavens like a curtain" (Isa. 40:21). To many "He" is the great protector, someone who responds to our prayers, judges our actions and who "sets us free from sin" (Rom. 6:18).

However, as we stressed earlier, most Mystics on the Margins have rejected as hopelessly out-of-date the phrases and stories that portray the Divine as person-like. Rather than believing in a being who issues commands and watches over our fate, we talk about sensing "an impersonal presence" a "a deeper reality behind reality" or a "being and at-oneness." James Finley, clinical psychologist, faculty member at the Living School at the Center for Action and Contemplation and a student of Thomas Merton, describes it this way:

> *There isn't some infinite being called God who exists. God is the name that we give to the beginning-less, boundary-less, infinite*

plenitude of existence itself. I am who I am. God is that by which we are (Kohls, 2023).

Rather than a figure who intervenes in our everyday lives, our sense of such a transcendent plenitude grows out of our experiences. If we use words like "God" or "the Lord" at all, most of us use them to point to the qualities of peace, a vastness or a flow that we (or someone we trust) might sense. Or as Anna Christina put this, "when people say 'God,' they're pointing to the experience of surrendering into the *flow*."

Philosopher and psychologist Eugene Gendlin has an excellent way of talking about these impulses and feelings. He talks about "a felt-sense" that shimmers beneath our words, emotions and understandings. To him,

> *a felt-sense is not a mental experience but a physical one. Physical. A bodily awareness of a situation or person or event. An internal aura that encompasses everything you feel and know about the given subject at a given time—encompasses it and communicates it to you all at once rather than detail by detail. Think of it as a taste, if you like, or a great musical chord that makes you feel a powerful impact, a big round unclear feeling... A felt-sense doesn't come to you in the form of thoughts or words or other separate units, but as a single (though often puzzling and very complex) bodily feeling* (Gendlin, 1981).[1]

We identify a "felt-sense" by attending to what we feel in our bellies, shoulders or elsewhere in our bodies. As we respond to people and situations, we may become aware of some feeling or what the body "knows." Such bodily knowing, Gendlin argues, is deeper or more primal than the words to which those feelings might give rise. We feel things in our shoulders and hearts much more immediately and deeply than we understand them.

For example, if someone used the word "God" or "The Lord" in an interview, I would listen for the felt-sense to which they seemed to be pointing. I might ask, "what is that for you?" or "what's that like?" As I did, I discovered that these words were consistently used to express a felt-sense of the kind of mysterious reality that Christine, Doug and Stephanie described, and that you probably remembered when I asked you to bring to mind your most meaningful experiences. As Birgitta, another Swedish contact, noted:

> It's an experience in and of the body in relation to the "Whole." It reaches out to something bigger, to a kinship and friendship with All.

Again, not one single person offered some theological theory or talked about how Jesus was "fully God and fully man." To Mystics on the Margins these words point to their past or present experiences of openness, peace or perhaps their sense of the vast "beginning-less, boundary-less, infinite plenitude of existence itself."

"EFFING" THE INEFFABLE

If we have a felt-sense, a feeling in our body, it's not generally verbal or something whose meaning we can immediately know. It's a "single (though often puzzling and very complex) bodily feeling." It's beyond what we can explain. That is, it's *ineffable*, i.e., beyond expression in words, unspeakable. Birgitta continued:

> "Whatever-it-is" seems to just fall over me, something I perceive more with my shoulder and belly than with my head or my words...

"BEING AND AT-ONENESS"

Then she concluded, "there are some things I just cannot explain." In this, I think she's correct.

Kevin P., a forty-something Christian from Vermont, agreed about ineffability. Kevin grew up as a scientific materialist, uninterested in spirituality, but through a long path he found his way to Christianity, where he found, especially in prayer,

> *something happens between God and the soul that you don't get to know about... I don't need to know what it is. I just trust that it's happening and that there is something about that that's enough.*

Whatever this mysterious "something that happens" may be, we "don't get to know...what it is." This "non-sensory reality" cannot be clearly defined, characterized, or named. Christine Anders told me this in especially poetic language:

> *The truth of the matter is that we can't really know the nature of the non-sensory reality. We can't even know its name. I say "God" but what I really have is a feeling: like a star shining over me.*

These vague feelings of some ineffable reality are, like stars shining overhead, way beyond what any of us can know. We can't capture what they're about with an image. We can't grasp them in concepts. For the spiritual reality is beyond thoughts, beyond words and beyond precise descriptions. In the face of such ecstatic and sensory encounters we stand mute and unknowing, driven by a sense of we-know-not-what. As Elizabeth Young put it, "It's like a wind... It's all around us. It's unbounded. But it's unknowable. I don't understand it."

Indeed, most of my interviewees prefer to leave a mysterious reality mysterious, i.e., *ineffable*. The president of ProgressiveChristianity.org, Fred Plumer, put it this way:

We believe something but it is a great mystery, beyond our understanding: the infinite mystery, something beyond our comprehension. So, we can't give qualities to it. We choose to call this something God or the Infinite Mystery (Plumer, 2012).[2]

Despite the fact that the mystical feelings or sensations of such a reality are wordless, despite the fact that we cannot "eff" the ineffable, people have struggled throughout the centuries to describe or make sense of the reality that they experience, using their various terms. As we've seen, different folks focused on various elements of their encounters. As I told you, when I asked them, "What was that like for you?" sometimes several times, I couldn't help but hear a strikingly similar sense of depth and a wide-eyed opening into "something more." Different descriptors and words were clearly pointing to experiences of a similar or even the same reality.[3]

We can portray this phenomenon—a deeply consistent set of experiences of an indescribable reality with different descriptors—with a Venn Diagram:

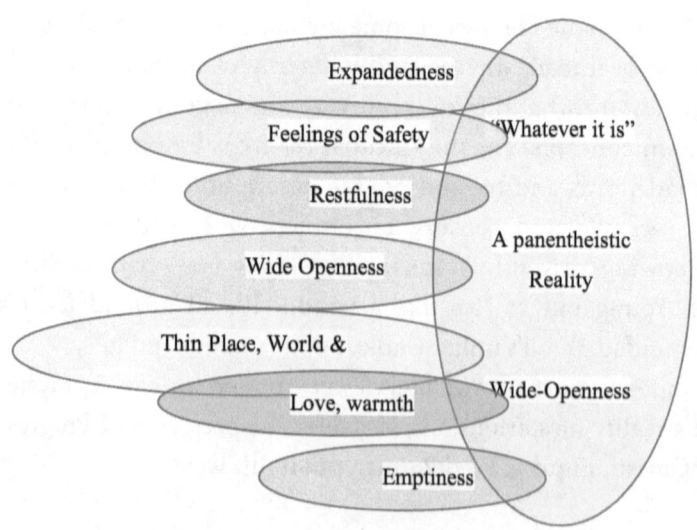

"BEING AND AT-ONENESS"

There's a problematic irony in these accounts. We sense a similar or identical panentheistic whatever-it-is; we know it's "ineffable." Indeed, in *The Problem of Pure Consciousness, The Innate Capacity* and my *Mysticism, Mind Consciousness*, we argued that people throughout time and around the world have been experiencing a similar sense of a depth, an openness to or an alignment with a "something more." And yet over the centuries and continents, people have described it using the endlessly varied descriptors from their cultures and eras, none of which are definitive (Forman 1990, 1999).[4]

Traditions all around the world have supplied a cornucopia of names for such experienced reality. To traditional Christians these have been experiences of "God," "Christ," "the Holy," the "Divine," "the universal life force," "Abba," "Father" or the like. As we've seen from our interviews, this reality has been described as an "impersonal presence," a "Ground of Being," "a transparent reality," "a feeling, like a star shining over me," and more. Marcus Borg used the dryer, more technical "non-sensory reality."

To my friends that do some Hindu-based meditation, it is the wordless and contentless "transcendental consciousness," "*Kaivalya*," "*turiya*," or when permanent, "Cosmic Consciousness." To Buddhists we become "one with the Buddha-mind," "*shunyata*" (emptiness) or "*nirodha samapatti*." To Sufi Muslims it is "*fana*," and so on. To psychologist Mihaly Csíkszentmihályi, these experiences are something like being in a flow, i.e., being nearly effortless in some sense of deep alignment while we're active. To jazz musicians, it's being "in the pocket" or "flowing with the band." A dancer in the New York City Ballet told me that ballerinas called it "being danced by the angels." In my book *Enlightenment Ain't What It's Cracked Up to Be*, I described such a sense as "the Vastness." To catch both its interpersonal character and its felt-sense, today I prefer the term "Openness."

None of these terms are final or definitive. Some of the Christians I spoke with told me that they use the word "God" "only as a focal point…not as a description or name of whatever it is I'm experiencing."

Let's add this cornucopia of traditional names to our Venn diagram:

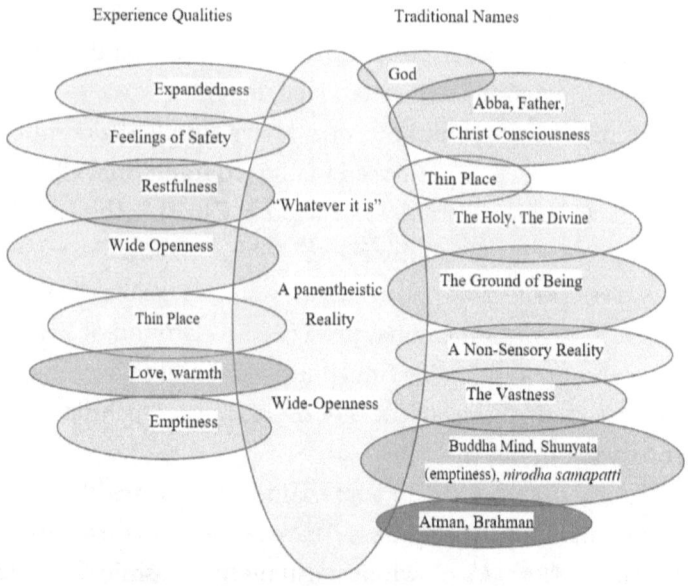

People from churches, synagogues, Zendos and temples report quite similar or identical experiences of an ineffable, cloudlike, "panentheistic reality." But such a reality is described and named with words and images that are as varied as the human cultures that have named it.

Which leads us to religious conservatives. I used to think they were profoundly different from the Mystics on the Margins. I began to change my mind when I was invited as a chaplain to the bedside of a shockingly skinny, wan and obviously weak woman, Patient S, in my hospital's Progressive Care Unit. When I introduced myself as a chaplain, she lit up and described herself as "an evangelical Christian." Then she told me, with a weak but confident smile, "God came to me."

"Oh, wow!" I said. "That sounds beautiful! Tell me about it."

"It was a few months ago. And I just knew it was God! I felt so peaceful, so calm that I just knew it was God."

"That must have been wonderful, to feel so peaceful and calm." Then I wondered aloud, "What was there about it that led you to know that it was God?"

"Well, when He was with me, I just wasn't worried at all—not about my diseases, not about dying, nothing. I was so at peace. I just knew!"

It wasn't some theory or story about God that had so moved Patient S. It was her calm, non-anxious sense of peace that told her that this was "of God." That experience, those feelings, convinced her in her bones of the reality from "another dimension."

And, she went on, it was clear that her brief experience had become a touchstone for her. When she or someone else spoke of God, she said, she'd bring to mind that sense of peace. When people read the Bible in church, she understood the stories in its light. Her memories of that settledness will, for the rest of her life, remain the shimmering core of her religion. And her life.

I believe that similar experiences drive other conservative believers as well. When I had interviewed a number of them, I told them that I was interested in their experiences in church. Generally, they began by talking about Jesus, "being saved," or something of the like. From doing many interviews over the years, I've learned that most people, especially in a tight group, first want to tell me all about their belief system, their "framework." Typically, conservative Christians have done this, first giving me their "rap" with their familiar jargon. When they did, I always listened attentively, for their "rap" was always full of unspoken meaning and implications. After they offered their system, I would then explore it. I might ask them: "Oh, you experienced Jesus. Wow. What was that like?" Or if they said they'd "been saved," I would wonder aloud about it. Since I really didn't know what they meant by these terms, I typically asked what experiencing Jesus was like, or what being saved felt like. Or perhaps, "How did you know you'd been saved?" I'd keep gently probing until I came to sense or understand the on-the-ground experiences or feelings to which such terms were pointing. Chelsey, for example, a lively twenty-something we've met before, who attends a Texas evangelical church, told me how she encounters God in her church:

> Sometimes, being in church the presence feels heavy. Heavy not in a bad WAY, but like the best hug ever and just safe. Like this big hug from which I feel, "Just give me whatever you've been worried about." Sometimes I just want to cry... If I walk into church emotionally just wrecked, I know I just feel safe there. It feels like home.

Always, always, I've come to believe, there are important, often life-changing, experiences at the living heart of a religious language. Much as the Mystics on the Margins do, conservative Christians, including the Evangelicals and Pentecostals that I met, refer back to those rare moments in which the veil lifted—sometimes briefly—and the ineffable openness revealed itself as "the presence," a calmness, a feeling of safety or a sense of some wide-open reality.

Chelsey and Patient S both used "God" to refer back to their experiences of calmness or of safety, along with a sense that there was "something" beyond themselves in which they were participating. Such experiences came with a sense of connection, of warmth, of love.

In short, though we use different words and frames, both Mystics on the Margins and conservatives like Patient S seem to share more than I ever expected. The spiritual encounters I heard described in both camps are not, at heart, all that different. And such encounters often become touchstones. People on both sides of the religious divides are having everyday experiences of a mysterious goodness and an unconditional love, or what we might call "peak experiences." Some call them experiences of "grace," others "experiences of Christ" or just a peak experience of "something more." But all are pointing to a strong sense that one is encountering or being held by "something greater," a "Divine Spirit" or participating deeply in life.

Though I don't have room to explore this here, the fact that these profound experiences are so similar may help us bridge our culture's seemingly unbreachable religious divides.

Now what should we call the kind of approach to religion that we're developing here? First of all, it's *phenomenological,* by which I mean it's about the study of awareness itself or how things appear to us, how they feel inside our bodies, how they come into our consciousness. Phenomenology focuses not on some theory of the ultimate, but rather on what Gendlin calls a *felt-sense,* what a spiritual experience is like in our awareness, how we can best foster it, and how it relates to the world and to our lives.

I call our approach then "Phenomenological Theology," understanding that by *theos,* the root of "theology," we mean the sense of a Divine that's not person-like but more abstract or field-like. Phenomenological Theology focuses not on the thoughts or beliefs we might have about the Divine but rather on the direct feelings that we might have in our muscles, legs, belly, back of the head or whatnot as we encounter such a reality. If we hear such terms as "God," "Jesus," "Yahweh" or the "Ground of Being," we can use our "soft focus" to sense how these words might relate to our or someone else's direct consciousness of such a panentheistic reality.

That such a reality is not person-like doesn't mean that we Mystics on the Margins don't seek out something of "God" or of "the Divine." Not at all! We just understand what we're seeking in our own way. Rather than looking for protection from some person-like being, for example, most of us seek to be conscious at some level of the "non-sensory reality" or Cristina's "being and at-oneness." This does not demean the word "God." Quite the reverse! By reimagining the centuries of tired analogies, suppositions, inferences, and dubious claims that the word has fostered, we're bringing the focus back to the lived experiences and heartfelt yearnings for this non-sensory reality around which the religion has always whirled.

HISTORICAL CONTEXTS

Now why are we seeing this experientially oriented approach to the Divine today? To answer this question, we'll have to think about the differences between the way ancient people talked and thought and the way we do. For, as I used to teach in university class after class, in general religions grow out of and give voice to then-current frameworks, especially the then-current view of the physical universe.

We've suggested that people throughout time have been enjoying similar ineffable and joyous experiences of a mysterious, panentheistic reality. If we're correct, then people in ancient times also experienced, and wrote about in their idiom, a sense of flow or a loving and boundless "something." I fully agree with Brother David Steindl-Rast, who suggests that fluid and wordless experiences of a "something more" are what the tradition—and perhaps all traditions—has *always* been about!

> The religions start from mysticism. There is no other way to start a religion. But I compare this to a volcano that gushes forth...and then...the magma flows down the sides of the mountain and cools off. And when it reaches the bottom, it's just rocks. You'd never guess that there was fire in it. So after a couple of hundred years, or two thousand years or more, what was once alive is dead rock. Doctrine becomes doctrinaire. Morals become moralistic. Ritual becomes ritualistic. What do we do with it? We have to push through this crust and go to the fire that's within it (Steindl-Rast, 2005).

I would go one step further than Brother David: the nonmaterialistic reference to "an ineffable reality beneath reality" could *only* have begun when someone or several someones experienced something like "an ineffable reality beneath reality." Long, long ago and far, far away the hairs on some person's neck must have stood up. Long, long ago and far, far away, some sensitive soul must have sensed him or herself to be surrounded by an ineffable reality.

We don't know where, when or in whom that initial spiritual "volcano" may have erupted. Perhaps it was around 64,000 BCE in the early Maltravieso Cave in Spain; around 12,500 BCE in the Gobekli Tepe temple; or maybe it happened around 1800 BCE at Ur, Mesopotamia or perhaps in some unknown time and place. We also don't know if it happened to Abraham, Sarah, Solon or, more likely, to some unnamed cave dweller. We'll never know. But some human being(s) somewhere had to have a sense of something mysterious, lively and ineffable to give such vivid depictions of something mysterious, lively and ineffable. Otherwise, we would all be strict materialists, talking only of things we could see, touch, smell or hear. Without foundational ecstasies, the blood of living faith that flows in so many millions of veins would be dry as dust. And we'd all be rational materialists, full stop. The more ineffable overtones of the term "God" must have had its start in, and ultimately it's grounding in, the kind of lively human spiritual experiences I asked you to ponder in the Introduction. And there must have been others who recognized the reality of this lifeblood and began to talk of it. Sister Gail Worcelo, the very open-minded and thoughtful abbess of a Vermont convent, put this poetically:

> *The womb out of which theology came is prerational, ecstatic and fluid. It's too deep for words.*

Behind Christianity's heady theologies, she's saying, fluid and wordless connections, those "prerational, ecstatic, wordless encounters" with something larger, have always vibrated.

Marcus Borg put this thought even more elegantly: "in the beginning was experience."

If ancient religious founders had a non-verbal sense of some mysterious reality, as we're suggesting, they would probably have assumed that it had a human-like source. After all, in 5000 BCE or even the first century CE (when the Gospels were written) the only source of governable power people knew about was human: human beings caused controllable movement, human beings made objects with intention. So inevitably, as Reza Aslan showed in his excellent *God: A Human History*, they would have turned to the metaphor of a person as the source or expression of such a mysterious power. And it was probably just as inevitable that this ancient and widely accepted metaphor of a human-like figure who "sat above the circle of the earth and...stretched out the heavens like a curtain" (Isa. 40:22) would shape for many centuries how people thought about the infinite. Or that such a figure would come to be thought of as a lawgiving, super-powerful general who controlled the roulette wheel of fate and who "bore you on eagles' wings" (Ex. 19:4). Or that "He" would "Father" a "Son." Given their worldview, this would all make perfect sense!

Alas, we know that over time this seemingly obvious metaphor has had incredibly destructive side effects! Only if we think of the non-sensory reality as like a Dude (or Dudette) can we imagine that "it" could etch a tablet, dictate a book, lead an army or ask people to obey its commandments. Only if our ethical codes are enforced by a quasi-human being who sits in judgment over our foibles can we imagine that the non-sensory reality could declare that "you *must* not fornicate" or "you have sinned." Even worse, only a person-like figure could declare that because "the thoughts of [humanity's] hearts were evil" they should all be drowned in a great flood (Gen. 6:5). Only such a person-like figure could inspire priests to declare that "you're a heretic and must be burned at the stake!" In short this seemingly natural and innocuous-sounding metaphor—that the infinite energy is person-like and that our ethical rules were dictated and enforced by such a person-like fellow—became the ultimate justification for mankind's history of religious cruelty, hegemony, misogyny, genocide, shaming, misfit-shunning and ultimately murder and war in "His" name. These unintended consequences turned out to be the bane of not only Western religions but also of Western civilization as a whole.

But today the worldview of Mystics on the Margins has shifted. Not only do we now think in terms of Quantum Physics, viruses, antibiotics, automobiles, gravity and TVs, but we've become far more experientially oriented. That is, we now regard experiences —what we feel, sense or give our hearts to—as nothing more and nothing less than experiences. We Mystics on the Margins no longer cling to the old metaphors that were once used to explain our unusual experiences, i.e., that God or the devil was causing them. Instead, again according to our modern worldview, it seems quite possible to have an important and transformative religious or spiritual moment without attributing it to any ancient force or some human-like agent. Though conservatives continue to use the comfortable word "God" to speak of their mystical moments, these days both liberal and traditionalist Christians as well as many religious "nones" can also talk about having a spiritual experience or responding to a ritual with tears or the like.

Because we now hold experiences to be experiences, we can use our "soft focus" to re-imagine the kinds of ecstasies and transformations that vibrate *beneath* some of the antique words and models. By listening "beneath the lines" or by attending to what we can sense in the rituals and gestures, we may be able to sense the mystery from which the words once burgeoned.

SHIFTING THE METAPHOR

I cannot overstate the importance of this metaphorical shift! If the ultimate reality is more an abstract, field-like reality than a human-like one, the whole picture of the Divine shifts radically! A "cloud of unknowing," a panentheistic "Ground of Being" or a "mysterious, impersonal ultimate" is unlikely to be mythologized as commanding an army, dictating an ethics, condemning a heretic or controlling someone's fate. The Ground of Being is simply an unbounded field and an energy with which we might align.

I am well aware that this unusual, even radical, view runs counter to the traditional Christian approach. Frankly, it's high time! For over the centuries Christianity has become a famously intellectualized, word-centered tradition, marked by heady theological debates about the nature of Christ (*Christology*), about the relationship between "the Father," the "Son" and the "Holy Spirit" (*Triune Theology*), and about how evil arises when God is both powerful and good (*theodicy*). It has been obsessed with its words and its doctrines, but not so much with the lived sensibilities toward which, I believe, those words have always pointed.

I'm suggesting that rather than their being primarily about a purported first cause of the universe or a final arbiter of our destiny, terms like "God" and "the Lord" are some of the traditional Christian ways of talking about what are, at heart, direct experiences of the ineffable, the nonpersonal Divine or the "something more"—either our own or those of someone we trust.

To be clear, Mystics on the Margins don't *believe* in a Divine or a Ground of Being. Instead, we *encounter* it, or seek to encounter it, through our legs, hearts, heads and lives. And we know that if we lose our connection with it and become lost in our ego, we can use our struggles as a jumping off point for a process of spiritual growth and hopefully reconnect with its flow.

One caveat about this approach. Short-lived experiences of the sacred like those we've pointed out are neither the be-all nor the end-all of anyone's religious life. They are temporary events and, at best, pointers. What we Mystics on the Margins are after, if you will, is a changed *life*. We seek to live more consistently and more often with a heart that's as wide open as it was in our "peak experiences." We seek to live with the sense that we're aligned with the Flow of reality. We seek to be aware of the non-sensory reality more of the time and more deeply, and use our struggles as part of that process. That is, whether we call this "God" or the "Ground of Being," we seek to open our hearts ever more consistently to it, to become ever more compassionate, and to live ever more available to ourselves and to others.

1. Gendlin, pp. 32–33. Full disclosure: Gendlin was a professor and mentor of mine, and I've taken Focusing training, which has no doubt played into my views here. Gendlin argues that we can pay attention to our bodily feelings, which are *separate* from our words. It is only as a secondary act that we allow the words to emerge out of that felt-sense. I am herein suggesting the reverse process: hearing words and seeing actions in a ritual sometimes causes feelings or felt-senses to emerge.
2. CF Plumer 2016, p. 31
3. Of course, we can approximate but never *prove* that their experiences were similar or identical. For any description contains a background of beliefs and understandings that could always lead the philosopher to point to differences in description and claim differences of experiences. But through empathetic and careful listening, we can make the leap into largely sensing another's direct experience.
4. It would be beyond scope of this book to establish this. I believe that people around the world and across the traditions have been seeking and experiencing similar felt-senses of the infinite energy in their worship and rituals. It is my conviction that spiritual experiences have always shimmered brightly beneath traditional religious words. This is not to say, however, that the actions to which those religious words have led have always been wise, ethical or benevolent!

CHAPTER 7

ELECTRONS, QUARKS, THE OMNIPRESENT FIELD AND LOVE

I was driving through the mountains of Colorado recently on a gorgeous, sunny afternoon, enjoying the piney hillsides, the ranch houses and the waving wheat fields. At some point something about the scene seemed strangely different, so I pulled onto the shoulder and got out. Whatever this newness was, I could feel it more than see it. I sensed something like a thin *cloud* around everything. It spread over the split rail fences. It rested between the long horns of the cattle grazing on the field. Down alongside the road, it was in the burbling stream. And far over there, it wafted up the side of the mountain. It was everywhere I looked. I could almost touch this cloudy "stuff" and twirl it between my fingers. I could feel this expansive something with my chest, belly and legs more than I could see it.

At some point I realized that this cloud-like "stuff" was not only *around* the mountains and longhorns. It seemed to course right *through* the cattle. It reached *inside* the granite grey mountains and *through* the ranch houses. This hush, velvety and quiet, penetrated everything I could see.

Finally, with a start, I realized that it ran right through me as well. "Oh, of course," I laughed to myself, "if it's everywhere, it's got to be *in me* too!" The cattle, the fence posts, and the hard grey granite were all the same "stuff" as me, as my own very consciousness! The mountains, ranch house and road were all the same "stuff" as I could feel coursing through me. Everywhere I looked I could feel this shapeless expanse with my chest, belly and legs more than I could see it. Weirdly, I was sensing the fences and the mountains that were yards and miles away in my own chest. What was in me was also very much *in* the world.

I got out of the car, leaned on a fence rail and felt into the scene for about half an hour: Cloud through the grasses; Cloud-like "something" beyond the clear sky; a Ground beneath the valley floor. I couldn't possibly have missed it!

We've seen how, in addition to enjoying connections with our church mates, many Mystics on the Margins have had some important, non-ordinary experiences like that, where they've sensed within things some seemingly unlimited reality. While floating in her swimming hole, Cristina had a sense of "being and at-oneness." In the desert Doug encountered an "impersonal presence that is greater than me." I saw around and within me a "velvety and quiet cloud that penetrated everything." And we're certainly not the only people who have sensed ourselves as part of some widespread mysterious "something."

But what is this mysterious "something?" While we cannot say just what it is, one thing we can say is that such a "non-sensory reality" didn't strike any of us as merely some subjective chimera. It always comes as something real, not imagined. But if this external and real "stuff" is not a quasi-person, as we've stressed, then what *is* it?

ELECTRONS, QUARKS, THE OMNIPRESENT FIELD AND LOVE

The hypothesis I'll develop in this chapter about this "eternal and real stuff" is in part an amalgamation of what I've learned from other Christians Who Doubt and in part the result of my own research and thinking. As this chapter touches on physics, it'll get a little geeky, especially in the first half. If you get bogged down, please skip to the chapter conclusions.

THE OBJECTIVE APPROACH

Modern physics teaches that hidden within or beneath *electrons, quarks, photons, atoms and everything we see is* a field of energy. A "field of energy," just to be clear, is an invisible physical field that extends through space in which some kind of object or process can produce force on another object or field. For example, objects like a magnetic rock, a toy magnet or an electrical rotor all generate magnetic fields around themselves. Though such magnetic fields are invisible to our eyes, they can be measured, they can move metal objects, and they can push or resist other magnetic fields. Similarly, a gravitational field produced by a massive object like a star or planet can influence objects and fields that are many millions of miles away.

Nobel prize-winning physicist Werner Heisenberg suggested that underlying all matter was an indivisible yet unseen energy, which he dubbed *Potentia,* from which objects spring into being when viewed by an observer. Quantum physicists have gone on to develop this intuition by identifying a field which is even more fundamental than magnetism, electricity or light. Although this field is in itself without form or shape, it is omnipresent, existing throughout matter, stars and even the vacuum between the stars. Its energy, sometimes called the "zero point energy" or "vacuum energy," is thought to be present throughout all space. Unlike the magnetic field, which weakens with distance, this field is believed to be everywhere equally. Let's call it the "Quantum Vacuum Field" (QVF).

This QVF field has one surprising feature. This can be seen when physicists pump all the molecules, heat and energy out of a cylinder, thus creating a near perfect vacuum and lowering its temperature to conditions that are found in outer space, i.e., nearly absolute zero. Now, we would expect that when we reduce the temperature in some unit of space to absolute zero, so that all the electrons, quarks and photons slow down to their lowest level of activity, there would be only silence and empty space left. But something always remains: a faint but constant level of activity at the tiniest, quantum, level (Physics Notes).[1] That's why this residual energy was named "zero-point energy." In other words, the Quantum Vacuum Field is everywhere. And no matter the temperature or how perfect the vacuum, it always remains lively.

This field is constantly fluctuating. Sometimes these fluctuations ripple into, say, embryonic electrons or photons, which dissipate within nanoseconds. Constantly flashing into and out of existence, these quasi-entities are called "virtual particles." It's believed that when pairs of oppositely charged "virtual particles" wink into existence, they get annihilated in an instant. Here then is the unexpected character of this Quantum Vacuum Field: even when we've reduced the temperature so much that no atoms, electrons or quarks are active, this field is not at all quiescent.

This Quantum Vacuum Field is described by physicist Dr. Hal Puthoff as "a wildly dynamical medium." "It's more like the base of a waterfall," he said, "with a lot of frothy, seething activity going on, rather than just something like placid, empty space..." Princeton Professor John Wheeler dubbed this ceaseless activity "quantum foam." In itself, this Quantum Vacuum Field has no particular shape or form, but it is omnipresent and simply "frothing" everywhere (Pas, 2023).

ELECTRONS, QUARKS, THE OMNIPRESENT FIELD AND LOVE

This notion that the Quantum Vacuum Field is dynamic is, by the way, not some fringe concept. It is so accepted an element of modern quantum theory that it was highlighted, for example, in Dr. Wilczek's 2004 Nobel Prize lecture in physics (Wilczek, 2005).

To give nonphysicists like me a sense for what happens in the Quantum Vacuum Field, I recommend two brief films.[2] You might find that images can help you visualize these infinitesimal disturbances as they emerge and disappear in a kind of quantum level pandemonium. These colorful figures move like a lava lamp constantly, while flashing into and out of existence.[3]

This frothy field, like the base of a waterfall, contains within itself potentially enormous energy: just one a cubic centimeter of empty space (i.e., of the Quantum Vacuum Field) has been calculated to be one trillionth of an erg (or 0.6 eV) (Carroll, 2006). That might not sound like much, but John Wheeler calculated that in a mere coffee cup's volume of empty space "there is enough energy to evaporate all of the world's oceans" (Physics notes, s.d.).

Recent experiments have gone on to show that the tiny fluctuations, the "virtual particles" that rapidly appear and disappear, can, if stimulated in different ways, become the quarks, gluons, photons and the host of fine particles which in turn become matter, light, electricity and gravity (Battersby, 2008).[4] Every biological microorganism, every flower petal, every raindrop, every piece of steel, every human being, and "even the molecules of wood that form the chair on which you are sitting" are expressions of this energy. In short, this dynamical QVF is *the* foundational reservoir of our universe.

A newer way to make sense of an unseen energy is "string theory." According to this theory, beneath all objects and all space exists an omnipresent realm which is filled with infinitesimal, vibrating rings and strings of pure energy. These rings and strings vibrate at wavelengths so small that we cannot measure them with our instruments. The theory is that all matter and all energy in the universe emerge out of the interactions of these vibrating rings and strings, even space itself. Again we have an account of a lively, omnipresent but unseen field of energy beneath reality.

THE SUBJECTIVE APPROACH

I found myself thinking about all this when Tony, Trinity Church's big teddy bear of a minister, gave a rather scientific-sounding sermon. "Everything that exists in the universe," he began in his rich baritone,

> is made up of energy. Every atom has electrons, subatomic particles that carry an electrical charge, which orbit around the atom's nucleus. It's all energy. There is an omnipresent field of energy that lies at the heart of electrons, quarks, photons, atoms and everything we see.

So far so good. Any physicists in the room would no doubt have been nodding their heads, for his "omnipresent field" was clearly referring to the Quantum Vacuum Field. But then Tony went on: "Not only are the subatomic particles, electrons and atoms in a blade of grass" *made* by God,

> they are part of God himself... Every blade of grass, every raindrop, every animal, every human being, every biological microorganism, every molecule of wood that forms the chair you are sitting on is GOD. Not just part of God, but IS God.

I was fully with him that there's an omnipresent field of energy. But why, I wondered, lay over this well-established theory a reference to "God himself?" Why did he characterize

ELECTRONS, QUARKS, THE OMNIPRESENT FIELD AND LOVE

such an omnipresent quantum field of energy with the image of that Old Testament figure who issued commandments, judged and responded to peoples' behavior, talked out of a burning bush and fathered a son? Why conflate our modern scientific model with a three-millennia-old "king of the universe?"

I think Tony and other scientifically minded priests and ministers want to weave the idea of an omnipresent energy field into the antique doctrine of a God to harmonize Christianity with modern physics. The religion would seem more current, relevant and "with it." But in truth we weren't alive 3000 years ago and we don't think as if we were. Reasonably educated, practical people like me and my interviewees are quite comfortable thinking of an abstract field of energy as...well...an abstract field of energy. And as disconnected with God-talk. We just don't personify physical fields. Nor do we hold that our laws and social rules come from such a personified field. Our laws, as we'll see in Chapter 12, were written by representatives, lawgivers and judges. Human beings all, not God.

The problem with Tony's analogy is this: though calling it "God" may be familiar and comforting, personifying a mysterious phenomenon can easily become both confusing and dangerous. Given our complex world and our scientific frame of reference, to declare that some energy field or some "impersonal presence that's greater than me" prefers our group, leads an army, writes some laws or tells us how to act seems just fantastical. It is people who write books, draw up ethical codes, lead armies and do physics.

However, Cristina's sense of "being and at-oneness," Stephanie's "deeper reality behind everything" and my own "velvety and quiet cloud that penetrated everything" all point to something field-like that is sensed around and perhaps through us. These are all versions of some sort of panentheistic and energetic field-like "something" that is "below" our everyday perceived reality. Many call it the "Ground of Being."

Since none of us experience it as limited or bounded, we say it is *omnipresent*. To all of us, this "deeper reality behind everything" comes across as lively, creative and energetic. Finally, for all of us (not to mention all mystics), it bears a positive, loving emotional tone.

THE ANALOGY

Here's the point: the field that Cristina, Doug, Stephanie and others experience *subjectively* sounds strikingly parallel to the *Quantum Vacuum Field,* doesn't it?

- *Omnipresence.* The Ground of Being is perceived as boundless, with no spatial limit to it. So too, the Quantum Vacuum Field is everywhere, even within the empty space between the planets. Both are understood or sensed as *omnipresent.*
- *Fields of energy.* Both the ineffable "reality behind everything" sensed by the mystic and the Quantum Vacuum Field (QVF) are described as "fields of energy." Both are in themselves energetic.
- *Source of Objects.* As the Quantum Vacuum Field ripples into photons, quarks and other particles, it is understood as the source of the objects in the universe. So too, the Ground of Being is sensed as "the source of" objects of reality as well as of the human mind and consciousness.
- *Formless into form.* Both the mystic's Ground of Being and the Quantum Vacuum Field have no "particular shape or form" in themselves. Yet both manifest into form, i.e., into the differentiated world. The omnipresent QVF ripples into quarks, electrons, photons and thence into our world. The omnipresent Ground of Being is perceived as being

"beneath" or "within" our world and "manifests" into everyday objects.
- *Consciousness itself.* The Ground of Being is sensed as connected with our consciousness itself: "the cattle, the fence posts, and the hard grey granite were all the same 'stuff' as me, as my own very consciousness." Recently, scientists have theorized that human consciousness is directly connected with the Quantum Vacuum Field. Nobel prize-winning physicist Roger Penrose and anesthesiologist Dr. Stuart Hameroff developed the Orchestrated Objective Reduction theory, the "Orch OR Theory" (Hameroff and Penrose, 2014). This well-regarded theory posits that consciousness is a quantum process that takes place in microtubules within brain synapses. You will recall that most quantum processes take place only near absolute zero. But physicist and oncology professor Dr. Aarat Kalra have found that even though brain matter is obviously warmer than absolute zero, quantum waves can indeed persist within it (Kalra, 2023). The implication is that human consciousness may indeed be directly involved with the Quantum Vacuum Field. This is, of course, only a theory. But if something like it is true, then the connection between human consciousness and the Quantum Vacuum Field may be more than an analogy.

Several further bits of evidence tend to reinforce the hypothesis that the Ground of Being and the Quantum Vacuum Field are one and the same. These are less well accepted claims:

- *Levitation.* There are many accounts of people who have been said to levitate (Harvey-Wilson, 2006). It was said that St. Joseph Desa of Cupertino (1603-1663), the famous "flying friar," would levitate when stimulated by light and prayer (Grosso, 2015). St. Theresa of Avila was known to levitate during prayer often enough that it became embarrassing. Other nuns tried to keep her earthbound (Adey, 2017). Indian "saints" like Nagendranath Bhaduri were reported to levitate. Yogananda quotes his friend Upenddra Chowdhury: "I SAW [Bhaduri Mahasaya of Upper Circular Road] remain in the air, several feet above the ground, last night at a group meeting" (Yogananda, 1946). Among the laity, the levitations of Eusapia Palladino (1854–1918) were witnessed by suspicious Italian, French and Spanish scientists, including a Nobel Prize winner, Charles Richet (Dennett, 2007).[5] Probably the best recorded levitations were those of Daniel Dunglas Home (1833–1886), whose ability to levitate was demonstrated and verified some dozens of times by scientists around the globe (Dennett, 2007).[6]
- *Manifestation.* Certain spiritually exceptional figures like the late Sathya Sai Baba were widely reported to be able to manifest concrete objects by dint of consciousness alone. Most famously, Sai Baba allegedly manifested sacred ashes *(vibhuti)* into the hands of devotees. Many people claimed to have witnessed this ability. There are videos that purport to show him doing it. However, other videos purport to show it as trickery.[7]
- *Parapsychological Studies.* Numerous parapsychological phenomena also reinforce this hypothesis. There is good evidence for telepathy

(Leder, 2005), clairvoyance Rhine, 1954), or remote viewing (Targ, 1977), psychokinesis (Radin, 1977), and precognition (Tart, 2009).[8] Each is supported by dozens of rigorous experiments.[9]

I am in no position to confirm or deny claims of levitation, the production of objects, or parapsychology. But if it turns out that some people, possibly spiritually "advanced" men and women, can actually levitate, manifest objects by means of consciousness alone, know what someone else is seeing or the like, it would tend to confirm a link between human awareness and the external world. It would suggest that what we subjectively perceive as the Ground of Being is indeed none other than the Quantum Ground Field beneath physical reality.

There are, of course, other ways of looking at quantum physics and at the parallels between the subjective and objective approaches that might also provide an explanation for this sense that we have. Nonetheless, I am convinced that the "nonmaterial level of reality that we can sense all around us" (*subjectively* described by Mystics on the Margins and others), and the Quantum Vacuum Field (objectively described by physicists), are like two sides of the same coin.

However there is one important distinction between these two modalities of perceiving such a foundational field. The Quantum Vacuum Field has never been associated with any particular emotion. This is to be expected, since such a field is identified by computers, spin detection devices, cosmic background imagers or just deduced, none of which register emotions (Carrol, 2006).

But *subjective* experiences *are* often emotional. Think back to the "most meaningful experience" that I asked you to recall earlier. Most would say that it did have an emotional quality, i.e., that it was positive, pleasurable, loving. As most who have had an experience of the Flow or an experience of being utterly present to a friend in a sacramental conversation can tell you, such experiences are among the most enchanting moments of our lives.

The positive valence of the Ground of Being has been variously described around the globe. To the Hindus it is *Ānanda*, the bliss of the freed soul (jiva). To the Buddhists, the Pure Land of Amida Buddha, *Sukhāvatī*, is "pleasure filled." To the Christian it is *sōzō*, being "saved," as if one has been "rescued from a dire situation."

To the Doubting Christians it is loving as well. To Anna Christina for example, "God is the experience of love, of deep truth, of presence." Elizabeth said that "it is love." Christine Anders told me that in such experiences "what I have is a feeling, like a star shining over me... It's a way of expressing the feeling of love."

As we noted in Chapter 6, when we pay attention to someone or to something unhesitatingly, we often feel ourselves connecting with this sense of "something more," or of a field beneath reality, a Ground of Being. And it is nearly always joyous. When I am having a deep conversation with someone, I feel much the same loving quality. In fact, I have come to think that being deeply present—to music, to a conversation, even to motorcycling—carries the same sense of welcoming openness as when I am experiencing the mystical openness of the Ground of Being. Doing so is an encounter with the selfsame field. Sacramental conversations whisper the transcendent. And a dose of love.

In other words, when this underlying reality is encountered subjectively, it often, if not always, carries the emotional tone of bliss, joy or love. Never does it come across as angry, unhappy or *cold*. Instead, it tends to be captivating, connective, alluring

ELECTRONS, QUARKS, THE OMNIPRESENT FIELD AND LOVE

or sublime—all very positive emotions. Almost always it is a joy to feel so undefended, so wide open! As the famous Catholic priest Bede Griffiths put this, "I encountered the void and the void is love."[10]

In a phrase, the Ground of Being is sensed as a field of love.

PHYSICS AND SPIRITUALITY

I recognize that it's tempting to make physics the final arbiter of what is real: "You see, physics proves it, so it's real!" But I do not make that claim. Rather, I am offering a hypothesis that the Ground of Being that we human beings sometimes experience is *none other* than the Quantum Vacuum Field that physicists describe. They are two modalities of encountering *one and the same field*. We can and should talk about such a field of energy objectively or subjectively, giving primacy to neither.

One implication of this analogy or possible identity: if all things are an expression of the QVF and/or Ground of Being, then all things are, in ways visible and invisible, fundamentally connected. Physics tells us that all matter and thus all people emerge from the same QVF. All our atoms and molecules, all our minds and bodies, are connected to and manifestations of one single energetic field. I'm connected to you and you to me, no matter our different religions, beliefs, races, proclivities and politics.

Just like that, my experience and that of mystics around the world and around the church is one of *sensing* these connections to each other and to the cosmos. This also implies that all human beings, all animals and all trees are actually cousins in spirit. We're all manifestations of the same mystical Ground of Being, the same Quantum Vacuum Field. We're all surrounded by and interpenetrated by the same One panentheistic reality. We may not recognize it; we may not sense it and we certainly don't always feel these connections. But we are all deeply interconnected.

Now, one important caveat: I cannot claim to be *certain* that the physicists' Quantum Vacuum Field is none other than the mystics' Ground of Being. As an erstwhile professor and a man who knows his limits, I must stress that we do not fully understand the Quantum Vacuum Field. Our knowledge of it is still too sketchy. And as someone who has studied consciousness and the mystical reality all his life (and helped found the *Journal of Consciousness Studies*) I am even more certain that our knowledge of both mysticism and consciousness is even less certain. We do not know just what consciousness is, nor just what the mystical reality is, nor whether all reality is in some sense conscious.[11] And we *definitely* cannot claim that the mystic's Ground of Being is *absolutely* none other than the Quantum Vacuum Field. We stand here at the edge of both our scientific and our spiritual knowledge.

But the parallel is striking, no?

So, here's what I can say with confidence: I *believe* that the Quantum Vacuum Field and the Ground of Being that I and others sometimes perceive are objective and subjective versions of the very same field. I am offering only a hypothesis, but a hypothesis that I *believe*. When someone experiences a mysterious energy at a church doorway or senses a vast energy stretching through a congregation or up and through a mountainside, I am *convinced* that they're experiencing the real and measurable energy that rests at the core of physical reality.

But the lack of certainty here and our inability to scientifically prove this parallel doesn't mean we have no educated intuitions or cannot offer a plausible hypothesis. I for one find this claim to be quite helpful in understanding both the world

ELECTRONS, QUARKS, THE OMNIPRESENT FIELD AND LOVE

and my mystical experiences, not to mention some of the obscure doctrines of Christianity.

Finally, based on the evidence from the world's mystical literature and my own experience, I *believe* that we can become aligned with the energetic Flow of that field.

---

1. In Physics Notes, "Physicist Dr. Hal E. Puthoff notes that the 'vacuum' is a vast reservoir of seething energy out of which particles are being formed and annihilated constantly. When quantum theory was developed, it became absolutely clear that space, if you look at it in a microscopic scale, is more like the base of a waterfall with a lot of frothy, seething activity going on, rather than just something like a placid, empty space. In fact, John Wheeler likes to point out that in a volume of empty space equivalent to a coffee cup, there is enough energy to evaporate all of the world's oceans. This is, by the way, is a basic underlying concept in modern quantum theory." See also http://www.subtleenergies.com/ORMUS/research/puthoffv.htm.
2. The first is at https://www.youtube.com/watch?v=G5yBXKvu7L4. Or you might take a look at Australian Professor Derek Leinweber's computer simulation of the appearance and disappearance of "virtual particles" very slowed down: https://www.youtube.com/watch?v=9TJe1Pr5c9Q&app=desktop#. This same illustration can be found at *http://www.physics.adelaide. edu.au/theory/staff/leinweber/VisualQCD/Nobel/index.html*. Both of these simulations can be found on our website, www.ChristianityReimagined.org.
3. You can see a different AI rendering of the foamy quality of the Quantum Vacuum Field here: www.ChristianityReimagined.org.
4. *See also* Ray, Chapter 10.
5. Dennett, pp. 121-131.
6. Dennett, pp. 107-112. Dennett reports on dozens of such cases. Adey views levitation as a cultural or religious statement only.
7. See https://youtu.be/ZXqBg1Uirbo. See also https://www.youtube.com/watch?v=lnCwebH0gyk
8. Tart, pp. 131 -149.
9. For an excellent summary of these experiments, see Tart, pp. 99–189.
10. According to his disciple, Greg Darling, in my private interview with him.
11. See the decades-long debates in the *Journal of Consciousness,* which I helped found.

RUMINATIONS ON THE VERTICAL

Over those years I've been going to churches, I came to see that I *do* believe in something "kinda sorta" like God. By this I mean that I and many others have encountered "something more" and that we can sometimes sense ourselves as part of or connected with a greater (dare I say cosmic?) energy. I know that many of us seek to, and seem to be able to, align with some greater Flow.

We come to these experiences when we let go of that to which we've clung, let go of our egos, or allow our hearts to open with little defense. If we can let go like this, if we can travel the *via negativa*, we can sometimes open our hearts more to the congregation, be less defended with others, and be readier to allow in that "something more." Opening ourselves, letting go of our defenses, we can grow our capacity to really trust.

Sometimes this openness of spirit leads to a deep gratitude for simply existing. Sometimes it means being truly present to a friend. At other times it morphs into an experience of beauty so intense that we cannot but weep, or into a tender sense of a moment as a blessing. Or it leads to gratitude for something utterly simple. Or it turns into an unusually intense sense of being conscious. Or it comes as a recognition that we're standing beneath or within "a Vastness" or a "nonmaterial reality." The seed of openness sprouts endless shoots.

Sometimes it comes as an experience of being awake, as the merest "I am." This is of course reminiscent of what God told Moses to say about him to the Israelites: "tell them that 'I am' has sent me to you" (Ex. 3:14). Perhaps that firsthand sense of "I am" is just what the term God pointed to from the start.

More recently we've learned about the Quantum Vacuum Field, the omnipresent energy field of "foaming" virtual particles at the basis of our universe. It is surprisingly parallel to the unbounded field that some people sense as the Ground of Being. I've hypothesized that these are one and the same field, encountered subjectively or objectively. Whatever energy we're sensing, we sense that—and physicists argue that—in some way the world emerged and emerges still from that fundamental energy. If we can ignore the syntax, we could say that "it created" the cosmos.

But how different this is from the thought that "In the beginning…God created the heavens and the Earth" (Gen. 1:1). This model may have made good sense 3000 years ago, but though it seems poetic, it is no longer realistic. We have to unpack such poetry to discern that when they wrote that God created the cosmos, they were unknowingly pointing towards quantum creation.

Tony, the priest, seemed to understand something like the Quantum Vacuum Field as "God," as might other traditional Christians. But I and other Mystics on the Margins can't see how it's like a human being, must less like a Father. But no matter what we believe, we *can* all accept the biblical authors' underlying intuition that the universe *does* have a single creative source, a One, abstract though it may be.

If we think of this creative source as like an energy field or a "ground," however, it's difficult to integrate the thought that this fundamental energy is watching over us, or that "God will deliver you from the deadly pestilence" or that "under his wings you will find refuge" (Ps. 91:3—4). The president of ProgressiveChristianity.org, Fred Plumer, speaks for most Mystics on the Margins when he said:

> *We don't believe in a theistic God, a persona, something that has human qualities, that is thinking about us all the time and intercedes in history. It is time to let that go (Plumer, 2012).*

This is not to say that prayer can have no effect. Prayers can and do work sometimes, as we'll see in Chapter 12. But to most Mystics on the Margins, "it is time to let go" of the thought that our prayers rise up to the creator of the stars and planets who will intercede for us. To Mystics on the Margins the Divine is the cosmos-wide but neutral energy behind *all* reality, be it good and bad, win and lose, lucky and unlucky. Our task is not to request things *of* it but to align our hearts and our lives *with* it.

On the bright side, by re-imagining the person-like metaphor in terms of an ineffable, omnipresent and energetic reality, Mystics on the Margins have found a way to protect the baby—the shining experience of the Divine—while tossing out the bathwater of the religious sectarianism, dubious science, Christian hegemony, bigotry, and nationalism that has done so much harm over the years. We can protect the baby while avoiding the dangerous claim that any one group can claim to be the one that really knows what God "wants."

By reimagining these ancient images, we can continue to center ourselves in the vibratory core of the religious life—the experience of opening our hearts to one another, to our community and to the world—and aligning ourselves with a grand vision of the transcendent.

PART FOUR
JESUS REIMAGINED

CHAPTER 8
JESUS OF NAZARETH

We've seen Mystics on the Margins talking about their church experiences, about making deep contact with one another, about their sense of the Divine and about their experiences of the transcendent. It's time to look at how this plays out in how they think about Jesus, "The Christ," and the resurrection. As we do so, we'll also begin to answer a question I've often been asked: "How is this Christian?"

Traditionally, of course, Jesus was thought of as "The Son of God" or "the Messiah." His death was "payment" for human sin, and if one believes in Jesus they're assured, after they die, of eternal life in heaven. But although I asked about Jesus in every interview, not one person offered these traditional phrases. No one asserted that Jesus was their "personal savior," that he "died for our sins" or that believing in him "saves us." Nor did any of them believe that he walked on water, was born of a virgin, or the like. To the Christians Who Doubt, he was a human being. Unusual perhaps, spiritually connected no doubt, but in the end, human.

JESUS: A BIOGRAPHICAL SKETCH

No interviewee offered what I would call a thoroughgoing portrait of the man. So, the following account is my best guess as an interviewer, as a former professor of religion, and as a man who has studied and been involved with spiritual processes all his adult life.

As we begin, we must keep in mind that his story is at best obscure. The Gospels, our main source of biographical data, were written three to six decades after his life, and were written in Greek, a language that neither Jesus nor the apostles spoke. They were testaments of faith, not chronicles of events. No CBS News stories these. To get to the historical version, then, we'll have to do some educated guessing and some leaping of imagination.

Once upon a time there lived a young Judean named Jesus who grew up in Nazareth, about 20 miles from the Sea of Galilee. Although today many wonder about this,[1] none of my interviewees said they doubted that he was a real person. We can confidently say little of his childhood, despite the centuries of children who dressed up for Christmas pageants, except that both his birth and his youth were probably in Nazareth. He had quite a few siblings and was a carpenter (Mark 6:3). At about 30, he purportedly was baptized by John, and during or near that event he seemed to undergo what William James would call a "conversion" experience. Whether due to that experience or stemming from some meditative prayer practice, deep reflection, scripture study, grace or just good genes, Jesus began talking publicly about religious matters and became renowned as a healer.[2] He was, according to the Gospels, the kind of fellow that people just wanted to hear and follow around. He soon developed a small but devoted set of disciples and followers. After a few exciting years he was killed at the hands of the Romans. Half a century later, and shaped no doubt by their respective communities of faith, a few people starting writing down stories about him. None of the Gospels were written by the people after whom they're named, except perhaps Luke. None offer eyewitness accounts of the words or actions of the man. What we have are testimonies of faith shaped and influenced by whole communities of faith.

These are just about the only facts about Jesus of which we can be pretty sure.

Jesus probably had quite a few rich and possibly permanent spiritual experiences of the Divine, the Ground of Being, the Flow, or the like—so much that he would dare quote the passage from Isaiah 61:1 that "The Spirit of the Lord is upon me." [3] (Matt. 3:16) Probably growing out of such a deep spiritual connection, combined with what must have been his quick wit and very appealing personality, he came into adulthood with enormous charisma, wisdom and personal presence.[4]

That's less unusual than we might think. Devotees of many great spiritual teachers—Ramana Maharshi, Swami Muktananda, Rajneesh, Zen Roshi Shunryu Suzuki, Sufi Sheikhs and the Trappist monk Thomas Merton, not to mention Moses, Muhammad, Lao Tzu and others—describe similar feelings. I myself used to feel something like that in my 20's when I was around my guru, Maharishi Mahesh Yogi. He had a heart-opening presence unlike anyone I've ever met, before or since. When he would walk into a lecture hall, we could all feel it. Conversations would just halt. When he began to speak, it was as if the floor and the walls of the lecture hall had dropped away and the space inside had become vast. In comparison with whatever he was, our worries or anxieties just seemed to float away. He was remarkable!

People must have sensed something much like this when Jesus walked into town. It must have been sublime just to be near him! Along with his personal magnetism, he brought remarkable verbal and metaphorical skills. He offered obscure but provocative parables that taught compassion, standing up for the poor and a love of the Divine. He consistently challenged his listeners' assumptions. Politically, he often spoke of confronting authorities, be they Jewish or Roman, on behalf of the excluded and the downtrodden.

As for his name, his fellow Judeans probably called him Yeshua ben Yosef, (Jesus Son of Joseph). Outside of his town he became "Jesus of Nazareth." However, no contemporary ever called him Jesus *Christ*. "Christ" is the English version of "*crystos*," the Greek translation of the Hebrew מָשִׁיחַ (*mašíaḥ*, messiah). *Mašíaḥ* originally meant one who is anointed or "touched with oil." *Something* about Jesus—his charisma? his defiance of authority?—must have led people to want to acknowledge his leadership by touching him with oil; *something* about him must have led his disciples to think of him as a (spiritually oriented) *political* or *military mašíaḥ*. But the term came to signify the expectation that Jesus would be like a previous *mašíaḥ*, Judas Maccabeus (190—160 BCE), who led the Jewish revolt against another powerful ruler, i.e., the Seleucid Empire.[5]

To be clear, no one in the synoptic Gospels ever called him "Jesus the *mašíaḥ*."[6] It was Paul, a man who never met Jesus and who wrote his letters two or more decades after his death, who first used *crystos* in this way. In order to bring Gentiles into the early cult, Paul taught that by identifying with the death and resurrection of this *crystos*, "one can be united with him."[7]

Over the months and years after Paul's missions, *crystos* and *mašíaḥ* morphed into something far more grand: the one and only Divine manifestation, *the* savior sent by God. After many centuries it became to Eastern Orthodox thinkers the *Pantocrator*, the omnipotent lord of the universe. To Western theologians it became "Christ in Majesty." Again, such grandiose images were foreign to, and certainly not used by, the humble carpenter from Nazareth nor by his fishermen apostles. Nor did he ever claim that he would "die for the sins of the world."[8] To our modern ears it still sounds obsolete and implausible.

For these reasons, I'll use "Jesus of Nazareth," not "Jesus Christ." (Unless I continue to shriek at my dumb typos!)

THE ETHICAL JESUS VIEWPOINT

Most Doubting Christians, and many traditional Christians, would agree with the above biographical sketch. Beyond this, however, we have to distinguish between two interrelated viewpoints of Mystics on the Margins about Jesus and the resurrection. The first perspective, the "Ethical Jesus View," tends to focus on the ethical teachings and actions of the living, talking Jesus, which some call the "pre-Easter Jesus." The second group, the "Mystical Jesus View," tends to affirm this view, but focuses additionally on his mystical life and what may have happened to him after he died. These people take more seriously what's called the "post-Easter Jesus."

Elizabeth Young, who joined the United Church of Christ as an adult, clearly holds the Ethical Jesus View. She told me that she has a "learned, historical view of Jesus that doesn't at all match the Sunday school version":

> *I don't believe in the Jesus that I learned about in Sunday school... I don't believe in the immaculate conception, for example, the stone in front of the tomb being rolled back or that he came back from the dead... But I believe in his teachings. They can serve as a grand blueprint for a way to be. They teach about encompassing love and about love itself.*

Elizabeth values Jesus as an ethical teacher. What matters to her are his messages about loving, about being true to one's deepest self, and about "doing unto others." She doesn't need the miracles, she told me. "His teachings are enough."

New York Times author Nicholas Kristof has a similar view. "I consider myself a Christian, for I admire Jesus' teachings." But he "doubts the virgin birth, resurrection and other miracles." (Kristof, 2020)

Mary Anne Grammar holds much the same view:

> I believe that Jesus of Nazareth existed. I believe in his teachings and those of the Gospels. I follow the path on which they guide me.

Exponents of this "Ethical Jesus" view tend to discount his supposed miracles. They focus on the earlier chapters of each synoptic gospel, i.e., on what he purportedly said and did during the three years of his activity. To them he was an ethical teacher of the first order, a teacher of wisdom, a social prophet and perhaps a leader of one of the Hebrew revitalization movements. He taught and modeled compassion and love. He connected with people across society's divisions and distinctions, even if it meant crossing ritual requirements like the Sabbath rules, in service of his connection with the Divine energy. And he presented his teachings as expressions of or a path towards the Divine.

Jesus taught that we have all been in bondage to the dominant cultural values—which persist still—of achievement and success, attachment to money, physical attractiveness, addictions of various kinds and the like. He was constantly encouraging his listeners to grow beyond such conventional values towards a life that was centered on connecting with each other and with the Divine. He spoke of liberating ourselves from such destructive attachments and living with greater compassion, communion and self-transcending action.

Martin Thielen, a fundamentalist Christian pastor who became a progressive Doubting Christian, probably captured this viewpoint best when he wrote that he has a huge affinity for the Jesus who loved sinners, extended grace, welcomed outsiders, blessed children, exhibited compassion, engaged in acts of kindness, challenged fundamentalist religious leaders, and demanded justice.

Then Thielen continues:

I believe in Jesus's call to love, serve, care, and practice compassion. I believe in Jesus's example of inclusion and grace. I believe in Jesus's example of breaking down human barriers and prejudices. I believe in Jesus's challenge to forgive people who harm us. I believe in Jesus's command to seek justice in the world. I believe in Jesus's overwhelming love for the poor and marginalized of society (Thielen, 2024).

This "Ethical Jesus" view stresses this "love, serve, care, and ... compassion." Many mentioned his "second great commandment"—"You shall love your neighbor as yourself."

The Ethical Jesus Viewpoint, then, focuses less on who or what Jesus was as a spiritual being and more on understanding, honoring and following what he purportedly said and did while he was alive. Many also appreciated his encouragement to let go of that which constricts us, and to align with the flow of the Divine.

THE MYSTICAL JESUS VIEW

Every mystic on the margins would agree with these "Ethical Jesus" claims that Jesus was a first-rate ethical teacher. Every one of them takes guidance from his example. However, the "Mystical Jesus View" adds that Jesus was a remarkable being who probably had unusually deep spiritual experiences and may even have resurrected.

Rev. Ted Harris in Stockholm, for example, said, "Jesus was someone who lived and manifested the love of the

Ground of Being and shows me how I can live my life." Sister Gail Worcelo agreed that it was probably "because of his spiritual development" that the tradition came to see Jesus as a "central figure of wholeness and stability, holding a central line." He must have been "one with the source, something vibrational."

Stephanie Bradbury speaks particularly elegantly of this stance:

> God is the flow, being in the flow is what it's all about. There is no separation between me and the flow of the Divine. Jesus said, "the kingdom of God is within you." We're all both physical and this ultimate energy. We might lose track of our true nature, we might forget it. But we remain both. We're physical and spiritual beings learning to live into the flow of the Divine... Jesus is the one who figured this out.[9]

Finally, theologian Marcus Borg was probably the most famous advocate of this "Mystical Jesus" view. He remarked in a lecture that Jesus was a "Jewish mystic," by which he meant "a person for whom God, or the Spirit or the sacred, is an experiential reality":

> The evidence that Jesus was a Jewish mystic is early, widespread, and persuasive... His relationship to the Spirit was utterly central, or foundational, to everything else he was. Jesus, I am convinced, knew the immediacy of the sacred in his own experience. He knew the reality of an unbordered relationship with God in his own experience (Borg, 2000).

People with this "Mystical Jesus" view tend to hold that through some sort of process, Jesus came to sense that "I and the Father are One" (John 10:30).[10] His use of the intimate term "Abba" (Father) for the Divine energy suggests that Jesus came to sense himself as near to or immersed in the quasi-palpable sense of "something more."

Informants who hold this "Mystical Jesus" view tend to have had one or several mystical experiences themselves, or to have been graced with something spiritually unusual. Some may have sensed "an impersonal presence that is greater than me," known "a kind of being and at-oneness," heard the voice of someone they "couldn't have" or had some other non-ordinary experiences. In part because they have, they are probably more open to the idea that Jesus spoke out of his experience of the mystery than are many. As progressive minister Pastor Dawn put it,

> *[Jesus] was a fully human person who had a fully Divine experience or series of experiences. How he got there is open for questioning... [but he] began to teach after he had many of his own experiences of the Divine... He began to realize that there are no enemies, no strangers, no people that were different than him...all of us have Godness within (Pastor Dawn, 2012).*

Many spiritual teachers and practitioners from across the ages and continents—even today—are believed to have similarly frequent and vivid experiences of such a non-sensory reality. Some enter *momentarily* into a non-ordinary state of consciousness, others see it shining throughout tangible ordinary reality *longer term*. A few live within it *permanently*. We might call such permanent infusions of spirit "enlightenment," "becoming God-infused," "aligning with the Great Flow," being "immersed in a non-sensory reality" or becoming a "mystic."

According to this "Mystical Jesus" view, Jesus of Nazareth was, like history's mystics and many of my informants, a highly evolved spiritual person. He apparently sensed, lived and spoke out of the spiritual reality on a day-to-day and permanent basis. His visions of the heavens opening, his visions in the wilderness, and his long fasting prayers all suggest that he was such a soul. He may even have had deeper spiritual capacities than many other mystics. Saying that "I and the Father are one" suggests that he experienced no borderlines between himself and the Divine.

According to some of my interviewees, he was a "spiritual way-finder" whose ethical teachings and parables grew out of his considerable spiritual depth. He forged a path that all can follow. As Stephanie put it, we are all "physical and spiritual beings learning to live into the flow. Jesus is the one who figured this out." Exponents of this viewpoint seek to manifest in their own lives both his ethical teachings and the spiritual depths he apparently knew and lived.

JESUS IN SPIRITUAL CONTEXT

Now there is one claim that I and the Mystics on the Margins who hold either viewpoint simply cannot accept: that he was "the *only* Son of God." Here we must part company with the traditionalists. To us, this "only son" claim has been the source, over the centuries, of the religion's sectarian, divisive and dangerous abuses. It's led to an uncrossable line between Jesus and the rest of us, to dangerous claims of Christian hegemony and to far too many religious wars. But to *no* Mystic on the Margins was Jesus the *only* "son of God" nor the *only* "spirit-infused human being."[11] Marcus Borg:

> To affirm that Jesus is the decisive revelation and disclosure of God need not imply that he is the only manifestation of God... The sacred has also been known...in the major figures of the biblical tradition such as Moses, Elijah and the prophets, and...in other religions in addition to Judaism and Christianity (Borg, 1998).[12]

The claim that he was the "only Son of God" was first

recorded in the first chapter of John (vs. 14), which was written between 90 and 100 CE. As for why this tendentious claim may have come up, it probably began at the very beginning. When people first met Jesus of Nazareth, he was so highly charismatic and astonishing, such a creative teacher and someone who spoke of the Divine so intimately that he must have come across as utterly unlike anyone else. They must have thought, "Wow, he's the *only* fellow who has ever existed that's like that!" And that innocent and plausible thought was probably the beginning of the claim that he was the one and only son. He must have seemed unique, *sui generis,* one of a kind.

After all, some 2000 years ago, people in dusty Judea were probably unaware of any other such folks. They no doubt had never heard of Indian, Tibetan, Chinese or any other culture's sages or gurus. They were unlikely to be aware of the 6th Century BCE Gautama Buddha, for example, or the third century BCE Dharmarakṣita, or of the authors of the Hindu Upaniṣhads like Uddālka, who also must have been similarly evolved. They probably had no knowledge of the 4th Century BCE Chinese sage, LaoTzu, the purported author of the Tao Te Ching (Dao de Jing). In other words, though there were no doubt similarly "evolved" human beings at and before his time, his apostles no doubt never had heard of them. They had no way to know that though Jesus was probably a "highly evolved person" or an "enlightened being," he was simply *not* the one and only such human being!

In other words, I can understand what might have led the early disciples and the author of John to think that Jesus was the "only" such man. People who encountered him must have thought, "man, there's just nobody like him!" But if they did, they were simply wrong.

Again, in the course of human history there have been lots of other "fully enlightened people." Even today we have heard of or even met many enlightened priests, gurus and spiritual teachers: Tich Nhat Hanh, Maharishi Mahesh Yogi, Tomas Merton, the Dalai Lama, Gandhi, Martin Luther King and many others. Countless men and women today have been meditating for half a century or more. There are also "old souls" who just seem to have been born wiser than the rest of us. Indeed, there are so many enlightened people today that scientists have found enough of them to draw conclusions about their brain mechanisms (Hanson, 2014).

If he appeared today, people would probably call a fellow like Jesus "an enlightened being," a "highly evolved soul" or perhaps a "great teacher" But never would we say he was the *only* such!

That this claim of *sui generis* was inserted into the creed— "We believe in one Lord, Jesus Christ, the *only* Son of God" (emphasis mine)—was probably also political. Constantine the Great summoned the First Council of Nicaea in 325 CE in order to resolve the competing theological approaches within his wide-spread territory. The claim that Jesus was the "one and only" was part of the council's way of ordaining their way as the one true way.

Given that I hold that Jesus of Nazareth was not the "one and only," I've come to regard descriptions of him to be, at heart, descriptions of *any human being* who has achieved something like that level of spiritual development. So too, I've come to think of the word "Christ" similarly. As noted above, the word is a translation of the Hebrew *mašiaḥ*, which originally meant "the anointed one," as anointing was the Judean sign of leadership. Jesus was no doubt given this title because of his charisma and his apparent connection with the underlying Ground of Being. I take the word "christ" as applying also to any person who is so connected, i.e., who taps into the high voltage wire that is the Divine Energy, and who endeavors to lead from it.

For example, I see "I am in the Father (i.e. the Divine

energy) and the Father (the Divine energy) is in me" (John 14:11) as describing anyone who is experiencing a panentheistic reality. Similarly, "before Abraham was, I (in my wide-open Vastness), I am"(John 8:58) describes the sense of being beyond time that is an element of such non-ordinary experiences. These are reasonable descriptions of any man or woman who feels that connected. Or when Luke's Gospel declares that "the spirit of the Lord was upon [Jesus]"(Luke 4:18), the text is actually describing just what it's like when anyone feels themselves filled with the spiritual reality: it's as if their chest is so full, so overflowing with spirit that they can scarcely breathe!

One of the things I learned from Rev. Stephanie Bradbury is that we human beings don't tend to respond to abstractions. We respond in a more heartfelt way to stories, especially stories of someone. So, Christianity wisely *personifies* abstract principles though its stories of Jesus of Nazareth. Stephanie said,

> *Jesus was a master of making the spiritual sensible. He was the master of taking the spiritual into the concrete. "This is my body and this is my blood" is a way of talking about something spiritual and complex and making it tangible. In sharing it we are saying that we are already the Divine. We are this!*[13]

By focusing on stories of one man, Jesus, who was apparently in alignment with the larger energy, Christianity is describing the spiritual path for *anyone* who seeks to walk, interact and live within the spiritual reality. For the Ethical Jesus camp, the path is principally ethical, social and perhaps political. For the Mystical Jesus viewpoint, the path is an ethical one plus coming to live long-term within the reality that he exemplified. By personalizing this principle, the tradition is showing us all what it is to live a spiritually healthy life. The actions and words they attribute to Jesus of Nazareth are modeling what it is for any of us to follow either path.

Most Doubting Christians find church meaningful, beautiful and emotionally freeing and so we attend regularly. All of us revere and model ourselves on the teachings and actions of this crowning figure, Jesus of Nazareth. To answer the question that we asked at the chapter's beginning, because we follow the examples and teachings of Jesus, we Mystics on the Margins can rightly call ourselves "Christians."

---

1. According to a 2015 survey, some 22 percent of British adults don't believe Jesus was a real person. https://talkingjesus.org/wp-contefhearent/uploads/2018/04/Talking-Jesus-dig-deeper.pdf
2. Perhaps his fasting in the desert for forty days, mentioned in Matt. 4:2, had something to do with his development, though this account was probably a reference to Ex. 34:28. In any case this alleged fast happened *after* the extraordinary baptism.
3. To be quite correct, Jesus said "the spirit of God is upon me because he has anointed me to proclaim good news to the poor." Luke 4:18. That is, the spirit is upon him because he is moved to preach. But the unbelieving pilgrims who quoted this take it in a more spiritual sense.
4. We are told about the crowds in Luke 9:12 &14. In Luke 19:3–4 we are told that as Jesus walked into Jericho, the crowds were so thick that Zacchaeus had to climb a tree to see him.
5. Judas Maccabeus was called a *mašíaḥ* because he brought the Jewish people to safety from the Seleucid empire; it was hoped that Jesus would help the people find safety from the Romans.
6. Cf. Carmichael, p.188. The more recent Jesus Seminar denies that any of Mark 8: 27–30 represents the words of Jesus of Nazareth.
7. Rom. 6:5. English Standard Version.
8. I have not been able to find any Biblical source for this oft-used phrase!
9. Stephanie Bradbury, personal communication. N.B., "The kingdom ... is within you" is taken from the ancient King James translation. The NRSV has this passage "the Kingdom of God is *among* you" and the Jesus Seminar's translation has "God's imperial rule is right there in your presence."
10. I don't make it a habit of quoting John, since the Jesus seminar doubts that any of it was actually spoken by Jesus. However, this phrase is so close to "The Spirit of God is Upon Me," quoted above, that I choose to use it.
11. As theologian Marcus Borg describes him.
12. Borg 1998, pp. 84-5.
13. Stephanie Bradbury interview.

CHAPTER 9
RESURRECTION REIMAGINED

I confront the Easter story humbly, since it's been so deeply important for so many millions of believers. But confront it I must, because it is central to the religion, because most Doubting Christians have had to confront it, and because there is so much confusion about it.

We all know the basic outlines: Jesus was a spiritually oriented mystic, ethical teacher, cultural gadfly and leader. He was crucified, according to progressive Christian Carl Krieg,

> because he was a troublemaker...Jesus had started a movement that threatened the power structure, the established economic/social system that benefited the rich and powerful, and so he was eliminated (Krieg, 2023, pt. 1).

After Jesus died in that famously gruesome manner, according to the Gospel accounts his body was wrapped and carried into a cave or tomb, in front of which a rock was rolled. A few days later people began to claim that the rock had been rolled back and his corpse had vanished. Sometime later, a further tale also spread that a few people had "seen" him alive.

Though the church teaches these tales as facts, indeed miraculous facts, few people actually believe this story (Paul, 2017).[1] The survey that found that 57% of people who attend church once a month or more do believe this tale, implies that some 43% of churchgoers don't! A mere 17% of all people in once Christian Great Britian accept the Biblical account of the Resurrection (BBC News, 2017).[2] Surprisingly, one in four Evangelicals are not convinced that the resurrection of Jesus was a real historical event (Ligonier Ministries, 2014). Given this, it's hardly surprising that most Doubting Christians don't accept the Biblical account at face value.

I heard two interrelated ways to make sense of the Easter claims, which were of a piece with our two "views" of Jesus.

THE RESURRECTION-AGNOSTIC VIEWPOINT

Not one person with whom I spoke was sure about what happened "in those days" or what it meant. Even though they all attended their respective churches regularly, not a single interviewee or hospital patient volunteered that because Jesus was resurrected, their "sins are forgiven" or "they are saved." No one thought that appeasing a God who was angry over humanity's sins required satisfaction, or thought that Jesus's death had done the job. Virtually everyone I spoke with was at best "agnostic" about the claims of resurrection.

Elizabeth Young was perhaps clearest about her agnosticism:

> *I can't believe in something as weird as the resurrection. There are an awful lot of things we don't understand about it. However, I've decided I don't need to know what I believe about it... It's a long way from believing that the crucifixion happened to believing there was a body in a tomb that rolled back the stone, dead but alive.*

Pennie Curry similarly said, "I wonder about the video version of the resurrection. It's a mystery I can't explain. But I stopped trying."

Rochelle Willingham, a Catholic from Texas who was a graduate student in religion, offered a particularly lyrical way to think about it. She encounters it not as fact but "as if it's a book of fiction. I derive inspiration from it, even if I don't believe it's real." Seeing it as a metaphor like that suggests that St. Paul was wrong that "if Christ has not been raised, our preaching is worthless, and your faith is in vain." (1 Cor. 15:14) For even if it's but a "book of fiction," this saga has been incredibly inspiring to many millions, whether or not one sees it as allegorical.

Pennie, Elizabeth and Rochelle are all, we may say, agnostic about the "video version" of the resurrection. And this makes sense because its claims are both so implausible and so unprovable. But I also note that such agnosticism allows a churchgoer to enjoy the tale while both sidestepping the question of truth or falsity and avoiding confronting fellow churchgoers who hold it as "gospel."

On the other hand, like Rochelle, most Mystics on the Margins take it as a rich metaphor. Jennifer, a Unitarian, was perhaps the most poetic about this:

> I have trouble believing the stories of the immaculate conception, walking on water or the resurrection. But these stories have a largesse. They're immense and unexpected. They represent the immensity of grace-filled love. But you don't have to believe them. I take them as metaphors.

I think all would agree that the stories do indeed bear a "largess," and that they represent the "immensity of grace-filled love." I heard many nuanced versions of that "largess." Because of our egos, our self-orientation we fall out of alignment with the Divine Flow. When we do, we suffer over pain, difficulty or death of our hopes. In the face of that pain, we must let go of our egoic way of being. Letting go and then letting go some more is called the *via negativa,* the path of negation. One author cleverly describes this path as "adding to your life by subtracting" (McKay, 2015). If we do let go and let go successfully, we can become transformed, i.e., resurrect. We can be reborn into a new way of living, a way that is more deeply aligned with the Flow of the Ground of Being.

Just as Jesus died to his old life before being reborn, so too, before we can take on a new way of living we must die to our old way of being. Like Jesus, if we can let go of a narrow way of seeing and living, we can then "resurrect" into a wider frame of reference, one that includes others' needs more, while staying deeply connected to the Flow of the Divine. Just as Jesus had to go through pain, loneliness and darkness before he got to rebirth, so too we will inevitably encounter pain and loss. Similarly, just as Jesus faced death and walked unhesitatingly towards it, so too must we.

The implications about the resurrection are as endless as the sermons about it. This whole tale then offers a model for engaging self and others, even unto death, while letting go of clinging to our fantasies of how things "must" go, avoiding change, or fearing loss.

THE MYSTICAL-RESURRECTION VIEWPOINT

Everyone who holds the Mystical-Resurrection viewpoint is similarly agnostic about the video version. But some of us (I say "us," for I am in this boat) add the possibility that something more supernatural, more mystical, may be involved.

Margareta is one such. After declaring her agnosticism—"I don't know about the resurrection...and I don't much accept it as factual"—Margareta makes room for the possibility that Jesus may have had remarkable spiritual "skills":

> *I accept that there's a mystical side of religion. And I respect that there are things I cannot explain. I've had enough mystical experiences to know that people could "see" Jesus. And that things can unfold in unexpected ways.*

Ted Harris concurs: "We know only 5% of reality. I can't pretend to grasp the eternal or what might have happened."

This viewpoint is particularly alert to claims of uncommon capacities. This may be because many of us have ourselves experienced some of these unexpected abilities. Many of us have had experiences that reach beyond the everyday. Some have been thinking about someone "just before they called." Others have known inside that a loved one is in danger, or known the moment when a beloved relative has died (Pew Research, 2023).[3] In addition, many of us have read about children who know details of a supposedly previous life (Stevenson, 2000). Some mentioned even more unexpected human abilities, like levitation "by consciousness alone," psychokinesis or moving objects merely by intention, and the like (Dennett, 2007; Tart, 2009).

As we'll see in Chapter 16, several Mystics on the Margins suggested that both Near Death Experiences (NDEs) and accounts of Reincarnation provide evidence of some sort of existence after we die. We're with William James here:

> *the world of our present consciousness is only one out of many worlds of consciousness that exist, and...those other worlds must contain experiences which have a meaning for our life* (James, 2009).[4]

Given this, the people that hold the "Mystical View" suggest that we should save room for the unexpected and the ununderstood. In truth, we just don't know the limits of our spiritual capacities.

The agnosticism of the Christians who wonder about the actual events is certainly understandable. Nonetheless, the evidence we have seen suggests the possibility that death may not be merely a blankness. Taken together, Near-Death Experiences, the recall of past lives and other evidence suggests that after we pass away, the consciousness of Jesus of Nazareth may have continued in some way.[5] Perhaps Jesus was, in some way we do not understand, able to capitalize on such an ability.

THE VIDEO VERSION: A BEST GUESS

We will never know just what happened "in those days." The "video version" is long lost behind the mists of time. But considering the emphasis traditional Christianity puts on the Easter narrative, it behooves us to thoughtfully consider what may have happened. So below I offer my best guess as an interviewer of Mystics on the Margins, a former professor of religion, and a spiritual explorer.

First, let's dispense with the pernicious account that the Jewish authorities condemned Jesus to the cross (Matt. 26:57-68; Mark 15:1-15). It is highly unlikely. After all, the Roman authorities had all the power and controlled all the means of execution. Consulting with any non-Roman group about punishment would have seriously diminished their authority. And there's not a shred of non-biblical evidence—in either Roman or Jewish records—of their consulting the Judean Sanhedrin about Jesus of Nazareth.[6] Few scholars—and not a single interviewee—accept this antisemitic trope.

Now, no matter who condemned him, according to the stories that we have, Jesus was nailed to a cross and soon died. His body was then taken down and put in "a rock-hewn tomb"

(Matt. 27:61; Mark 15:46; Luke 23:53) or in "a garden and in the garden a new tomb" (John 19:41). A rock was then rolled across the opening.[7]

Then the account continues that a day or two later, at "the end of the Sabbath," Mary Magdalene and Mary the mother of James returned to the tomb. Much to their surprise they found the rock rolled back and no corpse.

Since so much of Christianity's claims and history rests on this pivotal moment, let's pause here. For the accounts are jarringly inconsistent. In Mark, which is the earliest account, Mary and Mary see the stone rolled back. They see no body but instead see a "young man dressed in a white robe" who is "sitting on the right side" (Mark 16:5). Mark tells us nothing about this young man, who he was or where he came from, only that he informs Mary and Mary that Jesus has "risen."

At that point the two women "fled from the tomb, for terror and amazement had seized them; and they said nothing to anyone, for they were afraid" (Mark 16:8).[8] They were so freaked out that they didn't tell a soul. I certainly wouldn't blame them! They must have been utterly confused, doubting themselves and disbelieving their own eyes, wondering if he didn't actually die. (In Mark 16:9 ff, by the way, Jesus appeared and spoke to them. But since according to the *New International Version* "the earliest manuscripts and some other ancient witnesses do not have verses 9–20," this was probably a later addition. Even from the earliest times, the accounts were mushrooming.)

Now, Mark was written around 66–70 CE. Luke was written some 10–15 years later, around 85–95 CE. By Luke's time the white-robed young man had morphed into *two* men who were "in dazzling clothes." They give the two women a longer explanation about the missing corpse (Luke 24:4–5). By Matthew's time (85–90 CE), the tale had mushroomed again into something even more astonishing. First, there was a "great earthquake." The two dazzling fellows now became "an angel of the Lord, descending from heaven... His appearance was like lightning and his clothing white as snow." (Matt. 28: 2–3). The whole tale was now even more astounding, suggesting perhaps the author's hope for creating what today we would call "buzz."

Now rather than fleeing from the tomb and "saying nothing to anyone," as Mark had it, Matthew offers just the opposite: the two women "ran to tell his disciples" (Matt. 28:8). By the time of Luke, the two Marys had mushroomed into more than four, "Mary Magdalene, Joanna, Mary the Mother of James and other women!" Furthermore, in addition to "seeing an angel of the lord descending from heaven," Luke adds that as they left the tomb Jesus appeared, "said 'Greetings'" and they "took hold of his feet and worshipped him." Jesus then says, "go and tell my brothers to go to Galilee" (Matt. 28:9–10). Quite the concatenation of accretions!

Given these widely varying accounts, it's hard to know just what actually might have happened. It may have happened much as one or another account has it. Jesus may have come back to life, rolled back the stone, walked out and left a white-robed caretaker to hang out in the tomb, as some people believe. Or he may have sent an angel down from heaven to explain.

But I and other Mystics on the Margins tend to wonder. First of all, was he actually laid in a nice, newly hewn tomb? The corpses of practically everyone else the Romans crucified were "ripped and consumed by wild dogs and birds" (Krieg, 2023, pt. 2). But even granting that he was actually entombed, did Mary Magdalene and Mary the mother of James actually find the right tomb? If Golgotha was anything like it is today, it was something of a maze and the tombs were not marked. Is it possible that in their urgency they found the wrong "cave?" Or might some devotees have "stolen away" the body as the authorities feared? (Romans were worried that "his disciples [might] steal him away, and tell the people that 'he has risen from the dead'" (Matt. 27:64, Matt. 28:13). Might some devoted apostles have indeed spirited him away before Mary Magdalene and Mary the mother of James even showed up?

Whatever they actually saw, the story of a corpse-less tomb soon spread among the devotees.

Such a phenomenon is hardly unparalleled. Members of small religious groups are famously susceptible to "mass hallucinations" or "brainwashing" (West, 1993). In small religious groups, one member's claim to have "seen" something can lead to the whole community's "seeing" it. The clearest example of such a mass hallucination comes from professor of religion Dr. Scott Lowe. In his youth he was a member of the small community that had gathered around Franklin Jones, a.k.a. "Da Free John." One day, someone in the community claimed to have "seen" that the sun had been ringed for several hours by a purple corona. Lowe himself had not seen anything out of the ordinary that afternoon, nor had anyone pointed to the sky or mentioned it at dinner that night. But several days after the "event," Dr. Lowe relates, "the community was buzzing with increasingly dramatic tales of the astronomical marvels." Over the next few days, Lowe asked several devotees what they had seen, but no one offered a "satisfactory answer." He concludes that even though many members asserted that they had seen it, "it seems most likely that no one actually saw the marvel in the sky." Nonetheless, agreement with that purple-corona claim became a marker of the "real" devotees. Those who hadn't "seen" it were soon expelled.

Since such mass hallucinations are most likely to happen at times of communal stress—and certainly the death of their leader would qualify—perhaps something like this was at work among the apostles after the death of their charismatic leader.

In any case, the story spread like brush fire. On the one hand, as many firmly believe, these stories spread because they were all true. On the other hand, perhaps something else was at work. And here we can take a hint from the famous modern study, *When Prophecy Fails* (Festinger, 1956). In it, Leon Festinger and his colleagues studied a small, cultic group in early 1950s Chicago, "The Seekers," who prophesized that life on Earth would end in a great flood around Christmastime, 1954.

The floods didn't come, of course. But the Seekers didn't just say, "Oops, no flood, I guess we were wrong," and quietly fade away. Instead, they came up with an altogether new and self-justifying message: they "had spread so much light that God had saved the world from destruction." Soon they began an energetic campaign of talking with others, calling newspapers and doing what they could to spread their newly transformed message.

They did this, argues Festinger, in the unconscious hope that by convincing others, their beliefs and life commitments wouldn't seem so embarrassingly wrongheaded. The principle of group psychology, Festinger suggests, seems to be that the more people who believe a new story, the less preposterous it seems—both to themselves and to others. The deeper one's commitment to their original beliefs, says Festinger, the harder those commitments are to relinquish and the greater the participants' need for self-justification. And that's what the Seekers did.

Perhaps like the Seekers, the disciples revised their message from that of Jesus's ethical, activist and perhaps political teachings into their more audacious claims about his death and miraculous reappearances. We've seen how, much like the Seekers', the Apostles' accounts and message rapidly evolved and grew in glory, importance and supernaturalism. They found parallels in the Hebrew Bible, especially in Isaiah, and they, especially Paul, soon began an energetic campaign of spreading their now-revised message to both Jews and Gentiles.

1. See also BBC News, April 9, 2017 and *Premier Christianity,* April 5, 2023, "Why the 25% of Christians Who Deny the Resurrection Aren't True Believers."
2. ComRes surveyed 2,010 British adults by telephone, between 2 and 12 February 2017. The research was commissioned by BBC local radio for Palm Sunday. The survey suggested that 31% of all Christians believe the Bible version word-for-word, rising to 57% among "active" Christians. Exactly half (50%?) of all people surveyed did not believe in the resurrection at all while only 9% of non-religious people believe in the Resurrection, 1% of whom say they believe it literally. https://www.bbc.com/news/uk-england-39153121.
3. Alper found that 38% say they have had a strong feeling that someone who has passed away was communicating with them from beyond this world.
4. James, p. 392.
5. Indeed some 46% of Christians in 2023 believe in some form of life after death.
6. As Aslan points out, the Jewish authorities would never have gathered on a Sabbath, nor would they have gathered in the "High Priest's Courtyard" (Matt. 26:57). The Gospel writers of the late first century may have been trying to shift responsibility for Jesus's death from the shoulders of their Roman converts and hosts.
7. John, written last, is the most highly mythologized account. But if there was a tomb, it was no doubt *some*place.
8. The New Revised Standard Version of Mark 16:8 says "some of the most ancient authorities bring the book to a close at the end of verse 8. Later versions include verses 9–20, but are marked as being doubtful." I focus here on the earlier version.

RUMINATIONS ON THE STORY OF JESUS

One phrase that several interviewees mentioned was the famous line that Jesus purportedly uttered during the last meal: "Take, eat, this is my body." (Mark 14:22). Though these are probably not his words,[1] several of my friends who are Christians Who Doubt read this as saying that even the tiniest morsel of food or drink is a manifestation of the same invisible and sacred reality within which Jesus purportedly lived. He saw the wafer as food, yes, but at heart he saw it as the vast and sacred reality that he lived within. He was saying, "This too is sacred."

It would take a very clear and deep consciousness to see a morsel of pita or a sip of wine as an instance of the infinite spiritual reality (or the Quantum Vacuum Field). If he or anyone said this from their experience, as we would hope, they must have lived within a very wide-open vision of reality. Anyone who saw him or herself as the same 'stuff' as a piece of bread must have had an awareness which penetrated to the deepest levels!

Reading these words in this light requires however that we approach them in an entirely new way. The stories and words of Jesus are taught by the church as historical *facts*. However, most liberal ministers take the stories not so much as facts but as *metaphors*, which is no doubt more reasonable than taking them as a "video version."

Nonetheless, the church and even the most liberal ministers do not often ask about the underlying vision or level of consciousness that might have allowed a man to see at such a level, i.e., far deeper than most of us. Even if we don't accept that he was the one and only human who was permanently connected with the Divine, Jesus was clearly seeing at a much deeper level than most of us. He embodied what a God-infused human being looks like. And the whole point of his ministry was to encourage us all to live as he lived and love as he loved, both of which grow out of seeing as he saw. Far too few people recognize that there must have been an underlying depth of consciousness that allowed him to see as he saw and be who he was.

Unless the church promotes and proclaims that these stories are scraps and hints of an inspiring man's level of consciousness, and unless it asks how we might gain the same, it misses the whole challenge. The real question about Jesus has to do with the mystery within which he must have lived. His stories and his words grew directly out of the connection that he must have known, the state of consciousness that he must have lived. His healings came directly from that state. His stories and parables seemed to grow from that state, and they challenge us to discover *that* for ourselves. Recovering a similar level of awareness is the real task that he left us: to find and live an equally wide-open soul as the author of those lines.

To be clear, unlike many I don't see the Gospel stories as *metaphor*. I see the whole account as a *description* of what it is to be a human being who is deeply connected with spirit. I'm with Doug Kruschke here:

> *On the journey to realize the highest potential, there are challenges. We must let go of lower-self which feels like a death. In the face of that danger, we must be willing to stand up and be in the flow. Doing so requires that I'm willing to go through danger and travails. If I do, I can begin to live anew after the death of my ordinary life. The Easter story tells me that Jesus lived in the flow, even unto death, and so can we all.*

However mythologized they may be, the Synoptic Gospels (Matthew, Mark and Luke) are *describing* what it is to live in the flow. As such, they're offering an invitation to the *"Imitatio Christi,"* i.e., an invitation to align ourselves at a similar depth with the Ground of Being.

As for the resurrection, I see the tale of Jesus's death as an account of how a spiritually evolved human being might encounter impending death. Luke has him uttering the touching lines, "Father, forgive them, for they know not what they do," and "into thy hands I commit my spirit" (Luke 23:46). These words demonstrate the presence of mind and depth of compassion out of which such a man might speak. They suggest that he passed away, like so many other renowned spiritual leaders, as wide-open and ego-free as he was in life.

This Easter story was certainly not history's only such noble death. According to the Buddhist tradition, the Buddha recognized he was dying, laid down, and, unafraid, offered some wise final words to his followers. The twentieth-century guru Ramana Maharshi was said to have chosen to forego treatment for cancer and died peacefully and in full lotus meditation posture. Ramakrishna is purported to have said to his wife as he was dying, "Why do you cry? Because the one who is, is not going to die." And to his disciples who begged him to eat he said, "Why depend on this body? This body is gone and rotten."

The point of the Gospel account, as well as these others, is that just as Jesus remained compassionate, centered and connected to the Flow unto death, so too *we* can reach beyond our egos. We too can transcend our fears and abide in a similar wide-open Divine awareness. We too can live and die without inner grasping and stop clinging to our old ways of being.

On the other hand, Mark has his last words a discouraged *"Eloi Eloi lama sabachthani,"* "My God, my God, why has thou forsaken me?" (Mark 15:34, found in Ps. 22:1 and Isa. 49:14) which might suggest that his ego may have finally given in and he temporarily fell out of his connection with the Ground of Being.

Whether he fell out of connection with the Divine or not, Mystics on the Margins consistently told me that they read the account of Easter as an "immense and unexpected" story of getting caught in our ego-needs, letting go the grip of those egos, caring for others and living a life in the Divine Flow.

Even if our analogy with *When Prophecy Fails* is correct, and even if the apostles were indeed caught up in a group hallucination, considering their success, the Gospel authors seemed to have tapped into some deep vein of truth about life, death, hope and spiritual connection. The noble death of Jesus, the inspiring visions of him, the possibility of his appearing again, and so much more seemed to tap into untold depths of human possibility.

Taking the Biblical story neither as fact nor as metaphor but rather as descriptive of a level of consciousness runs counter the *traditional* way to understand his death and resurrection. The very idea of relinquishing our attachments to ourselves, transcending our fear of death, letting go our grip on our fragile egos, and living in the Divine Ground even unto death offers a truly astounding vision of possibilities! It challenges us to raise our consciousness, to self-transcend in alignment with the Divine energy, even beyond death.

And whether one believes firmly in the historical details of this tale or refuses to deny the laws of biology, we can all hold that some or many human beings can self-transcend and align with the Divine energy. Neither our tears, our being emotionally affected, nor our sense of encountering a greater reality disappear if the story of the resurrection turns out to be true or a highly mythologized tale that early believers told in order to strengthen their cult. For no matter the truth of the "video version," Christianity's central claim that it's possible to be as awake as was Jesus, awake enough to transcend death, still remains and inspires.

The resurrection story is, above all, claiming that it is possible for a human being, for anyone, to reach beyond the visible and beyond death.

In this light, the resurrection story may be taken as a single instance of a larger set of claims about the kind of wide-open life that is possible and that Jesus probably lived. Whether we believe that Jesus was fully awake or not, we can all affirm Christianity's core insight that some or all human beings may actually become wide-open, in life and perhaps after. It points to the claim that becoming fully alive is possible and that death may not be the final end.

---

1. According to the Jesus Seminar.

PART FIVE
CHRISTIANITY'S COMPONENTS REIMAGINED

CHAPTER 10

REIMAGINING SIN AND SALVATION

Livingston Van De Water (Van), a tall, handsome sixtyish professor of cell biology, is a warm and kindly soul who also thinks clearly, like the scientist that he is. The United Church of Christ in which he came of age wasn't a fire and brimstone church, but he still heard a lot in it about "sin" and "salvation." He told me,

> Without really realizing it, I was carrying this burden that I'm going to hell. That I'm going to be damned in some way for whatever I'd done without knowing it. We all carried a load from this. Some of the churches have done some horrendous stuff to the kids. And so people think, I thought, 'thanks anyway, I have all the religion I need!'

"Sin" is probably the most loaded word in Christianity. The burden he carried from it was a huge part of why, in his 20's, Van abandoned the church. Indeed, this one word probably sent more people fleeing Christianity than any other! It's a sin to "commit adultery." It's a sin "if a man lies with a male as with a woman." Getting drunk, being effeminate, masturbating, gossiping, being covetous, being haughty... The list of things that have been called sins literally goes on and on. Break any of them and you would (supposedly) "be an offense to God" (Mortal Sin, s.d.).[1]

The Gospel of Mark lists fornication, theft, murder, adultery, avarice, wickedness, deceit, licentiousness, envy, slander, pride and folly (Mark 7:21–3). In his letter to the Romans (1: 29–31) Paul adds envy, murder, strife, deceit, craftiness, gossip, slander, god hating, insolence, haughtiness, boastfulness, inventor of evil, rebellious towards parents, foolish, faithless, heartless, ruthless. The Catechism of the Catholic Church (CCC) enumerates 38 "sins," which adds to the above lists: adultery, anger, avarice, blaspheming, coveting, defrauding the workingman of his wage, drunkenness, emulation, extortion, gluttony, hatred, heresy, homosexuality (which includes other sins like sodomy, lying with a man and being effeminate), idolatry, indifference towards charity, ingratitude, lusting, murdering, neglecting our Sunday obligation, obstinate despairing of hope for salvation, presuming that we can live without God or that we can be saved by our own power, showing pride, sedition, sloth, strife, taking advantage of the poor, stealing and being unclean... "Those who do such things shall not inherit the Kingdom of God."

That's a *very* long list!

Van left the church, like so many, because so many of the rules in the New Testament or in the Catechism of the Catholic Church (CCC) seemed to him, as to most of us, downright offensive! For example, the Bible's assertion that it's a sin for "a man to lie with another man" is, frankly, homophobic. The claim that a "heretical" statement is a sin smacks of brainwashing. An offense to drink? An offense to masturbate? Sheesh!

Supposedly all these rules were declared "sins" by God or Jesus, and then codified by some priestly committee. But who on earth were those priests or those bishops, many of whom turned out to be or to be coddling pedophiles, to instruct us about ethics? Their harping on sin comes across as moralistic, judgmental and blatantly hypocritical. Perhaps more important, the ancient concept of "sin" has lost any connection to our actual struggles such as our neurotic anxiety, our sense of oppression, our haunting malaise, or our sense of meaninglessness. And it's left countless decent people like Van worried that they're going to Hell!

In part as a result, Mystics on the Margins have long since abandoned the word "sin." No longer do we see our failings as about breaking one of these specific priestly rules. No longer do we hold that ethical rules—be they 38 or 10—are given to us "from on high." And we certainly don't accept the idea that if we masturbate, get drunk or love someone of the same sex, we're unacceptable in the larger scheme of things.

Now, I want to stress that on the whole, we Doubting Christians are a reasonably ethical bunch. Few of us murder, few of us steal. We don't need the priestly list to tell us what's immoral or wrong. We are well aware that some actions are wrong, but we don't see our moral code as God-given, or that if we break one, we "shall not inherit the kingdom of God."

So, here's the question: on what basis have we become decent, ethical people? Whence cometh our ethics?

As I've pondered this mystery and researched the ancient terms, I've come to think that we *do* have a good reason to be ethical. There *are* core principles and sensibilities that stand behind and drive my own ethical behavior and those of other Mystics on the Margins. And I believe that these are roughly the same principles that originally drove the religion's notion of "sin."

SALVATION, SŌZŌ

Let's start with "salvation." The seventeenth-century King James's Bible used this word to translate the Greek σώζω (*sōzō*). *Sōzō* originally meant to *protect* or *heal* someone, to foster *thriving* or becoming *whole*, or to *deliver* someone from a dire situation.[2]

Well, what's it like to feel "protected," "healed" or "thriving"? What happens to us when we get "delivered" from some dire situation?

Imagine that it's about a century after Jesus died (which is when the New Testament was being developed), and you're a farmer outside some dusty village near, say, the Greek city of Philippi. Imagine further that today the sun is brilliant, your wheat is blowing in the breeze and your day of farming and tending your flocks is going well. Suddenly you see a marauding gang of Roman thugs thundering up your drive and racing to your house, swords, shields and javelins a'clattering.

"Quick," you shout to your family, "hide in the cellar!" Everyone runs to the house and rushes pell-mell down the ladder and cowers behind the bags of barley, quaking.

Talk about a "dire situation!" You would be utterly terrified, afraid of what might happen to you, your spouse and your kids! Hyperaware of every sound on the floor above, you're conscious only of danger. Your brain is going haywire, thinking fast and anxiously, or maybe it drops into a kind of brain-freeze.[3] Your amygdala is ringing out 'threat!' and all you can think about is running, grabbing a sword or silently cowering. Your heart is pumping faster, your breathing has shallowed, and a fist of anxiety has risen into your throat. Your fight, flight or freeze response is hard at work.

All the lessons you've learned from your scrolls, all the good feelings you had over dinner the previous night, all the cute things your baby did—have disappeared from your awareness.

Your whole world, your very consciousness, has shrunk down to the thumping of sandals overhead, the breaking of pottery and the fear in your breast. Pulled away from all that's good in your life, you know only your breathing (rapid), your feelings (terror), and your gut (sinking).

But eventually, the marauders grab the crockery and, in a cloud of dust, thunder back down the driveway. The terror is gone! You're delivered! Hooray!

You grab your children and your spouse and hug them. You feel exhilarated! Your mind and heart begin to slow back down. Your shoulders and chest relax. Your mind and your feelings let go of the fear. Your consciousness and your world slowly return to normal. You laugh. You hug your kids again. Slowly you become your old complex, complete, whole self.

This is what it's like inside when we go from confronting "something dire" to experiencing being "delivered," "healed," "protected" and "whole." This then is what it's like to feel "sōzō." Whereas we had been preoccupied with danger, in sōzō we've become more open and ready to flow with life. We've let go of our self-protective instincts, let go of our anxieties. Things just become less conflicted. We are more open to life and one another.

I've really learned about this quality of sōzō, salvation, as a hospital chaplain. As I've talked with my patients about their spiritual lives, some of them, even some very sick ones, told me that they've been "saved." If so, I routinely asked them, "What's that like for you?" Over and over, they've told me that "being saved" leads to the feeling that life is easier, more effortless or weightless. They feel "supported," many said, like they could live "without having to work at it so much." It's like they felt they were being carried down a river, I heard, more in the "flow."

For example, one young man with diabetes quoted the famous line from Luke, "Consider the birds of the air—they neither sow nor reap, they have neither storehouse nor barn, and yet God feeds them" (Luke 12:24). "Birds just fly," he said sanguinely. They "never worry, are never self-conscious. They just live, effortlessly. No matter what, we can relax like them, we can live as effortlessly as they fly." This then was his felt-sense of "*sōzō*." It's much as we might feel after those marauding thugs had gone.

But recovering from a short-term terror like the marauding horsemen is only the first step. If you really let go of the sense of danger and come to feel truly safe, you may experience a longer-term second step, what Professor Csíkszentmihályi calls the feeling of Flow. He defines "flow" as a deep sense of enjoyment or alignment with what we're doing. It comes when someone feels fully competent and focused (Csíkszentmihályi, 2024). When we're in such a flow, he goes on, things seem right just as they are. We may come to feel as if we're born along by the streaming waves of some greater Flow of life. And *sōzō* signifies just this as well: "to thrive" or "to do well."

Most of my readers can probably remember at least one such moment. It's the kind of thing I asked you about in the Introduction. Perhaps you felt it when you were in "runner's high." Or when you were "in the zone" and just couldn't make a mistake. Maybe you felt it on a hike, when the leaves, the mountains, the world and the dappled light seemed just perfect.

I often heard descriptions of being open and feeling like we're in a flow in my interviews. Kathy Clausen said it was like "an ease, the feeling of being loved, connected to something deep and peaceful." It's like something was holding her up. Others told me about "riding on the wind" like this in their church. One respondent talked about this in terms of flowing:

> *In the experience of flow, I become large. Something like an uncoiling happens. I open up. It's like I was holding my breath, but I*

start to take it in. I can receive light and love. I feel there is something larger than us, and I get comfort from it.

When he has moments like these, Csíkszentmihályi tells us, he feels that he

almost doesn't exist. I've experienced this time and again. [The hand that's doing the work] seems devoid of myself, and I have nothing to do with what is happening. I just sit there watching in a state of awe and wonderment. And it just flows out by itself (Csíkszentmihályi, 2024).

The key to "flow," he continues, is that there's a fit between what the world is calling for and what we're offering, like a hand in a glove. Poet Denise Levertov best catches the felt-quality of *sōzō* in her poem "The Avowal,"[4] when she writes that such a state is like floating without effort, the water bearing us up, in the deep embrace of the Divine Spirit.

When we feel as if we're floating in the "cosmos's all-surrounding embrace" like this, we feel that we are somehow aligned with the rhythms and needs of the cosmos, supported by "that all-surrounding grace."

And, adds Csíkszentmihályi, such effortless moments of flow are found in every age and culture, including that of Jesus. Perhaps this sense of being free in our lives, doing what we do effortlessly, being open enough to sense a flow was the very sensibility that led originally to the notion of *sōzō*.

So, to answer our earlier question about the felt-sense behind the term *sōzō*, we can say that originally it probably pointed to this quality, this inner sense of effortlessness that is quite like what we feel when we've been "delivered from danger." For the Mystics on the Margins, to be *sōzō* is to experience the effortlessness, freedom and open heart that defines the sense of flow. *Sōzō* implies that we're attending to our own needs and that of others such that we feel we're aligned—without struggle—with some greater energy. It's the quality of life that my patients were pointing to when they were really "letting go and letting God," i.e., trusting their destiny without struggle. When we're saved, *sōzō*, we sense ourselves as living in alignment with the greater Flow of things.

SIN, HAMARTÁNŌ

Of course, almost no one—believer, Doubting Christian, saintly nun or secular atheist—lives with such an effortlessly open heart forever.[5] Though Jesus may have been an exception, we human beings inevitably fall *out* of such openness and become ego-centered and small again.

Let's return to our scenario. Imagine that it's now some time after those thugs have grabbed the pottery and silver and thundered away. Your heart has long since stopped thump, thump, thumping and you're feeling pretty safe. You've hugged your spouse enough and your kids are okay.

But alas, a nasty thought soon worms its way into your brain: "Will they come back? Next time will they grab *all* our money or *enslave* our kids?" Nothing outside has changed, of course. It's only a thought. But inside, that wide openness you had been enjoying is suddenly nowhere to be found. Your insides have become all knotted up again. Whereas before you could allow Levertov's waters to effortlessly "bear you up," you find yourself no longer able to "float." Preoccupied with self-protection and worry, what was once effortless flow has become anxiety and dread. Dang!

Here's where that nasty word "sin" comes in. "Sin" was the King James translation of ἁμαρτάνω (*hamartánō*), which was originally an archer's term for "missing the mark." *Hamartánō* was also used in Greek tragedy to point to the dark *inner* qualities or feelings that drove someone to act with pride, ambition, anxiety, self-protection or the like.

These very "dark inner qualities" as well as an obsession with wealth, the need to seduce or the craving for fame are some of the impulses that *drive* us to skew our behavior. We might crave to prove to ourselves that we're the best athlete, the smartest student or the most popular, all in order to convince ourselves that we're good enough. Our cravings make us small and afraid. They lead us to "miss the mark," and get in the way of our dealing with people in an upright, non-egoic, way. We become separated from the depths that we've sometimes known.

Janet Zimmerman, an Episcopal priest, said:

> *There's a force in the world that's always trying to make us smaller, afraid, timid. With it, I want to guard what's mine. It is always concerned about just what's right here.*

Note how different is this notion—that it's our cravings that are the problem—from the traditional view that the problem is doing one of the priestly-defined "bad" acts. In our modern, psychologically astute minds, the real spiritual problem is not some bad act. It's what *drives* the bad act. The *exterior* action is the result of some *interior* drive. The problem is not that the businessman "defrauded the workingman of his wage." It is that his selfish ego *led* him to cheat. It's not that she had the affair, but that she was driven subconsciously to *have* it, or that some unacknowledged inner fantasy told her that the affair would finally make her feel worthwhile. There's always some self-involved obsession that leads us to such self-aggrandizing actions. To the Mystics on the Margins, our real failings have to do with our self-involvement or our underlying drives. Again, some acts are illegal or immoral, and are wrong. But the real "sin," if you will, is our being trapped by the inner cravings that shrivel us down and make us selfish enough to do such deeds. The "sin" is the unconscious drive that causes us to "miss the mark."

And we know it when we're off. As Birgitta put this in our interview, sometimes you just...

> *know inside when you're wrong. When you're not honest, when you're gossiping, for example, you just know you're off. Your conscience tells you. I have something like an inner compass. I get an uncomfortable feeling. I feel it more acutely these days. Sometimes it's almost unbearable.*

Her sense that she's "off" is her inner recognition that she hasn't taken the needs of others, herself or the larger world into account. If I've pursued my needs and forgotten yours, or conversely if I've been focused on your needs and forgotten my own, I carry this sense of being "off." It's almost physical; we feel it in our sinews and bellies. And we'll carry a degree of shame or guilt inside, consciously or unconsciously, at least until it's resolved. Birgitta again:

> *Every time we are hurt or do something we regret, that hurt lives in our bodies. It's a lifelong journey to remove the effect of those stories and wounds in the tissue of our bodies.*

When we obsess or when we do something that we sense we shouldn't have, we "just know" that we're off. Because of the inner shame, pain, embarrassment or guilt, we just can't quite relax.[6] We just can't let go. As Lincoln reputedly said, "When I do good, I feel good. When I do bad, I feel bad."[7]

At the end of the wonderfully intense 2016 film *Hell or High Water*, Marcus, the gruff Texas Ranger, comes face to face with Toby, the young bank robber, after his bank robbing has come to light. Marcus says in his gravelly-voiced wisdom, "four people died in the course of [your actions]. And that will haunt you for the rest of your life." He's right, of course: Toby, a fundamentally decent fellow, will always know in his bones that he's "off." He will be *hamartánō*.[8]

As with *sōzō*, this meaning of *hamartánō* may be close to what was in the minds of the Biblical authors. In Paul's "Letter to the Romans," *hamartánō* doesn't point to breaking a specific, externally defined rule like committing adultery or lying. It points to Paul's *inner* sense that he hates something that he's done: "I do not do what I want, but I do the very thing I hate" (Rom. 7:15). And it is very close to what Mark put in the mouth of Jesus,[9] i.e., that the failings that "defile" us aren't our exterior acts. Rather "the things that come out [of someone] are what defile... All evil things *come from within*" (Mark 7:21-23).

When I have a sense that I've done something to another or to myself that feels "off," if I've done something illegal, the only tool I know that can cure it is to acknowledge the failing and to take my lumps. And in the case of harming another, the only cure I know is to tell myself and/or apologize to the person that I've hurt with the real, unvarnished truth. I need to drop all the self-justifications, the rationalizations or the lies I've been telling myself and / or someone else. I need to stand up straight and acknowledge the simple truth about what I've done without averting my eyes even a little. I need to face up to how and why I've been small and hurt another.

As Psalm 15 puts this, "Who speaks the truth from his heart, There is no guile upon his tongue." We need to say the real truth aloud and then say it again. And we need to make amends to those we've harmed if possible, and then change our behavior.

> *Happy are those who sins are forgiven...*
> *Happy are those...in whose heart there is no deceit.*

> *When we keep silent about our wrongdoings, our lives disintegrate with worry and guilt (Ps. 32:1–3)* (Longhurst, 2024).

Alas, such self-reflecting, honestly admitting our selfishness, or facing without hiding from how we've harmed another can be scary. No one *wants* to acknowledge their shameful or embarrassing truths. But acknowledge them we must, if we are to overcome our sense of wrongness, our inner "hauntings."

REIMAGINING THE PATH

Growing spiritually in this way, however, is primarily *our* work to do. We are too psychologically aware today of our dysfunctional childhoods, our unrealistic self-images, our addictions and our obsessions to think that anyone but we ourselves can see into them and cure our dysfunctions. Nobody, no person-like deity, can "forgive and restore" us. The real work of forgiveness and self-cure is ours. And it's hard.[10]

Like most of the Mystics on the Margins, I've been trying to do this work—self-examining, self-reflecting, self-analyzing and working to change—all my life. I'm with Gregory of Nyssa, that the only real sin "is the refusal to grow" (Rohr, 2011).[11] And I'm certainly not the only one who's been working to let go of self-involvements, arrogant certainties or obsessions!

It is my sense that this impulse to say the real truth aloud, to utter what we don't want to acknowledge, is probably the very same impulse towards humility that led to Christianity's much-maligned practice of "confession." Saying the real truth to ourselves and/or to someone else, even in a ritualized confession booth, may actually help. Speaking out our secrets, identifying our shortcomings or our self-delusions and making apologies can release the hold of virtually any secret, any neurosis. Bringing what is hidden into the light of day can help bring those secrets out of the shadows. Doing so can help us reenter the flow.

I've found that asking for forgiveness in a ritual setting, turning to one another, reminding ourselves of our failings and asking for help from "something more" can itself help. It can help us feel safe in the face of fear and pain. But for someone like me, the idea that a Divine being will zap me out of such pain, or out of my obsessions or that uttering "Hail Mary, mother of God" or "most merciful God, we confess that we have sinned against you" (the "confession of sins") will cure my neuroses is, at best, a chimera. We need to do the work: take up psychotherapy, attend our AA meetings, travel to weekend workshops and self-reflect. We need to take responsibility to "do the work."

One other traditional word here: "repent" is the King James translation of the Greek μετάνοια (*metanoia*), a compound of μετά (meta), "change," + νοέω (noeō), "to perceive, to think." To the two young evangelists who accosted me recently in an airport, "repent" was about "accepting Jesus as my personal savior." When I pressed them to explain, they told me to stop doing "sinful" things like sex outside of marriage (which I wasn't) and to come to a church like theirs. But these are exteriorizations. The key of meta-noeō is to "change" the "way we think," i.e., to make an *inner* shift. The real juice of *metanoia* is about transforming ourselves—from being defended and closed off to being as undefended and wide-open as we've been in our deepest experiences. *Repentance* is about transforming a defended heart into a vulnerably soft one, about moving from living small to living with open arms, both towards others and towards what is more. Telling the real truth and seeing ourselves as we really are can help free ourselves like this.

On a social level, *metanoia* is about going beyond the customary social rules or ritual regulations in order to become more humane and compassionate. Jesus was famous for deliberately breaking social conventions: loving the tax collectors, welcoming the Samaritans and the prostitutes, healing on a sabbath. He denied that any group of priests had the right to determine who was eligible for Divine favor. He consistently asked people to stretch and then stretch even farther, to push open social protocols and the boundaries of the sacred, to topple yet another wall. Over and over, he taught us to expand more and more until, perhaps, we might cross the final frontier and come to exhibit a truly wide-open heart.

---

1. The CCC references Gal. 5:19–21; cf. Rom 1:28–32; 1 Cor. 6:9–10; Eph. 5:3–5; Col. 3:5–9; 1 Tim. 1:9–10; 2 Tim. 3:2–5.
2. Sōzō was translated into English as "to be made whole," to "protect" and "to heal" (Mark 3:4, Mark 5:23) and "to thrive" or "to do well" (John 11:12).
3. Re the freeze response, see Seltzer, 2015.
4. https://allpoetry.com/the-avowal
5. It is open to debate whether the so-called *enlightened* do. See Forman 2011.
6. This we might call shame, the inner sense of having done something wrong. It often extends to a more global feeling about ourselves as flawed. Guilt, on the other hand, is more specific, involving the sense that something we've done has injured someone else.
7. Though this has been repeatedly quoted, I have not been able to find its source.
8. Of course, let's not forget Toby's response: "Poverty has destroyed my family's souls for generations. I just saved them." So, he sacrificed his own soul —without redemption—to save his children's souls. Nonetheless, he knew and would remain aware that in the process, four people died, and that will still haunt him.
9. I say that Mark "put this in the mouth of Jesus" because the "Jesus seminar" maintains that though these words are attributed to Jesus, they were most likely not his.
10. In our emphasis on our inner drives, we doubting Christians may be rediscovering what Mark meant when it said that our failings, which "defile" us, aren't our exterior acts. Rather "the things that come out [of someone] are what defile... All evil things *come from within*" (Mark 7:21-23). Note that the "Jesus seminar" maintains that these words are not Jesus's.
11. Mentioned in Rohr, 2011, p. 51, but without a reference.

CHAPTER 11
REIMAGINING ETHICS

SOURCES OF ETHICS

In the last chapter we saw that we Mystics on the Margins don't tend to see our ethical rules as God-given. Since we experience the Divine as a field-like foundational energy, it makes no sense to claim that "it" dictates anything, much less commands behavioral "laws." Energy fields just don't speak. An energy field, no matter how powerful, can lay down no rules about "right" beliefs, about sex before marriage, about being kind to one's neighbor, about abortion, or about any human concern.

No mystic on the margins would ever declare that their personal morality or favored political position is "God-given" (except perhaps in some vague or analogous sense). *Certainly, none of us believes that if we don't follow certain ethical rules we'll go to hell.* Rather than deriving our ethics from Paul's list or from the 38 sins in the Catechism of the Catholic Church, most of us work out of a more intuitive, less absolutist ethical process. And it seems to work: most Doubting Christians are reasonably moral and compassionate people.

However, this still leaves us wondering—where or from whom might we derive our guidelines? From where do we derive our sense, however vague, that this act is right and that one is wrong?

In a word, from *many* sources. This I learned from the retired Swedish businessman Bengt Johansen. Bengt, a lanky, charming and intelligent fellow, grew up in a moderately Christian family in the Swedish countryside. As a teenager he was quite involved with the church, but grew skeptical of any story that, as he put it, "could not be scientifically proven." Bengt offered that he doesn't derive his ethical principles primarily from the Bible. Rather, he's acquired them from a range of sources over a lifetime. "Most people who are not traditionally religious," he said confidently, "are ethical, but they don't turn to a religion for guidance. It's not our main source." Bengt went on,

> Both non-religious and secular people draw our ethical codes from many sources: state laws, political positions, social customs, readings and teachers, parents, our own sense of right and wrong and the like. You don't need to be religious to know not to murder. You don't need a Divine commandment to treat others well, i.e., as you'd like to be treated.

Bengt is suggesting that we derive our ethics from a wide range of personal, cultural, legal and countless secular and religious sources.

Kathy Clausen agreed and added that the process of becoming ethical begins when we are children:

> It starts at birth. People just want to connect. It comes from our experiences in community. Ethics grows out of that, for connection brings both love and conflict. Our morals come from the sand box, from school, our roommates, sports fields. Without connection, we

get alienated from one another, and that leads to selfishness and evil.

We began to develop our ethical sense on the playground, when we learned to care for one another, to scratch each other's backs and to not bite. God help the poor child who doesn't have the opportunity to learn how to get along with others, for he or she will grow up self-involved, selfish and lonely!

And as we became adults, our sense of ethics grows out of our total life experiences, especially of love and conflict, religious or otherwise. Through it all, we develop a "conscience," a voice that just knows when we've done something that hurts another, that just knows when we're "off." As Margareta puts this:

When you do something about which you have conflicted feelings, you just know inside you're wrong. You sense that you're not being honest, for example, or that your gossiping is somehow wrong. You just know you're 'off.' We say your conscience tells you... I feel when I'm off more acutely than I used to. Sometimes it's almost unbearable. I have something like a compass, I get an uncomfortable feeling.

Like Bengt, some mentioned that their sense of right and wrong was also shaped by the teachings of Jesus, who was someone who clearly had a deep spiritual connection with the Divine. Though no one regarded his words, actions or teachings as Divine *dictates*, Doubting Christians uniformly valued their insight as growing out of and pointing towards a deeply connected and compassionate way to live.

Several quoted Jesus's "greatest and first commandment"— "Thou shalt love the Lord thy God..." (Matt. 22:37, Deut. 6.5)— and saw it as pointing to being deeply connected to, i.e. "loving," the openness or the way things "want" to Flow. However, since by itself this commandment could lead to a life that was self-involved and unconcerned with the world, they also mentioned his second "great commandment": "Thou shalt love your neighbor as yourself" (Matt. 22:39; c.f. Lev. 19:18), the so-called Golden Rule. This maxim, holding others as human beings like ourselves with needs and wishes like our own, is another form of moving out of self-involvement. No one I know, and certainly no Mystic on the Margins, wants to align with the flowing of the Divine energy while *ignoring* or *harming* others. In fact, most of us would like to help others live fully and in spiritual openness. Our ethic includes watching out for other people *and* the larger world *as well as* ourselves.

SERVICE

This leads us into a key element of Christianity that was often stressed by many interviewees: service. As a youth, Janice was struggling, for example.

> *In my lowest point what lifted me out was service. It took the focus away from my self-centeredness, reminded me of us and that there's a world around us.*

She continues to actively volunteer to this day.

Service, social action and ethical behavior are stressed by most liberal and especially progressive churches. On the ProgressiveChristianity.org website, for example, recently some 3319 articles were devoted to service and ethics, whereas only half that number were devoted to the second most popular issue, worship. Virtually every liberal church bulletin includes countless posters and announcements about soup kitchens, aide to the needy, protest marches and the like. Rev. Kurt Strukmeyer captures this ethos well when he writes that the "way" of Jesus *is not a way of believing; it is a way of living. It is centered in human love for one another and is focused on compassionate action toward those in need. It involves our ethics, politics, and economics. The way of Jesus...is an appeal for a life of service, justice, and nonviolence* (Struckmeyer, 2023).

To this emphasis, many Mystics on the Margins add that we should be careful to not let this focus on service usurp the place of spiritual and emotional encounters with the Divine. Richard Beck points this out most clearly:

When faith is reduced to moral or political performance, life with [the Divine] is stripped of its strange, startling, sacred magic. Faith becomes being a good neighbor and voting well. Being a good person is a huge part of following Jesus...[but] beyond goodness, there is also the pressing problem that morality and politics do not heal the deep pain we're experiencing in the modern world (Beck, 2024).[1]

Most Mystics on the Margins would agree with Beck that while service is important, healing our deep pain comes primarily from experiencing and being oriented towards the mystery.

To Doubting Christians, compassionate social action grows out of our connection with the vast and mysterious reality. We see both as necessary elements in the full life. As the much-beloved priest Cristina Rathbone puts it in her pamphlet, *The Contemplative Imperative,*

Solitary and silent prayer helps us access the hiddenness of the unrevealed [mystery]. But being open to the mystery of the world though engagement with others helps make visible the hiddenness of [that mystery] (Rathbone, s.d.).[2]

To her, like many Mystics on the Margins, engaging with

others and experiencing the Divine are flip sides of one another. Christina goes on:

> Both solitary prayer and engagement with others can open us to our vulnerability...because plunging into the depths of [the Divine] through prayer, and plunging into the depths of [the Divine] through engagement with others are really the same thing in the end...one naturally, inevitably flowing into the other, inseparable, indivisible, changing and unchanging both.[3]

The underlying energy is vast and spacious enough to include others, especially others in need. If the Quantum Vacuum Field or the Ground of Being is the source of all reality, through it we are all connected. Engaging with others, serving others enhances and expands that deep connection and gives life to those Divine depths. It is the natural expression and completion of the vulnerable experience of that depth.

Stephanie, our priest from Lowell, adds that contemplation is crucial but not sufficient. It must be completed with grown-up responsibility and compassion:

> There's something I call "cheap grace." People should understand that even if they feel that they're loved, they're still on the hook. You can love and be loved but still recognize that there are consequences. The spiritual love is not all sweetness and light. There is a tension in it. You're precious and loved AND you're expected to behave and operate out of that love. Acting responsibly, caring for others, is part of the whole here.

Even with a sense of spiritual openness, we're still "on the hook" for compassionate action.

In turn, compassionate action can feed back to our experience of openness and freedom, if we do it right. Too often we unconsciously serve out of an unequal power relationship, when we serve another, say, or volunteer at a soup kitchen, as if we are offering gifts of food or time "from on high" to the disabled, the poor, the "other." Serving like this is shot through with ego and self-importance. If we want service to reinforce and deepen our sense of Openness, it must be ego-free. Christina suggests that

> if we approach others in need from a position of no power...of not knowing, and not presuming, and not composing redeeming patterns or superior causes, then...we are occasionally able to slip through our own projections to the fullness of life beyond them.

The inward movement of aligning with the Divine, she says, "naturally, inevitably" flows into the egoless activity of service. And vice versa.

Pennie Curry, also from the Berkshires, similarly extolled ego-free service:

> I used to think I was going out and serving someone. But now I think it's about coming together with someone else. Not doing service FOR someone, but connecting WITH them. To me now, serving someone is about standing alongside, being with them... Before there was more of a separation, like I'm the holy one and they're the needy one: "I'm doing this deed and I'm serving." But now it's how can I serve? What's your story?

Many a sermon has focused on doing "right" things in the world: caring for the homeless, watching out for the environment, etc. These are good deeds, and Mystics on the Margins are as concerned as anyone with improving the world and the lives of others. But our ethics also connect with *how* we engage such issues. We can show off how generous we're being, we can tell ourselves how holy we seem. We can do some action because we've been taught that it's "right." But such attitudes are secretly *transactional*. Truly ethical action arises when we engage with the world without ego. It's a product of being utterly open and undefended in what we do, so that we have no personal agenda. It arises when our view is wide enough and clean enough to take not only another person into account but the larger society and world as we do so. The ethical is not an attribute of the action that we do but of *how* we do it.

I discovered this non-egoic way of being with others the first time I served at a soup kitchen, about 6 years after all this began. I had helped a friend bake several strawberry cheesecakes and we took them to folks there. In the past when I offered something, I would have been subtly looking for something: a thank you, admiration, whatever. But that day, when I offered the men and women desserts,

> *I just didn't feel any of that. I served them with, well, no expectations. It was at that moment that I realized that I had never given anything to anyone without at least subconsciously expecting something in return—at least a 'thank you.' But that day I just served the men and women as I might have in my own house: "Do you want a piece? ...Here ya go..." Just giving like that without expecting anything back was, surprisingly, a gift to me. I felt sweetly connected with them. It was utterly effortless. I continue to offer what I can in that same spirit, just doing.*

Christina, Pennie and I are all trying to do service not so much as a doing *for* others, but rather as a being *with* others. Rather than seeing ourselves as "the holy one" who dispenses gifts from a position of power, we're trying to encounter people as friends, as guests, as equals. When we do, there's a largeness and minimal ego in the interaction. Just as we become wide open in contemplation, we're trying to remain wide open as we serve. That is, trying to "slip beneath" our need for power or approval and do what we do with less ego, we're seeking to help others as both an expression of the openness and as a simple gift.

Here's another way to think of this: When I'm acting in order to get something for myself, I'm not truly "clean." My actions are "dirty," with unspoken agendas. But when I am acting without ulterior motive, I feel "clean." Thus

> *Who shall stand in the holy place? Those who have clean hands and a pure heart, who have not pledged themselves to a falsehood nor sworn by what is a fraud, they shall receive a blessing* (Ps. 24:3–5).

To be "clean" in this sense is to act with simplicity, with no extra motives. For action that is minimally infused with ego, i.e., done with a "pure heart," is an expression of and an enhancer of our felt-connection with the Divine.

Service, by the way, is one of the places a spiritual community can help. It's easier to serve others when there are a gaggle of us. Mates and friends in our community, not to mention ministers and leaders, can help service happen, and can make it both easier and more effective. Our mates can also remind us when we unconsciously slip into those egocentric patterns of which we may not be aware.

In sum, and using the language of Jesus's twin "great commandments," we could say that Mystics on the Margins hold that we should "love God with all our hearts and minds." That is, we should live in such a way that we become spiritually open, uncomplicated in heart and undefensively open in our action. As a natural outgrowth of such egolessness, we should "do unto others as we would have them do unto us"—treat them as human beings with their own needs and wants. And if possible, help them do the same.

Here then is a simple statement of what I understand as the ethical approach of Mystics on the Margins:

> We seek to understand more, feel more and align ever more deeply with the loving Flow of the Ground of Being, while enhancing other peoples' ability to do the same.

CHRISTIAN POLITICS

Now we come to what is for many 21st-century people the most destructive side of Christianity: politics, especially Christian Nationalism. This is perhaps the main reason that most religious "nones" "stay the hell away from Christianity," as one put it. To many of my interviewees and to most of my liberal friends, just terms like the "Christian Right," "Christian Nationalism" or "Evangelical Politics" feel so loaded, so abhorrent, that even the very name "Christianity" has become repugnant. I hate to say it, but the Christian Nationalists have covered the name of this religion in slime—perhaps permanently.

I certainly used to think of Christianity this way! The very word meant all the politics I hated! But as you can tell, over the past eight and a half years I have discovered that not all churches and not all ministers teach those doctrines. Not all demand conformity of thought. Not all command that we follow their sexual mores. Not all are hypocritical. Not all espouse nationalism. When Mystics on the Margins choose to explore church as adults, we do so knowing that there are countless Christianities and we can and must first of all find a church that roughly agrees with our politics, our ethics and our morality. It's possible, I know; in fact it's easy! Take Boston psychologist Marc Roberts. When Marc chose a church, he did so because

> its very liberal ethics is congruent with my own. It's not preachy, not Bible thumping, very open to all races, ethnicities, genders, sexual preferences and the like. I get the positives of organized religion without the negatives.

Marc, like the bulk of my interviewees and I myself, was quite comfortable with the relatively liberal church that he found. He found a community that stressed an ethic of welcoming the marginalized or underserved, of helping the poor, and that espoused generally liberal politics. In most places, it is painless to find a community that is congruent with your own ethical and political stances.

It's also relatively easy to find a conservative church, if your ethics points that way. I interviewed several Texas evangelicals whose moral codes were very different from Marc's before they found a church. Rural Texas is "pro-life," for example, so the attitude towards abortion that my interviewees grew up with, and that of nearly all their friends, included the conviction that abortion was wrong, as it was "killing an unborn child." They also found a church that conformed to their ethical stances.

It turns out that the arrow of influence goes both ways: our life-long ethical stances shape our church's teachings. And our ministers and churches shape the way we think and act. But alas, this reflexivity is a matter for another book.

---

1. Beck p. 7.
2. The bracketed words are replacing the word "God" here.
3. p. 25.

CHAPTER 12
REIMAGINING PRAYER

Every now and again, I attended different churches than Trinity. Once I went to a United Church of Christ fairly close to my home. It was a lovely space. A man and two women, educated all, read their Biblical passages clearly and well. The choir was well-rehearsed, the music well done. The preacher gave a sermon about gun control, a hot issue about which he was knowledgeable and passionate. He shared with us his recent conversation about it at the White House. It was easy to be swept up with him!

Then the assistant pastor got up to offer a prayer. It was very long. She talked about the conflict in Somalia. She prayed about the horrors of gun violence. She offered and prayed for congregants' personal needs. She offered heartfelt prayers for parishioners in the hospital and for church members who had recently passed away. She had obviously thought about her prayer and had prepared it well, and only glanced at her notes. She did a very good job.

But it left me cold. For all of her good intentions, for all of her sincere feelings, for all of her carefully chosen words and movements, I had the feeling that I was *watching* someone pray.

Intelligent and carefully thought out though it clearly was, her words and feelings were *hers,* not *mine,* not *ours.*

One of the things that I have been learning the last few years is how deep the chasm is between understanding something and feeling it. Even more important, there's an equally deep difference between thinking or feeling something and being transformed by it. This intelligent woman clearly understood the moral issues in Somalia. She was sweet about the congregants in in the hospital. She clearly knew her tradition's doctrines, and prayed with apparent sincerity. But for all her good words and her gestures of blessing, I felt that I was watching her do *her* thing. Her words were good, but they didn't touch me.

I have often been struck by the difference between my understanding, which was so honed as a graduate student and as a professor, and my heart. I could talk for hours about various notions of trust, but it took years of weekly tears to begin to *experience* trust. I could've told you volumes about belief systems, but it took that phrase "it's just us" for me to actually *feel* the impact of that word. I've always known that there's a difference between thinking about God and feeling the cosmic energy, but again, only when I've sensed it burgeoning out of my chest has it really hit home.

I suspect that for the members of that church, their assistant pastor's prayer felt fine. But to me, her prayer made sense in our heads, which is profoundly different from touching our hearts. She offered good and moral thoughts, but missed the unsayable.

For me, the power of the church comes from a very deep, even pre-cognitive level. To have someone gently put food in my mouth touches me at just such a preverbal level! To have someone look into my eyes and help me drink from a cup, touches me in a way I haven't known since I was an infant. These things work on us not in a mental way, not in the way of intelligent thoughts. These things work in us in the catacombs of our deepest intuitions. The power of a church touches our secret places, well beyond words.

Most Doubting Christians who left their church as teenagers were taught as kids to pray. Praying was, as one told me with a chuckle, something like a long-distance call to a "Cosmic Bellhop" that they'd ask for stuff. Or negotiate with: One told me about a deal she made that if "He" made Grandma well, she'd never, ever go to another dance! If they prayed hard enough, God would smile on them and grant the blessing they'd asked for, be it Grandma's health or a new Nintendo.

But when people grew up and began thinking about things more scientifically and began noticing their spiritual connections and experiences, the image of the infinite energy morphed, however vaguely. As we've seen, it went from something like a person to something like an omnipresent energy field. As such, prayer made little sense: inanimate objects or energy fields just cannot be bellhops, cosmic or otherwise.

Growing up a secular Jew, I never believed in either the long-distance call or the "cosmic bellhop." Prayer seemed, well, kind of silly: all folded hands and asking for things. Janice Joplin's line, "Oh Lord, won't you buy me a Mercedes Benz" seemed to me to catch the idea and was...ahem...laughable.[1]

But today, we Mystics on the Margins have reimagined prayer. And it's anything but laughable.

PRAYER AND THE PRAY-ER

I began to understand this new take on prayer, ironically enough, with an atheist. Patient W, a slender 57-year-old man, was in the hospital with a very aggressive form of stomach cancer. When I knocked on his door and told him I was a chaplain, he was initially reticent to see me. He blurted out, "I'm an atheist!"

"That's fine," I assured him. Then I explained that we chaplains do not represent or promote any religious views. At that, he tentatively invited me in.

We chatted for a while about his situation. Then he leaned closer.

"I have a confession to make," he whispered. "I prayed the other day. And I felt badly about it. I felt dishonest. After all, I don't believe in God. I haven't gone to a church in decades. Truth be told, I've denied the whole thing."

Now on a roll, he continued, "I haven't earned the *right* to pray. What right do I have to turn to some God when I haven't supported any of it? What the hell was that?"

I just listened to him. After a while I said, "I'm not sure praying always has something to do with some God-figure. Personally, I don't think we have to know what we're praying to. To tell the truth, when I pray with a patient, I have no idea who or what I'm praying to. I just put out there what I've heard of their concerns as well as what I feel. I try to put into words their pain, their fears, their hopes and my feelings about what I've heard."

He found the idea that a prayer doesn't have to involve a God figure "really helpful."

Then I added, "When you prayed, you asked for help, right? How did that feel, asking for help?"

"You know," he said with a rueful grin, "it actually seemed to help. It kind of lightened things up."

"Seems to me that your asking for help was itself a damn good prayer," I said. "Just to be able to ask for help was a kind of gift. For when you said it, if nothing else, you were telling yourself what you actually felt, how much you needed help."

"You know," he said with a hint of a smile, "I have always

found it really hard to ask for help! I guess that *was* part of why it seemed to help."

"Yeah," I agreed, "I find it really hard to ask for help too. But doing so, just acknowledging that we need help, it's kind of freeing, isn't it?"

We talked for a while after that. He told me more about his prognosis, his situation at home and so on. When we seemed to be winding down, I asked him, "Whaddya think, should we pray together?" He nodded.

I took his hands, looked him in the eye, and said, "In the light of whatever forces there may be in the universe..." At that he smiled. I went on,

"Sometimes we just need help." ...Pause.

"Sometimes we feel like we can't do it all on our own." ...Pause.

"There are times we feel we can't carry the load all by ourselves." ...Pause.

"Sometimes we just need something to keep us going." ....Pause.

I don't know quite what I said after that. Something about hoping we can get through this difficult time... About being afraid... About needing to lean on something that we cannot name and so on. The only thing I know for sure is that I never used the word "God."

Then he said to me, "thanks for that. You had me all choked up. I teared up while you were talking." And he couldn't thank me enough for coming.

The prayer that Patient W offered, like mine in the Mahwah Cathedral so many years before, worked in large part because we spoke out our real pain. And we asked for help. Acknowledging that we can't do it all on our own was key for us both. For when he and I each cried out our unacknowledged feelings of helplessness and asked for help—from wherever or whomever—we opened ourselves vulnerably and spoke out our real truth.

Even when we ask for something in a prayer—"give us our daily bread"—there is a moment when we're directing ourselves not towards ourselves or our food but towards the very possibility of Divine openness. Even if we begin with a particular need, we remind ourselves of what is more.

PRAYING IN THE HOSPITAL

Towards the end of my chaplaincy visits, I usually offered to say a prayer. Most patients and families wanted one. If so, I would typically then offer them a choice, "Something we all know or something from the heart?"

About a third chose "something we all know." If they chose that, most people opted for The Lord's Prayer, which we would then recite together.

There's something ancient and soothing about those few stanzas. I don't buy its words like "heaven," "kingdom" and "glory," but I like that they encourage us to hold our worries in a wider perspective. The prayer encourages us to see our issues in the context of the larger Flow of life, and how these problems may be playing some sort of role. "Thy will be done" works much like that to help us trust this larger Flow.

But the power of "Our Father who art in Heaven," I think, has only indirectly to do with the words. The real power of a prayer like this comes with its poetry, its rhythms and its familiarity. The very rhythms of "thy kingdom come, thy will be done" or "hallowed be thy name" are downright soothing. Muttering these familiar cadences can be so comforting! As Episcopal Alice Anderson described this prayer, "these words are part of my soul." My Alzheimer patients often seemed comforted when they recited with me what they could remember of it. These rhythms offer the comfort of a beloved old friend. Learned through decades of recitation, such beloved prayers—the Lord's Prayer, the 23rd Psalm, the *Shema* for Jews[2] or the *Bismillah*[3] for Muslims—vibrate more in our bellies and bones than in our heads. Though the words and images are all about safety and decency, their real power emerges from deep in our unconscious. When we're scared, when we're grieving, when we're lost, these slow and familiar cadences comfort us as little else can.

The majority of my hospital patients, however, opted for the second kind of prayer. "Yes, please, something from the heart." In effect they were inviting me to come up with words on their behalf. I would begin these prayers with whatever phrase they'd be most comfortable with: "Dear God" or with a Jewish family "Barukh ata Adonai." With a religious "none" like Patient W I might began with "In the light of whatever forces there may be in the cosmos."

I would then try to put words around the fears, loves and hopes that they had shared with me or, more likely, were unable to say.

"...in times of trouble we can use your help..."

"...sometimes we feel so anxious about our children..."

"...when we must confront more than we possibly can..."

I tried to frame their concerns and hopes into words. The words I used seemed to come *through* me, not *from* me. And much like Patient W, patients generally found these simple prayers healing. Just to know that they weren't alone, that I had heard them and had spoken out what they had said and what they hadn't, seemed to help. I tried to speak out deep truths so that they heard them not just with the head but with the whole body. More often than not, they teared up or cried.

The tears and warmth of these prayers seemed to have to do with the connections that I had established with the patient or the family, the sense that I had heard them, and with the pain and fear that was so present. What I really offered was a loving witness, the linking of our hearts and the listening together into mystery.

The effects on the "pray-er"—of being vulnerable, of acknowledging unspoken truths and of listening for the terrors and hopes beneath our self-images—is clear. For at its most powerful, a prayer is a cry from the heart. It can help us discover the longings we've kept unconscious, feel the pangs we cannot allow ourselves to feel, or face that which we dare not face. In praying we acknowledge at some level that we cannot carry the load by ourselves, that we are scared, and that yes, that we need help! We're saying what we really, really want and what we really, really need, and if we're present, mean every word. A good prayer brings our desires and our barely known longings to consciousness.

There's something wonderfully healing about acknowledging such hidden feelings and exposing our secrets to the light. Saying them requires that we drop below our "I've-got-it-all-together" self-talk and become vulnerably honest with ourselves.

In a good prayer we relinquish our lifelong preoccupations with self-interest and begin to surrender into what is larger. When we do so, when we reach outside our everyday concerns and say out real truths, a prayer feels positively holy. It becomes a sacrament.

Such a prayer is different than a "sacramental conversation" or "being in the Flow of the Divine," for a prayer includes an intention, a request. In it, we ask for guidance or healing and, as Mary Meader put it, "we are open to a response." Mati Engel, one of the most sensitive and articulate chaplains I've ever met, put it this way:

> *Whereas meditation is like a deep listening or witnessing of the internal landscape, prayer has the audacity to seek a response. A prayer beckons. It asks that something be different than it is... It is*

audacious enough to seek to intervene, to interrupt reality. It says, please...please do some*thing.*

Such prayers seek to move the immovable.

In a sincere prayer we empty our minds of ego-laden desires and offer trembling and carefully chosen words of longing and of truth. When we do, when we speak out our honest yearnings, at the very least we get to hear them. We get to recognize how much pain we have been feeling, how lonely we have been, how deep is our thirst for connection and how much we long for love. A prayer like this is not a transaction with some Cosmic Bellhop. It is a cry from the heart about what we dare not allow ourselves to acknowledge.

Many have shared anecdotal evidence with me how praying has affected their lives. Melissa West, for example, a bright, lively and multi-talented sixty-something, was born into an actively Christian family. As a child she was serious about her Christianity, at one point seriously considering seminary. Today she considers Christianity a valuable element in her multi-traditional spiritual path and she continues to pray. If she can let go of "neediness and ego," she said, if she can hold herself and her life "in a comprehensive way," then she...

> *can ask for something that will help me, help us all, in a deep way. I don't mean asking for something in the old "gimme, gimme" way. Instead, I want to ask for something in an unconflicted way that will help me, help my friends, my family and the world—my whole ecology of connections—in a deep way.*

When she prays in such an inclusive way, she told me, a response generally comes. "I have to be open for guidance, open to the response I get. But I've seen it work." She needs, in other words, to not only be honest and unconflicted within herself, but to also be humble enough to be ready to receive guidance.

Several informants told me of putting out requests for more psychotherapy or consulting clients and the phone starting to ring. Another told me that he had put out a call for "friends I can really connect with," and a few such new friends soon showed up. One contact talked about asking his "spirit guides" for help, another turned to her spiritual "team." Others just "put it out there." For all of them prayers led to worldly responses.

Now, it may be that to ask for more clients or friends might just foster in the pray-er a readiness to *notice* when someone new walks in the door. That's certainly possible. But something more interesting may also be at work. Many are convinced that if they're really open to guidance, support or something unexpected, they actually do receive guidance, support or something "strange that can't be explained by science!"

Whatever the cause of these unexpected happenings, no mystic on the margins pretends to know from whence they come. Might these effects be caused by something in our unconscious or in the collective unconscious? Might the effects come from our "larger self?" Might there be some as yet unidentified "forces of nature?" No one claims to know the source of any responses. We Mystics on the Margins are comfortable not having all the answers. And we prefer to leave deep mysteries mysterious.

To go from the sublime to the heady, in the largest and most famous controlled study of prayer, Herbert Benson found that the greatest effects were on the person doing the praying (Benson, 2007).[4] He saw beneficial changes in metabolism, heart rate, blood pressure, breathing rate and brain activity. Another study found that prayer reduced stress-hormones (Coruh, 2005). Among Presbyterian ministers, more prayer was correlated with improved vitality, general health and mental health (Meisenhelder, 2001).

PRAYERS AND THE WORLD

Many people, like the assistant pastor at the UCC church, pray for people in endangered regions—wars, famines, floods, mass shootings and people subject to the endless litany of social problems. People pray for the hungry, for the hurt, for the dying and for those who have died. These prayers seek to heal our heartbroken world.

In seeking to heal our heartbroken world, we're hoping that our prayers will do, as Mati put it, *some*thing. We say our words in hopes that they'll change the world's trajectory or move the great wheel of fate. It is of course impossible to know what the measurable effects are on the inhabitants of some distant troubled locale, if any. But at the very least, they can help us feel like we're expressing our hopes and doing what we can.

There is some scientific evidence that prayer can indeed have external effects (Fincham, 2024). One study showed that when people prayed from a distance for women who were getting *in vitro* fertilization, their pregnancy success rate rose (Cha, 2001). In a 1999 study, heart patients who were prayed for by community volunteers suffered about 10% fewer complications (Harris, 2000). In a study of patients with blood stream infections, intercessory prayers were correlated with a shorter duration of fever and a shorter hospital stay (Leibovici, 2001). Another study showed that when a person in a romantic relationship prays for the wellbeing of the other, there are "detectable positive effects" on them. On the other hand, Herbert Benson found that while there were measurable effects on the person doing the praying, there were little or no measurable effects on the cardiac bypass patients for whom they prayed (Benson, 2007). Nonetheless, taken altogether some 57%

of trials of distant healing through prayer showed positive effects (Astin, 2000).

Dr. Larry Dossey, a distinguished Texas internist, became interested in the power of prayer when he kept running across what he called "miracle cures, patients who had healings or remissions that clinical medicine could not explain." As he kept studying this phenomenon, he discovered it was much more common than he knew.

> *Almost all physicians possess a lavish list of strange happenings unexplainable by normal science. A tally of these events would demonstrate, I am convinced, that medical science not only has not had the last word, it has hardly had the first word on how the world works, especially when the mind is involved (Dossey, 2000).*

Out of these discoveries came his book *Healing Words: The Power of Prayer and the Practice of Medicine*. Dossey suggests that prayer can indeed have effects, even from a distance. To explain this phenomenon, Dossey begins with the hypothesis that our consciousness is connected with the Ground of Being or the Divine "Force Field" (which is nearly the same hypothesis that I offered in Chapter 9). As such we are connected to this omnipresent field in ways we do not understand.

> *Consciousness and prayer are infinite in space and time... [i.e.] omnipresent. This implies that prayers go nowhere, because being omnipresent they're already there... [That is,] there is no directionality to prayer. This obviously conflicts with the ordinary Western view of prayer as being sent to the Divine and deflected from the Divine to the object of the prayer (Dossey, 1993).*

In other words, Dossey suggests that our consciousness is connected to an omnipresent Ground of Being. We dwell within, with, through and beyond it. If this is correct, then the conscious intentions that we express in our prayers can, as it were, "twang" that field. To pray then is not only to speak out our longings to ourselves but also to speak them into that greater field or towards those greater forces. A comforting thought, even though (so far) impossible to prove.

---

1. The song was actually written by Bob Neuwirth and Janice Joplin.
2. *Shema Yisrael,* Hear Oh Israel, The Lord our God, the Lord is One.
3. *Bismillah Al-Rahman Al-Raheem* (In the name of God the most Merciful, the Beneficent).
4. Benson, pp. 934–42.

CHAPTER 13
REIMAGINING BEING CALLED

My attitude towards the whole idea of "calling" and "being called by God" was shaped long before I found my way to a church. Fresh off a meditation retreat, I was driving down a country lane and stopped to meditate in a lovely country church high on a hill. It turned out to be empty, so I sat in a pew to meditate for half an hour. As I was coming out of meditating, a young man came in and plopped down next to me in the pew.

With no preface he said, "Have you accepted Jesus as your personal savior? Have you been called by God?"

Honestly, it made me nauseous!

It wasn't that I didn't even know him. It wasn't that he was rude enough to not even ask my name. What left me feeling ill was that he treated these questions so flippantly!

Whatever it is, asking if you've been called is not like asking if you've tried a new type of toothpaste or exercise equipment. It's not just something that you pick up half-impulsively. Choosing a spiritual path is perhaps the deepest choice we ever make. We're choosing what we consider to be the most real, the most important and the core matter of our existence! And sensing being called, whatever that really might be, is perhaps the deepest kind of mysterious guidance we human beings are ever privileged to receive. It's as if the infinite forces are talking to us, guiding our steps, pointing to what is probably our deepest truth. This stuff is so mysterious, so profound and so intimate that we can scarcely whisper about it.

And it's certainly not subject to a simple yes/no question!

That young man was probing into the depths of my soul—utterly heedlessly. That's why he made me nauseous!

EXPERIENCING BEING CALLED

To be called is traditionally viewed as to be chosen "by God" for a certain purpose. Some are called to the political arena, some to end human trafficking. Others are called to be pastors, teachers, worship leaders, Bible translators or a host of other roles. Thomas Tarrants, the President emeritus of the C.S. Lewis Institute, describes the notion of "calling:"

> God has a place of service for each of His children, whether they are at the top of society or the bottom or somewhere between. God will personally guide and direct us...to the meaning and application of His word to the circumstances of our lives and the situations we face (Tarrants, 2018).

The idea that God will show us where to go and guide our steps to get there is a wonderfully sweet and comforting idea! I *wish* there was something or someone wise and kindly enough to tell me what to do and powerful enough to make it possible!

But as we've stressed, we Doubting Christians just can't believe in such a someone. We've let go of the picture of a person-like God who "thinks about us all the time," who has a plan for our lives and who guides our steps.

It makes a certain kind of sense to say "God, who is like a

Father to me, called me to be a minister." Its syntax is clearly parallel to "George, my father, called me to come to dinner." But things change if we experience an infinite energy as an underlying energy field or as a loving Ground of Being. It makes no sense to say that a magnetic field called me to dinner. Nor does it make sense to say the Ground of Being "calls us" or it "guided me" towards a particular job or spouse. Only people (or perhaps dogs like Lassie) beckon. Fields of energy just don't beckon any more than magnetic fields can. Abstract fields of energy like the Ground of Being just are. However we understand the energy that underlies all reality, it has no plan for anyone's life.

And yet, and yet...

I and the Mystics on the Margins with whom I spoke actually do sometimes feel guided, pushed along or nudged in a certain direction. And it can be life-changing. We might call it "feeling guided," "pointed in a direction," "nudged" or the like, but not being "called." Jazz musicians famously report that when they get into the flow they feel as if the notes they're playing come from "someplace else." Musician George Michael suggests that he feels his music just comes "to" him fully formed:

> When I write a melody in my head something in the back of my neck just knows that I've hit it. It's almost like it was already there, but you hadn't spotted where it was yet. It's almost like it comes to you fully formed, and you just pulled it out of nowhere. And the feeling that you have that makes you shiver is that you found it.[1]

A professional ballerina told me that when their dancing became effortless, she and her friends in the *corps de ballet* of the New York City Ballet described it as "the angels were dancing me." I spoke with several ministers who told me how, when they were writing a sermon, they felt like they were almost taking dictation from someplace. Mountain climbers feel sometimes that their next move is "given" to them. So do chess masters. Atheists, agnostics and church-going doubters can all feel nudged or guided sometimes. But none of us attribute the nudges or impulses we may sense to a "Father God" or "His Son."

A few contacts told me that these hints or nudges sometimes come wordlessly: "I just knew I was going in a wrong direction," or "I just felt like I was off." Mati Engel, whom we met before, feels a nonverbal sense sometimes that she should "go this way, go do that."

> It feels like a magnetic charge or pull. You sense it or you feel it. I get a sensation of direction that "there is something for you there." I have felt it towards certain teachers, sometimes about a geographical place. It is an energetic guidance I feel in the solar plexus. It's heart centered. In a sense, it's an encounter with a liveliness. But never did I have the thought, "This is God talking." It was more just "go there."

Others sometimes hear a voice—loud, clear and insistent. On the night before her wedding, Mary Ellen Washienko, a Boston Episcopalian, was having eye trouble and had to put patches over her eyes. She then heard a voice that said, "When these patches come off, open your eyes to what you are doing." She knew instantly that while she had been busy with wedding details, she had been looking the wrong way, i.e., that she didn't really want to marry her fiancé. A few hours later, he phoned her to call it off. "I had no idea what that voice was, but it was right on!"

When she was young, one minister told me, she had been casting about in her life. One day she heard a voice that said, "Who you are and what you do with your life is important." That voice, as clear as a trumpet volley, served as a wakeup call to start taking her life choices seriously. Again, she didn't hear it as "God." "I was open to the message," she said, "but I didn't know who it was. It came without detail about who or what it was."

Elizabeth Young too has also felt guided sometimes. Generally, it's come to her wordlessly, as a nudge. Sometimes it seems to have a voice:

> *I have a sense sometimes of something that can direct my life in an ethical and meaningful way. It rises up clearly in me. I experience it sometimes as a voice or sometimes just as a direction. It feels essential and right.*

Sometimes the sense of direction comes to us in a religious setting. It's different from what a novelist or a musician might feel, for in a religious setting we open ourselves to such guidance somewhat *intentionally*. We might call it "grace." Becoming more present, we listen consciously for the impulses of wisdom.

Sometimes such guidance comes through another person. One of my Doubting Christians was planning to become a professional musician. He asked a favorite professor for her thoughts and she reflected aloud on what she saw as his natural talents. Much to his surprise, she pointed in the opposite direction. Her thoughts "rattled around and around inside," he told me. By a few weeks later it was hardly a decision at all and soon he found himself in graduate school in English Literature. It was as if she had cognized something that seemed to be in alignment with whatever larger forces there are in the world. Like Mati, it never occurred to him that this guidance was "from God." But wherever it was from, it turned out to be a perfect and successful choice!

When Christian traditionalists have a similar experience, they naturally assume it is "from God." When he was a teenager, David Knight attended a mainline nondenominational Christian church. Typically, there were "altar calls" in it. On one particular Sunday the pastor invited those who wanted to give their lives to the ministry to come forward. David had never been particularly interested in being a minister, but then,

> *I experienced some sort of a presence, as if something came up from behind and lifted me up from my seat. It wasn't scary or unfriendly. It was very real. The next thing I know is I'm standing up and stepping out into the aisle and walking down it.*

He went on to describe that what propelled him down the aisle as "something strange, intimate and powerful, but not unfriendly."

Jacob Melancon, an Evangelical guitarist in Texas, told me that he and his fellow musicians sometimes say, "We sing whatever God wants us to sing." But, he clarified,

> *when we say that it was God, what we're really saying is that 'something' is moving us. I might say to my church mates that I'm guided "by God," but really, I don't have the sense that someone, some figure, is zapping me with a lightning bolt from the sky. It's rather that I'm just singing whatever I'm moved to sing. Honestly, I'm just moved from my heart to sing this or that song.*

Though Jacob, David and Elizabeth all used traditional God language, they all were clear with me that it was just a shorthand way of talking about their strange sense of being nudged. They all left its source, in the end, unnamed.

FROM WHOM OR WHAT?

Several patterns in these accounts stand out. First, even without the notion that we're called "by God," these nudges all seemed to express deep wisdom. Their hints and nudges always seem deeper than the person could have come up with on their own. It's as if we receive wisdom and nudges from something beyond our thinking minds, and those nudges seem in the long run to be in unexpected and right alignment with "something more." Sensing such a nudge, people are moved to let go of their "smart" but limited ways of seeing.

Second, these moments of being nudged are different from just feeling in an undirected Flow, like a runner's high. When we feel actively guided or directed by something that seems other than us, we sense that some greater energy is nudging us in a particular direction. It's like being pushed *thataway* by a great wave.

Third, we experience whatever is doing the pushing as external to us. Mary Ellen was sure that the voice that told her to open her eyes to what she was doing was not *her* voice. Elizabeth said that one of her nudges is

> *different from my conscience in that it seems to be external, separate from me. It comes up through my belly and pushes me to do something.*

And the wordless sensation of direction that Mati sometimes senses also seems to come from some source not herself.

In other words, our nudges seem to come *to* us, not *from* us. Over and over in my interviews I heard people say that they have learned to take the guidance or direction that comes from "beyond themselves" very seriously. They somehow carry an unmistakable authority, an insistence, and a wisdom.

Now we come to the central question: Who or what told Mary Ellen to open her eyes? Who or what "lifted" David out of his chair and into the church aisle? If these voice or nudges seem to come from someplace or something external to us, from where or from what?

No one knows.

Many Doubting Christians speculate, of course. The psychologically oriented claim that such nudges come from our personal unconscious. The Jungians suggest that they blossom out of our *collective* unconscious. To those who cut their teeth on Eastern doctrines, they're an expression of our *karma*, our *dharma* or the *akashic records*. Others suggest that their source is an "impulse of nature," which is vague enough to satisfy almost everyone. But, and I stress this, no one claimed to know their source with certainty.

But this fact—that we *don't* claim to know, that we acknowledge uncertainty—is in itself something new among religious people. One thing that differentiates Christians Who Doubt from more traditional Christians is that we explicitly Doubt. None of us claim to be sure about who or what is doing the nudging. David Knight left it as just "something strange." Jacob, our evangelical guitarist, told us only that "something" occasionally moves him. He said,

> I don't have the sense that someone, some figure, is zapping me with a lightning bolt from the sky...but that I'm just singing whatever I'm moved to sing.

Mystics on the Margins are at ease with the ambiguity of not-knowing.

One of the few things we can say for sure is that these nudges seem to have a magnetic quality. Whatever their source —the depths of consciousness, the impulses of nature or whatever—they seem to propel us like a magnet towards a certain direction. In technical terms, these nudges seem to bear a "teleological draw." "Teleology" is the doctrine that things tend to move towards a certain goal, especially towards deeper self-knowledge. This might suggest that our nudges are "drawing us" towards greater self-realization. Many of us come to see our voices or nudges from a wider perspective only years later. If we do, we often see how they brilliantly led to something important for our lives or for the world.

Nonetheless, unlike the traditional Christian who has certainty about his or her calling's source, the Mystics on the Margins I interviewed seem to be largely content with such uncertainty. We just do not know—and we cannot know—what is guiding us.

"Disembodied voices or impulses from beyond" don't come with calling cards.

Fortunately, most of us are humble enough to recognize that there is much about life we cannot know, that we don't have all the answers and that we have a lot to learn. We are, once again, content to leave great mysteries mysterious.

In fact, being comfortable with not knowing may be the defining mark, the *sine qua non*, of Mystics on the Margins. Whereas more traditional believers—and alas!—Christian nationalist politicians might claim to know the wishes of what they call "God," we recognize the limits of our knowledge. We are content to leave the source of our nudges or the object of our prayers as "forces in the cosmos that we just don't understand."

We leave great mysteries mysterious.

I believe that most Doubting Christians would be comfortable with my summary of our attitude towards both prayer and being called:

> There may be forces in the cosmos—powers and impulses that we simply do not understand—that may sometimes guide us and respond to our prayers.

---

1. Quoted by Stephanie Bradbury, email correspondence, 8/15/2023.

CHAPTER 14
REIMAGINING THE AFTERLIFE

As a chaplain I walked in a very delicate space. I often attended to people who were dying. Only once was I present when someone drew his final breath, but the job had me often listening to men and women who were staring into the abyss. Some of my more traditional Christian patients told me that they were counting on the traditional promise that, though their life had been hard, they were confident that they'd "get to live forever with God and everybody they loved." No doubt that made the prospect of dying less terrifying. (Interestingly, although many mentioned heaven, almost no one spoke of hell—and only if they were looking to this chaplain for forgiveness.)

But no Mystic on the Margins mentioned heaven. None believed in the rapture. Nor did anyone accept the image of a God who judges their actions and assigns them to hell or heavenly bliss. "I just do not believe there is a place we go to after death like heaven and hell," Kathy Clausen said simply. "I certainly don't see any sense in purgatory."[1]

"I have *no* sense that there's a purgatory, hell or heaven," agreed Elizabeth Young. To Christians Who Doubt, who tend to be educated and scientifically oriented, a *post mortem* heaven or hell seems more fairytale than foretell. Elizabeth then went on,

> ...*Whatever happens will happen. I can only assume that whatever happens after we die, it is loving. The world I believe in has no need to be scary.*

It's my impression that for the Doubting Christians with whom I spoke, what happens after we die is just not the huge concern that it was a few centuries ago. Virtually none of my informants ask themselves whether they will go to anything like the cartoonist's pearly gates or the sulfuric fires of hell. This whole set of images has become so beyond the pale, so far-fetched, that we just don't worry over it.[2] As my Swedish contact Birgitta put it:

> *Death is not a big question for me. It's just not ours to know what death is like. I'm an agnostic about what happens after death. If we should know we would know. It's not for us.*

Our shrinking preoccupation with our fate *postmortem*, suggested Kathy, has probably been due to the changes in our life situation. For people like medieval peasants or today's homeless, she suggested, life tended to be poor, nasty, brutish, and short. So not surprisingly, they were very concerned with death and what happens after. "If you are not satisfied with your life, if you are not living heaven on earth here," she suggested, "you very well might cling a to heaven in the sky." But, she implied, compared to them, our lives are wealthy, comfortable, humane and long.

To Christians Who Doubt, the New Testament is not about predicting what happens beyond the grave. It's about transforming our lives and our consciousness here and now. The "pre-Easter" Jesus was exemplifying and pointing to just such a transformation in this life, not the next. According to the theologian Marcus Borg, his message was

> not really about how to get to heaven. It was about a way of transformation in this world and the Kingdom of God on Earth... Jesus wasn't very much concerned with life beyond death, either his own or that of others (Borg, 2003, p. 173).

Jesus was more concerned with leading a good life here on earth, being compassionate, finding and offering love, etc. So too are we. When he said, for example, that "The kingdom of heaven is at hand" (Matt. 10:7), he wasn't describing a place among the clouds to which we hopefully will go. He was pointing to a transformation we can each achieve in *this* life, i.e., coming to live in alignment with the Divine Flow. According to Borg, the traditional belief that heaven comes only beyond the grave is the expression of a long-standing and antique misunderstanding.

We Mystics on the Margins seek to become more fulfilled, to make the world a better place and to align with the infinite energies—in the here and now. When Jesus is quoted as saying, for example, that we should "become like children to enter" the kingdom (Matt. 18:3), he was encouraging his hearers to become simple, straightforward, honest and ego-free.

TWO FORMS OF EVIDENCE

Now, even though death is just not the huge concern that it was long ago, how *do* Mystics on the Margins understand what happens to us after we die? My interviewees pointed to two kinds of evidence that offer hints.

1. The first kind of evidence comes from *Near Death Experiences* (NDEs). NDEs are accounts of people who died and, after

being resuscitated, told stories about their experiences while they were clinically dead. Several interviewees referred to Raymond Moody's *Life After Life,* which first popularized the term, "Near Death Experience" in 2015.

Some referred to Dutch cardiac surgeon Pim van Lommel's *Consciousness Beyond Life, The Science of Near-Death Experience,* which offers scientific data about NDEs. Of the 344 patients in van Lommel's cardiac ward who were resuscitated, some 62 (18%) had specific memories from when their heart had stopped. This percentage was roughly confirmed by an American study that found that some 15.5% of resuscitated patients had NDEs. Two British studies found that of resuscitated cardiac patients, 11% and 18% had rich memories of what happened to and around them after their cardiac arrest.

Many saw a tunnel or a light. Some sensed deceased loved ones who beckoned to them. Many reported a process of reviewing their lives and judging their lifetime's behavior. Some saw their lives through their friends' eyes and judged it from their vantage point. Others reported sensing some sort of benign being which did the evaluating.

Every patient who had such an experience lost their fear of dying. Most Near Death Experiences are, surprisingly, *pleasurable*. In other words, as Mary Ellen put it, "NDEs show me that the life we lead now connects with a place of love."

NDEs, however, tend to be relatively brief, generally lasting only a few minutes or hours, though one man reported an NDE in a coma that lasted several days.[3] Such temporary experiences obviously don't *prove* what happens after we actually die. But they do they suggest that death is not like heaven or hell and not a blank darkness, but rather is, in some sense, lively, vibrant and strangely appealing.

On a side note, in addition to seeing a light, a tunnel and loved ones, many NDE patients also reported fairly detailed "out-of-body" experiences. They recalled veridical experiences of watching the doctors and nurses trying to resuscitate them, generally from a vantage *outside or above* their bodies. Pim van Lommel's book contains a lengthy account of a Pamela Reynold's out-of-body experience. While her heart and brain activity had stopped, she "just sort of popped out of the top of my head." Looking down from above her body, she saw "the instrument in the surgeon's hand; it looked like the handle of my electric toothbrush...it looked more like a drill than a saw..." Her surgeon later confirmed that this "corresponded very accurately to the saw that was used to cut open her skull...[which] does indeed resemble an electric toothbrush" (von Lommel, 2011).

The interviewee who has given the most thought to Near Death Experiences was our Episcopal priest, Stephanie Bradbury. I will let her tell us in her own words how she has come to understand the sense of divinity in NDEs:

> *Sometimes in an NDE, people sense themselves as brought before a loving entity, the Divine. They talk about it as like being in the light of 1000 suns, but it doesn't burn their eyes. And that they're infused with a love that is a million times bigger than anything they've experienced before, a staggering and overwhelming love. And when people come back from NDEs, they often talk about being homesick, because they feel like it was where they belonged. They were home there in this light and in this love, and they want to be part of it again.*

The idea that we persist after death is by no means a fringe concept. According to Pew Research, approximately four-in-ten Americans say they have sometimes had a strong feeling that someone who had passed away was trying to communicate with them. That includes 51% of adults in the historically Black Protestant tradition and 47% of Catholics. Smaller shares of Jews (31%) and evangelical Protestants (30%) say they have had a strong feeling that a dead person was trying to communicate with them. Among the religiously unaffiliated, 35% say this.

2. Some of my interviewees pointed to a second kind of evidence: *reincarnation*. Dr. Ian Steven and Dr. Jim Tucker, both from the University of Virginia Department of Perceptual Studies, documented numerous accounts of people, especially children, who demonstrated surprisingly accurate memories of previous lives. For example, some children knew their way around a distant town to which they had never travelled. Other children told stories that included vivid details of another life with which they had no contact, details which were later verified. Others offered details about a family unrelated to their own and about the layout of a house they had never entered. Finally, some offered veridical details about how they had died. Such accounts, of course, don't *prove* that we humans become reborn, but they do suggest that it's possible.

These accounts of NDE's and of reincarnation clearly suggest that after we die, we experience *something* other than mere blackness. They suggest that death is in some sense active. And again, none suggest a heaven or a hell.

Frankly, I wish I could go further. I wish I could offer an account of what happens after we die with greater specificity. But as I say, the facts here are well beyond what I or any of us can know with confidence. Most of us are with Birgitta, that such knowledge is just not for us. About death as about so much, I am, we must be, agnostic.

But I, like most Mystics on the Margins, actually don't mind. For as Kathy said, this question just doesn't loom large for us. Our fate beyond the grave is not something we tend to spend much time worrying about. And that's ok. The question just doesn't make it to the top ten list of our preoccupations. Like so many, I think that it's high time we as a species stopped pretending to know what we cannot, and make room for the mysterious.

One final note. Taken together, the evidence from NDEs and reincarnation suggests that after his gruesome crucifixion, Jesus may have been able to consciously survive his death. As we suggested in the Resurrection chapter, we know neither the limits of human consciousness nor of our human spiritual capacities. Jesus of Nazareth may have had some such unusual capacities. That's why we left room for the possibility that one young man who grew up in Northern Israel may indeed have been able to make himself seen *postmortem*. We'll never know with certainty, but he just may have been able to consciously resurrect.

I stress that we Mystics on the Margins have reached our conclusions about the afterlife not by accepting the ancient and confusing Biblical accounts. We have come to these hypotheses by broadening our evidence. Taken together, our evidence points to the possibility that, in some sense, we may be able to live a life that stretches beyond self, beyond ego and beyond death.

---

1. Moody found much the same when he interviewed people about their near-death experiences: "In all the reports I have gathered, not one person painted the mythological picture of what lies hereafter. No one described the cartoonist's heaven of pearly gates, golden streets and winged, harp-playing angels, nor a hell of flames and demons with pitchforks."
2. Paraphrased from Marcus Borg.
3. See Alexander's incredibly complex and rich account of his near-death experience during his days-long coma.

RUMINATIONS ON CHRISTIANITY

I have come to see over the past eight and a half years how much shifts if we come to believe that Jesus was not the only God-infused being.

No Mystic on the Margins sees Jesus of Nazareth as the *only* "Son of God." Most see Jesus as a deeply mystical fellow, a spiritually rich soul, who became a healer, political provocateur, wisdom teacher and prophet, but not the only such. We see him as a man among men, a human being, who resided in the openness that is the living experience of the Divine energy. Just as any of us can. We hold him as someone who was able to truly love. Much as any of us can. And we see him as a man who became a spiritual leader, guiding his followers towards a life in which he acted without getting triggered either by other peoples' judgments or by his fate. Just as have many spiritual teachers. We admire his teachings and his example of letting go and simply allowing. Much as we admire many others. And we recognize how he's all about trusting:

Look at the birds of the air; they neither sow nor reap nor gather into barns, and yet your heavenly father feeds them (Matt. 6:25–6).

Rather than thinking of Jesus as the "only one," the Messiah, we hold him as an *exemplar* of the evolved spiritual life. Rather than being the "one and only," we hold that everything that the tradition claims about him is also true, in a sense, of all of those rich souls who have become God-infused: Thomas Merton, Meister Eckhart, St. Theresa, Thich Nhat Hahn, Dalai Lama, Buddhaghosa and so many others. Most important, we hold that the Gospels challenge all of us to become such a "son" of the Divine.

Drawing this out, when the tradition described Jesus as "fully God and fully human," it is saying first that he was a material being. So are we all: we all have blood, bones, cells and mouths that can smile. It's also saying that we too abide within the Divine. The mute materiality of molecules and cells somehow gives rise to our stunning ability to be aware, to choose and to feel. That is, our bodies host the miracle of consciousness. It is also saying that just as he lived spiritual openness or Flow, so too we can live such a Flow. Just as he was familiar enough to call the Divine "Abba," (Father) so too can we know a similarly intimate connection by sensing ourselves as part of the vast Ground of Being, the Quantum Vacuum Field. Just as Jesus was "fully" aware of his own dual nature, so can we become conscious of our materiality and our connection with the vast "non-sensory reality" that is the Divine. In other words, we too can all become "*fully* God and *fully* human."

Jesus was said to be God's "son." In that we all are manifestations of the Ground of Being and can realize our link with it, the Mystics on the Margins suggest that each of us can realize ourselves as a "son" or "daughter" of the Divine. We too can experience and carry on our lives amidst the Vast sea of love.

When the tradition describes Jesus, in other words, it is describing a promise that *any of us* can realize. Everything the texts say of Jesus, as Meister Eckhart taught, is or can be true of any of us.

All that God gave his only begotten Son in human nature he has given me... Everything that Holy Scripture says of Christ is entirely true of every good and holy man (Forman, 1991, p. 129).

It is possible for each of us to live our lives in the effortlessness that is Holy, in unreserved love. We can thus live in the energy of the Christ.

The resurrection story dovetails with this vision of Jesus. Again, we've observed how Mystics on the Margins don't cling to the stories of the miracles. Rather, we see the stories as portraying what it can be if any of us, no matter the dangers, truly relinquishes our self-concern and lives in effortless openness. Just as Jesus went through hardship and pain while remaining connected to the Divine energy, so can we all. Just as Jesus "resurrected" into a new kind of life, so too can we all transform.

The implication here is that even if we hold that Jesus was not the one and only Divine being, we can be perfectly good Christians. Even more, dropping the claim of exclusivity is not a loss but a gain! We gain a great deal when we align ourselves with Jesus, and also experience our connection with the same spiritual energy that he lived. Experiences of the Divine are the birthright not only of Jesus, but of any of us.

Furthermore, recognizing that the experience of the openness that is the mark of the Divine is available to anyone, no matter what their denomination or religion, is an enormous gain. Such mystical connection stands at the shimmering spiritual core of virtually every spiritual pathway. This fact invites us to connect with sincere seekers across any doctrinal disagreements. Holding that we can all experience the Divine firsthand is indeed a gift, not a loss!

Even though the Doubting Christians don't accept the post-Easter Jesus story or the creeds, we admire and try to follow the teachings and example of Jesus of Nazareth. Some focus on his parables and teachings, others on his loving, on-the-ground encounters with outcastes like Samaritans and tax collectors, others on his lionization of the poor. But for us all, he is shining!

This more phenomenological approach to Christianity also affects how we think about our life's purpose. Traditionally, Christianity taught that life's purpose is to "know God" and to "follow God's purposes for our lives":

> *I know the plans I have for you, says the Lord, plans for your welfare and not for harm, to give you a future with hope (Jer. 29:11).*

And traditional believers are, of course, to follow "His" plans.

But the Mystics on the Margins I interviewed don't tend to talk much about their life plans as "God-given." We may develop life goals, but we ourselves have to listen for and discern them, fully aware that our individual purposes will probably change over our lifetimes. One's purpose may, for example, go from "finding my voice" in their twenties, to "being productive" in their thirties to "learning to love" in their forties to "loving my grandchildren" or "satisfying my bucket list" in their sixties to yet something else later on. We write our life plans not in stone but in pencil.

On the other hand, we Mystics on the Margins do see our life challenges as learning to align ever more deeply with the larger Flow of life and connecting ever more deeply with others. This means relinquishing our grasping after fame, power, wealth, control or the like. We are always challenged to relinquish our ego and then to relinquish it some more. We are always challenged to open our hearts ever more honestly and deeply to one another. And we are constantly challenged to align ever more deeply with our sense of the greater call. All this is much as a traditional Christian might feel. But where Mystics on the Margins differ is that we just don't claim to know the source of this call.

One caveat here and it's important: We could imagine someone taking on the task of aligning with the Divine Flow or unabashedly loving their spouse, while also being a nasty boss at work, embezzling at work or even shooting someone. To take a hackneyed example, consider a man who was a kindly and devoted husband who was also a Nazi guard at Auschwitz. Or an angelic teenage boy at home who became a mass murderer of his high school. Though it seems unlikely, we can imagine such a man or boy sensing a strong connection with the transcendent who also "felt called to shoot those people." This is clearly wrong: Any spirituality that focuses exclusively on one's own spiritual growth to the detriment of others is not spiritual at all. As Jesus reminded us in his twin commandments, the experience of loving the connective Ground of Being finds its fulfillment in loving one's neighbor. This is why the deepest aspiration of the Mystics on the Margins, as I have come to see it, is:

Understanding, feeling, letting go and aligning ever more deeply with the Flow of the Ground of Being, which is love, while enhancing, not harming, other people's ability to do the same.

Speaking of "loving one's neighbor," pretty much every Mystic on the Margins with whom I spoke engages actively in some sort of service: manning a soup kitchen, working on environmental issues, tutoring, singing in a choir, or the like. Service, as Cristina and Pennie stressed, is both a natural fulfillment of and a cause of our spiritual openness. It makes the love that comes with encountering the Divine visible.

I think Christianity lost a great deal when it abandoned its simple focus on living and acting out of the love that Jesus taught and exemplified. It lost a great deal when it became an institution, a religion, and developed fixed creeds and law-like behavioral rules. Jesus was about none of that. Becoming an institution was probably inevitable, but in doing so it lost much of what it was in the beginning.

In this sense the Mystics on the Margins are, I believe, recovering the tradition's original emphases, beginning with Jesus himself. When Christianity was "The Way" it was a path to develop participants' embodied spiritual connections ("to love God with all your heart..."), and their on-the-ground loving ("love your neighbor..."). Christianity offered then, and should offer today, a path that was focused solely on developing spiritual openness and loving one's neighbor. If we can stop getting trapped by the overtones of its antique and sometimes misleading models, if we can let go of the fanciful miracle claims, if we can put aside the great Christological debates, and if we can listen to the spiritual depths that once shimmered behind the ancient words and shimmers still, then we will find ourselves face to face with a truly believable, truly helpful Christianity.

PART SIX
FINAL REIMAGININGS

CHAPTER 15
TRANSLATING TRADITIONAL LANGUAGE

If it is to help modern, educated people create healthy church communities and deepen our lives under the vision of the Divine, the church will have to find new ways to make sense of its antique language. In this book we're attempting to do just that, to articulate the new ways of thinking that Christians Who Doubt the old language have been developing. I have listened to my interviewees' vulnerably honest accounts of their experiences and to their thoughts about how they reimagine the implications of those ineffable experiences in today's frame. Those experiences are, I believe, largely the same kinds of experiences towards which the early texts were pointing, so I am attempting here to translate—no doubt inadequately and unpoetically—two important texts from their fourth or tenth century religious worldviews into our twenty-first-century framework: The Apostles' Creed and the Collect for Purity.

THE APOSTLES' CREED

What follows are the words of the traditional Apostles' Creed in italics, followed by my own "translated creed," in roman type.

I believe in God, the Father almighty,

I believe that there is a mysterious and non-sensory field-like reality beneath everything that we can see, hear or touch. Some think of it as God, the Ground of Being, the Quantum Vacuum Field or many other names. The subjective experience of that energy field carries the tone of love.

creator of heaven and earth;

This energy field was and is the foundational reality within all matter. It is the source of quarks, electrons and other fine particles that are the source of matter, the earth, the stars and our own consciousness.

I believe in Jesus Christ, his only Son, our Lord

I admire and follow the teaching and example of Jesus of Nazareth, a highly illumined man. The texts suggest that he thoroughly relinquished his self-centered ego and became wide open, fully aligned with the Divine. I am committed to following a similar path to becoming equally open and aligned.

He was conceived by the power of the Holy Spirit
and born of the Virgin Mary.

Like all of us, Jesus was born into a material body from a mother. Also like all of us, his awareness was a manifestation of the fundamental energy field. His consciousness was simple in itself, and not solely the product of his material body, his brain cells or his history. His consciousness was connected to and aligned with the Divine energy, which was so intimate that he should call it "Father," "Abba."

> *He suffered under Pontius Pilate,*
> *was crucified, died, and was buried.*
> *He descended to the dead.*
> *On the third day he rose again.*

Like any human being, he suffered, died and was buried, but the Ground of Being with which he was aligned did not die with him. Stories spread that he had resurrected. He may have had the unusual spiritual ability to appear after he had died.

> *He ascended into heaven,*
> *and is seated at the right hand of the Father.*

As any illumined person can, Jesus became fully aligned with the Divine flow. That is, he lived with an ego-free, spacious wide-openness, i.e. "heaven on Earth." He lived, worked and taught out of that spaciousness to help others relinquish their egos and align with the Divine.

> *He will come again to judge the living and the dead.*

Though we have no external judge, we judge ourselves, often subconsciously and critically, when we do things we know to be selfish, wrong or detrimental to others. Unless we resolve those self-judgments, they will warp our spirits and our lives.

> *I believe in the Holy Spirit,*

I believe that we all carry a spark of the Divine, the "Holy Spirit." We encounter it in our mystical moments.

> *the holy catholic Church, the communion of saints,*

There is a worldwide community of churches whose task is to bring into community followers of Jesus's way in order to help them, individually and collectively, relinquish their egos and align ever more deeply with the Divine.

> *the forgiveness of sins*

I believe that telling someone truthfully about how I harmed them, and/or about my selfish, egoic or embarrassing behavior, is the best way to overcome whatever guilt or tension that I continue to hold.

> *the resurrection of the body,*
> *and the life everlasting. Amen.*

I believe that overcoming our egoic attachments can lead to aligning our bodies, minds and consciousness with the loving Flow of the Ground of Being and that doing so can heal us permanently and help create heaven on earth. Amen.

THE COLLECT FOR PURITY

The Collect for Purity is recited near the beginning of the Episcopal Eucharist ceremony, Rite II. Originally written in Latin as *Deus cui omne cor patet*, it was the product of a tenth-century worldview. It reads:

> *Almighty God, to you all hearts are open, all desires known and from you no secrets are hid: Cleanse the thoughts of our hearts by*

TRANSLATING TRADITIONAL LANGUAGE

the inspiration of your Holy Spirit, that we may perfectly love you.

This is a psychologically astute way to begin a ceremony. Think back to your deepest or most meaningful experiences. Experiences like these dawn when we've let our defenses go, so that we're no longer pulling away or holding back inside, i.e., so that our "hearts are open." When we pull down our inner defensive hands, our breathing becomes easier, our chests feel like they're opening out. We're not anxious, not afraid. When our hearts are open like this, we're peaceful and calm, which for Patient S were the signs of the Divine that she found so comforting.

One way to understand such non-defensiveness is that we have either permanently let go of the secrets that we deny to ourselves or have let them go for the moment. That is, we have let go of everything about which we've been feeling ashamed or guilty: we've dropped our hidden envies, our private angers, our secret longings, so that they're not bubbling up inside even a little. If we can do this, for the moment we are hiding "no secrets." Having swept everything about which we are conflicted away from our consciousness, we have "cleansed the thoughts of our hearts."

In letting our inner conflicts go, we are creating the key condition to opening ourselves wide to that "non-sensory reality," that Ground of Being. That is, opening our hearts allows us to connect with, to become one with the underlying source and "perfectly love" it.

As for the line that our hearts become clean "by the inspiration of your Holy Spirit," I'm afraid that the claim that we "inspire", i.e., "breathe in" the Divine makes it seem solely other-reliant. I resist the thought that such love is given to us *in toto*, that we can do *nothing* from our side. But that's wrong, we do, or should do, whatever we can from our side. We have to tell ourselves the real truth about our secrets, at least for the moment. We have to relinquish, at least for the moment, anything to which we cling.

But though we must work from our side, we cannot bring about true effortlessness solely by our own efforts. Here's where "inspiration" comes in. We cannot force effortlessness. Rather we're creating the soul-conditions for the ineffable.

Here's my underlying point about the Christian language. Creedal statements and foundational prayers are not metaphorical, as many preachers, both conservative and liberal, suggest. Nor are the Synoptic Gospels (Matthew, Mark and Luke) offering *metaphors*. Rather, the Gospels, the creed and this prayer are *depicting* or perhaps *provoking* the kinds of spiritual experiences and transformations that a sincere pilgrim—in any era—might have. Though its models are ancient and its language sometimes misleading, Christianity is *describing* or *evoking* a living encounter with the wide-open and ineffable reality.

CHAPTER 16
FINAL RUMINATIONS

SOLVING MY ENIGMA

I'm coming to the end of my eight-and-a-half-year process. It's time to answer the questions with which I began: How on earth can a religion whose words and tales people like me don't believe, so move us emotionally and spiritually, week after week, even to tears? Even without buying the words, what on earth is this religion *doing* to us? And *how*? And finally, to what, if anything, is this path inviting us?

More broadly, what, if anything, have we learned about the workings and the future of the church? Do the Mystics on the Margins have anything to say to it?

To understand what this religion is doing, let's begin by looking at the kinds of problems it seems to be addressing. The details will differ for each person, of course, since we each come with our own particular wounds and problems. But I believe there is a fundamental human problem at the core of this (and every) religion: the longing to be accepted, loved or simply OK just as we are. Some feel it as a longing to be seen or welcomed. Some hope to feel safe or just not scared. Some wish to feel accompanied, perhaps by a partner. Others hope to feel worthy, perhaps by caring for others, perhaps even to the detriment of themselves. Some seek to become worthwhile by earning (or stealing) money. Or by becoming famous. Or...

This core issue may even be *the* fundamental human problematic. As Goethe saw, we all carry a great burden.[1] None of us was born into a perfect family situation and we grow up carrying scars and hurts and feel, at some level, unloved, unworthy, unseen or unacceptable. We come of age struggling to counter all this and feel deeply welcomed, supported or connected. Others struggle later in life with a sense of failure, of shame or guilt, of being ugly, of being not good enough...

Whatever our issue, most of grow up afraid of the hidden, painful truth of it, and become afraid of our shadow. Few of us dare to trust another with our secrets. So, we become self-protected, defended, hostile or closed off, each in our own way. As I've interviewed people, I've come to see that I'm anything but alone in holding up an inner defensive hand. For the shadows we carry bring deep pain. And *that*—bringing down our self-protective hands enough to become truly open—becomes our core life's work.

Solving such life issues, healing such ancient wounds, is, in the end, the kind of deep work that Christianity, like most other spiritual and psychological pathways, is trying to accomplish. Its goal is to soothe our hurts, to let us each know that we're not alone, that we're worthy and that even though we hurt, it will be and is OK. And to help others realize that as well.

Meditative pathways face a similar challenge. But Christianity is unlike the typical meditative pathway in two ways: first, it is *communal*. It brings us together as part of the path. The group, the so-called "body of Christ," is emphasized again and again. In science-speak, we describe this "groupness" as its *HyperBrain*. Together, we breath, vibrate and feel together as we watch someone light candles, as we smell frankincense, as we mutter hopes and fears, and as we together recite prayers. As we stand up, sit down, kneel together we are forming a set of heart-to-heart and brain-to-brain connections beyond words. Perhaps most powerfully, as we bow down shoulder to shoulder and hold out our hands to be fed, we are subtly weaving ourselves together. We're in it *en masse* as a community. Every ritual gesture, every standing up and bowing down, every carefully orchestrated procession down the aisle expresses and promotes mutuality, connections, love.

Secondly, while the typical Eastern meditation path emphasizes the meditator's enlightenment, Christianity explicitly emphasizes "love." Though "nirvana" may imply a somewhat distant "compassion," the word "love" evokes not only "compassion" but an intimate relationship and personal connection as well. It is not surprising that the word "love" appears more than 700 times in the Bible: "God is love," "Jesus loves you," "You are loved," "love one another" and on and on. Its central thrust is to love the Divine and love others as we love ourselves.

I stress these twin emphases because I heard them so often from my interviewees and my patients. People told me how much less they distrust others, how they feel accepted in their communities, how they've come to love their community, how they've learned to love. As it fosters in us the *experience* of welcoming, of joining together in a great meal, it is teaching love.

I struggle here: writing that "God is love" or that "the Ground of Being is a ground of love" feels painfully hackneyed! But the sort of love we're talking about is not some schmaltzy hallmark-card love. It's not about being "nice, nice" or smiling beatifically. What the religion is about is feeling welcomed in all our irritable, ugly, curmudgeonly and vulnerable glory. At its best, Christianity is about giving, talking about, expressing and feeling human and spiritual *love* in the deepest, most honest sense. It's about the experience of depth, of soul-to-soul connecting, of deep centering. And it's about the oh-so-difficult realization that "I actually *am* worthy," that "I actually *am* lovable" or that I "actually *do* love." Christianity is about the kind of welcoming love that causes us to sob and sob in can't-catch-breath shudders. It's about lowering the hands that we've held up in defense all our lives and letting others *in,* really *in.* It's about opening down to the vulnerable depths of love.

Jesus was all about opening to the Divine and fostering deep connections in this visceral, on-the-ground sense. But over much of Christian history, I'm afraid, this oh-so-difficult heartful task seems to have been largely overlooked. Too often, loving one another within our respective church communities has led participants to see in terms of "us and them." And eventually to "us *versus* them." Which in turn evolved into crusades, into wars of reformation, into endless claims of supremacy, and on and on. What a travesty! These are the exact opposites of Jesus's invitation to "love your neighbor as yourself"!

Jesus was all about, and Christianity is (or should be) about learning to love, especially where there is no love. How simple! How difficult! Beneath every word of the ritual, beneath every prayer, beneath every line of its creeds and its songs, it is pointing to this *love*. And it does this in part by creating sacramental spiritual communities and rituals through which we might help one another foster it.

This love was an expression of, and a cause of, the mystical, the openness to the Divine and the love of neighbor that emerges from it. These experiences of an unhesitant openness are the vibratory source of it all. Jesus himself was clearly responding out of his own spiritual experiences. People like the desert fathers, beguines, benedictines and so on picked up on this Flow of the mystical.

But the church has rarely recognized this fundamental conflict between its original mystical fluidity and its creedal or doctrinal rigidity. Over its long history and especially from its fourth century political context, the tradition had to ossify itself. Beginning in Nicaea, the tradition boxed off what was once its unruly mystical side into a calcified framework of fixed and unbending creeds. There's a reason that so many Mystics on the Margins have gone quiet in their churches and put themselves on the margins. Or joined the ranks of the "spiritual but not religious."

The church would do well to refocus its energies on these experiences and this holy task in order to help people do their spiritual exploration in their way. Ministers simply cannot require that people buy into certain phrases or models while also expecting them to spiritually explore in their way. They would do well to create ways to support people who say, "I don't believe this but..." and to be genuinely open to their new language and interpretations. Rather than remaining attached to its comfortable but fixed models, Christianity must find a way to align with our modern, evolving worldview and ethos. If it does not, thinking people will continue to abandon it.

Yet I want to point out that, despite its flaws, despite its ossified creeds and doctrines, I would never have had, and no Mystic on the Margins would have had, any spiritual church experiences or any growing sense of transformative, collective love without the ritual, the community and the group meal. We had our experiences in and around the songs, the standing and kneeling, and the whole host of actions that were the product of the institution and its doctrines. This irony—fluid experience out of rigid doctrines—is paradoxically the axis around which our responses to Christianity swirl.

Now, some of my interviewees focused their path on being "present." When we are "really present to" something or someone, when we are truly attending to another, with them without distraction, we're not pulling away, even a little. In being truly present, in focusing on something other than myself, in letting go of my own needs and demands, I am fully with them, if only for a moment or two. Presence is a form of love.

Furthermore, as we've said, when we are really present to another like that, we are also being present to "something more." Christianity has always understood this. Jesus's "first commandment" was to "love the Lord Thy God." That is, he counseled opening to the mystical reality. That is why the desert mothers and fathers, the Trappist monks, St. Theresa, Thérèse of Lisieux, the Medieval Beguines and other sisters, and modern people like Thomas Merton, Thomas Keating and others would make opening to "something more" the primary focus of their lives.

When Christina Rathbone sensed in her swimming hole that "the usual realities of separation and struggles simply melted away and I was left in a kind of being and at-oneness," she was swimming without any separation within the loving and ineffable Divine energy. Her deepest experience of being wide open was her connection with the mystical reality. So too, Patricia was present to the mystical reality when she felt in her church that...

> the line between me and the world has become thin. I feel myself part of something bigger, a sense of some ultimate reality or level (this is my word for God) where I feel connected to the people around me and to everything.

And when Patient S felt "not worried at all" and "so at

peace" that she "just knew it was God," she too was sensing love in an uncompounded form, i.e., open to the Divine. And as I walk through those heavy wood and brass doors, week after week, I find a thin place as well. My chest opens, I let down my self-protective hand, and I become really present to—really connected to—the choir, the priest, the space, to my comrades in the pews and to the Vastness, the Ground of Being.

The weekly ritual is, to me, a mute drama about this opening. I can't say the words. I can't accept the resurrection. But every ritual gesture, every ritual element, speaks volumes about openness to the infinite and to each other. We stand and sit and listen and think and share with other people, all in service of an indescribable openness—towards each other and towards the spaciousness.

This then is the answer to my riddle. Every gesture of the ritual and every song of the religion are about expressing, visualizing and experiencing the kind of wide-openness, acceptance and love that is the answer to some of my, some of our, deepest wounds. In the way we are together, in the way we sing together, in the kindly way the priest offers the wafer and the acolyte the wine, I feel this love. In the quiet way that such a mute drama works, it is offering reminders to, and practice in, making space in my heart. The words they use may be confusing or obscure, but the point of the ritual is not. Week after week, I have been intuitively, often silently, receiving, speaking, giving and offering love.

Now, I know, and I believe that most of my readers know, what it is to open our hearts like this for short periods. It is the kind of short-lived experience I asked you to bring to mind in the Introduction. The real challenge is to live out of such openness and presence *long term*. Herein is the work of a lifetime. I believe that Jesus lived with such presence most or all of the time. I believe that he was pointing to just such a long-term experience of spiritual openness and love. His unmistakable compassion and openness epitomized living effortlessly with such a consistently wide-open heart. He apparently lived without raising that defensive hand, even in the face of danger and death, and has become our paradigm of open-hearted love. We seek to live such openness in a similarly long-term way.

Through their antique idiom, the Gospel writers were describing this level of vulnerable openness, this level of consciousness. They did so by portraying one man. They were depicting, again through their first millennium eyes, what it's like to open one's heart towards the infinite energy without pulling back and the love of others to which such an opening gives rise. Christianity offers words, music and actions that are designed to show us, and help us learn, what it is to live in such a level of awareness, and to achieve the impossible, wonderful task of becoming a whole human being.

BUT CHRISTIANITY? REALLY?

How paradoxical that I and the other Mystics on the Margins have rediscovered *Christianity* of all things! A decade ago, like most of my liberal and educated friends, I would have scoffed at the very idea! A tradition that was centered around a puppet-master God who rewards and punishes based on whom we had sex with?? A tradition that puts forward an "all-good" deity that allows pandemics, child abuse, wars, and genocide? And whose priests and ministers are blatantly hypocritical? *Egad! Never!!*

But behind the scoffing and the guffawing, when we threw out the bathwater of Christianity and of religions in general, we also threw out one helluva baby! For from where I sit today, tossing it had an unnoticed but enormous cost. For that baby offered something deep, valuable and irreplaceable.

Despite all our wealth, despite all our high-tech gadgets, fast cars, moon rockets and life-saving medicines, we have found no other way to foster a similar sense of depth, connection and meaning. The baby we Mystics on the Margins and others have rediscovered, what we have found in the churches, is a process and, yes, an organization that is (in theory) oriented around experiences of more and deeper connections with self, other, community and with the experience of "wide-openness."

Reimagined aright, Christianity can fill this hole and bring heart, meaning and sanity into our modern lives. Yes, *sanity*! Compared with a life of screens, bank accounts and football games, a life of connection, meaning and spiritual discovery is, above all, *sane*. For its balance and deepening is something that we human beings actually need. Desperately. And all our technological prowess cannot deliver anything like its depth of meaning, human connection and Divine openness.

Furthermore, this reimagined Christianity may solve some of the very problems left when our culture abandoned its religions.[2] For at its best, for both Christians Who Doubt like me and for Christians who don't, Christianity offers the invitation to be fully present to one another, to drop into vulnerable contact with each other, and to engage with the Divine without having to believe things we don't. And this, I believe, is why our Reimagined Christianity can help answer some of our culture's deep struggles with loneliness and alienation, suicide and depression, meaninglessness and the like.

No widespread system of meaning or connection has been able to fill the vacuum left when we abandoned the churches. Oh, we can cheer together for our football teams in our stadium-sized "communities" and dance together to Taylor Swift in loud coliseums. But America has few places in which we can link arms with one another to deepen our connections or to work together to help others all under a unifying vision. There are even fewer places that can help us deepen the ability to love. Losses like these are enormous. I believe that this reimagined Christianity can fill these social lacunae, both in us as individuals and in us as a society!

Again, I want to stress that the spiritual or mystical experiences and transformations that are the religion's life-breath don't come with fancy church doors, incensed processions or reciting a few words. They come with being present to one another week after week, listening to its wisdom or manning a soup kitchen. They come with helping with a ritual, with standing up, sitting down and kneeling with others, with breaking bread shoulder to shoulder, all under the felt-presence of the vastness of the Ground of Being. It is through action, ritual and service that we open our souls to that which is more, but through action to which we are present and without ulterior motives, or in which "our hands are clean" (Ps. 24). For it is effortless action that invites in the greater Flow.

I for one have experienced such openness primarily in relatively liberal *Episcopal* churches like Trinity. I'm not promoting it except to say that the progressive Anglican way works for me. It has provided me with a consistent and spiritually provocative ritual that provides a comfortable routine while leaving me free to think my thoughts, feel my feelings and open up my spirit, all in my own way and time. It has provided a safe enough haven for me to address some of my very old, very deep pains. I have no doubt that other denominations do something similar for their followers. I recommend finding the way that works best for you so that it can become your seminary for learning and growing in love.

So yes, despite the paradox, Christianity. A healthy church offers the welcoming love of a community, reminds us to love one another, and helps us see how we're standing under the canopy of what is More.

SOCIETAL ISSUES

When I began weeping in church while not believing any of what I was hearing, I honestly thought I was the only one.

After a few dozen long interviews with Mystics on the Margins, it became obvious that I am not at all alone! There were *lots* of folks who also don't believe the creeds yet are deeply moved. I may be weird, but it turns out I'm not the only weirdo.

Again and again, I heard how the Doubting Christians' church communities had become rich emotional and spiritual homes:

> *"I feel cared for, nurtured, loved there."*[3]
> *The community opens an inner well within me. Sometimes I cry at the mere beauty of it."*[4]

Some told me of feeling love from and for their fellow members. They told me of a kind of mystical bond, if you will, that arose in their church "fellowship." Some told me how their community had served as a springboard into an ineffable experience of the Ground of Being.

> *Singing together in harmony with others, being with others in this kind of quiet way, creates an openness... When I'm with people at these depths, I feel part of something bigger than me.*[5]
> *When I'm really present to the minister or to a church mate, when I'm really there, I feel projected into the transcendent through the other.*[6]

This then was my first sociological discovery, that there were lots of other nonbelieving churchgoers who also were having spiritual experiences in church while disbelieving the doctrines. And who were, like me, trying to make sense of—reimagine—Christianity.

My second ah-ha came a few years later. I had assumed this relatively small coterie of people "on the margins" were the *only* group who were getting something important from their church life without accepting the beliefs. But I came to realize how wrong I was. I've recently come to see that only 44% of mainline protestants hold that "Jesus Christ is my savior." About a third (some 28%) do not believe that they'll "go to heaven after I die." And just a fifth (20%) of young people believe that "if I confess my sins I will go to heaven" (Carter, 2020). This is to say that there are many, many people who are *not* on their church's margins who go to church, feel connected with their community and sense something of the Divine without accepting the ancient doctrines. And who are trying to make sense of it all.

Many people are like Patient S. and use the word "God" as a way to express the felt-quality of some meaningful experience. For example, when someone tells themselves in a hospital to "let go and let God," they're actually encouraging themselves to open their hearts to "accept my destiny without fighting it." Or they're reminding themselves to "allow all of their life to rest in that peace or spaciousness."

I've also come to recognize an even larger demographic: there are many who go to church and have some sense of self-transcendence and yet don't know how to talk about it. This I heard in many of my patients. Probably they don't notice that when they hear the word "God," or "confess their sins" something important is happening inside themselves without their being able to articulate it. They might have grown up thinking that the word "God" is really about the creator of the universe or the controller of their fate, but don't quite realize that they believe these things no longer. In fact, I've come to think that *most* churchgoers are in this boat. After all, as we saw, only 9%

of Christians believe in God, Jesus, salvation, prayer or sin in the way that the tradition presents them. Many of these people who remain committed to the language and models may have a more or less clear intuition that there is "something more" to which they are pointing but struggle to say it. I hope this book helps give new words to a few of them.

Finally, many hold to the belief system more tenaciously. For them a felt-sense of a transcendent reality may be there, but they use only traditional language for it, despite the awkwardness. They might sense the Divine in the wide openness they sometimes feel while talking with a good friend, and use the word "God," without caring that the anthropomorphic model doesn't particularly fit. I hope that this book helps clarify a few things for them.

THE "PURPOSE" OF LIFE

Does this reimagined Christianity have anything to say about the purpose of life?

Well, let's think what a traditional Christian might say about life's purpose. Here is a purpose statement from a conservative minister, "Pastor John," which is about as clear as any I've seen. He writes that our purpose is...

> to know God as he really is; and to enjoy him and all that he is for us in Christ; and to reflect in this dark world some of the light that he has shown to us when Christ...died in our place, precisely that we might know God and enjoy God in spite of our sin; and then one day to see him and know him perfectly unendingly. Let me say it again. The meaning of life is to know God, and to enjoy God.[7]

In simple terms, Pastor John is encouraging his flock to overcome sin and perhaps evangelize others so that they can "reflect the light," i.e., know and enjoy God "in spite of our sin."

It seems to me that as comforting as it may be, an answer like Pastor John's has two very deep flaws. The first problem has to do with its syntax. If we ask what is the purpose of a bowl, we know how to answer it: its purpose is to serve as a container in which to prepare, serve or store food. The purpose of a car is to carry human beings over distances. The syntax here makes perfect sense. We human beings make cups, automobiles and other things in order to solve specific needs.

But it's not obvious what specific need was being solved when we were created. We didn't come into existence to solve any specific purpose. Nor since we doubt the image of a great potter in the sky, it's not clear *whose* needs we solved. What seems easier to understand is that by some process like natural selection, humanity just came into being. No potter, no purpose.

The second flaw is that no matter its specifics, any firm statement that supposedly captures our purpose will almost inevitably lead a believer to emotionally attach themselves to it. If, for example, someone follows Pastor John and holds that their purpose is to "reflect the light" and "know and enjoy God," they are likely to invest a good bit of energy in those lines and connect this purpose with themselves. If anyone or anything challenges their sentence, inevitably they will feel threatened. Indeed, one of Pastor John's congregants, Abijah, experienced just such a threat when her comfortable sense of life's purpose was challenged. In the past, she told the pastor, she could face life's challenges with the assurance that God was in control and that she could trust Him. But when her life's challenges became hard...

> *I started to get really depressed about the whole meaning of life... My entire view of God and life has been shattered. I can't seem to get myself out of wondering why life is even a thing... Life often feels like it has no meaning.*[8]

FINAL RUMINATIONS

When we build our spiritual lives around a relatively clear answer, we will inevitably feel at risk when that answer no longer explains. As did Abijah's, our sense of meaning will shatter.

Thus, it was hardly surprising that when I asked Mystics on the Margins about the purpose of life, not one offered a clearly verbalized answer like Pastor John's. Nonetheless, I actually did hear a surprisingly consistent response. That was,

"I have no idea."

Virtually everyone could not or would not name life's purpose.

Now, at first take I thought they were just brushing off the question. But I've come to realize that there is far more to it than that. We Mystics on the Margins just don't feel the need to offer a clear, articulatable purpose. Nor would we know how to formulate one. We just know we don't know. And we're comfortable with that not knowing.

Yet I believe that in this claim of uncertainty is the clue to how we actually do answer the purpose-question. To declare that "I don't know," is to declare a willingness to live *without* a clear, articulated purpose. We have long ago given up on thinking that we can have complete knowledge. We have moved towards allowing in the unknown, and are comfortable with such ambiguity. This indicates, to me at least, that we are holding our life and our sense of meaning without clinging to any easy answers or formulations. Such unknowing is the beginning of our "answer."

This comfort with such ambiguity suggests that whatever we believe about life's "purpose," we'll hold it with the same curiosity and lightness that we hold the object of our prayers or what happens after we die. The desire for certainty is, to me, itself part of many a believer's problem, for it keeps people trapped in the bubble of their system.

I believe that the Mystics on the Margins' holding the

answer lightly is healthier. For it allows us to engage people who hold different beliefs with fewer firm beliefs that we have to defend. We can listen more openly and curiously and perhaps even find common (experiential) ground. As such, our religious differences may become far less strident.

Now, even though we don't cling onto a clear and articulable purpose, I and every Mystic on the Margins that I've ever met *do* see ourselves as on a path. Most are committed to becoming ever freer, ever less trapped in our viewpoints or beliefs. To become ever more fully alive, to overcome our emotional stuck places, to become ever more open and authentic and to live in ever more complete alignment with the divine is our ongoing life's work. It is our unending challenge. Perhaps we should say that our lifelong challenge to promote emotional fluidity and become more open to the spiritual reality is a kind of "life purpose." Thus, I might summarize that

> *Our purpose of life is growing towards and living ever more deeply in alignment with the ineffable and transcendent Ground of Being (Quantum Vacuum Field) to which our deepest experiences point.*

Note here that this "purpose" is more a vector than a goal, more a process than an end state. The "purpose" here is the path, the path the "purpose."

This lifelong "vertical" challenge towards the transcendent has a horizontal implication: as we saw in Chapter 11 on Service, as we become increasingly free and wide open, our path naturally comes to include helping others and helping our world thrive. Thus, part of our life's work is reaching ever more profoundly beyond our individuality by loving our fellow beings (human and otherwise), loving our planet, and forming ever more loving communities (creating ever stronger "Hyper-Brains"). Connecting these two ideas, our "purpose" becomes something like:

FINAL RUMINATIONS

Our purpose of life is growing towards and living ever more deeply in alignment with the ineffable and transcendent Ground of Being (Quantum Vacuum Field) to which our deepest experiences point. This we seek to do in part by loving our neighbors ever more deeply and forming loving communities (stronger HyperBrains), thus learning how to love, especially where there is no love.

To bring this exploration full circle, this statement parallels that of Jesus

The two greatest commandments are "Thou shalt love the Lord thy God with all thy heart and with all they soul and with all thy mind. And the second is thou shalt love thy neighbor as thyself" (Matt. 22:37-39).

This ongoing challenge can be seen as a modern reimagining of Jesus's twin commandments, but with two key differences. First, since we Doubting Christians recognize no person-like deity, we don't tend to use "interpersonal love" as our paradigm for our relationship to the impersonal Ground of Being. We tend to talk about aligning with such a ground or seeking an *openness* of psyche and spirit towards this nonsensory reality. Secondly, we stress that our challenge towards such openness is not a goal but a vector, not a destination but a path.

FINALE: THE CHRISTIAN OPTION

A friend recently called this book, half-jokingly, a modern version of St. Paul, who was dubbed the "Apostle to the Gentiles." But in this book, he added, you're an "apostle" to the doubters and the dubious. He was right: I have tried here to systematize what I heard from churchgoers who doubt the miracles and the models and I am being an apostle to such people. And I'm an apostle to the religious "nones" who are dubious about the whole religious endeavor.

Here's what I want to say as the Apostle to the Dubious who are "spiritual but not religious" or who are religious "nones":

Before my friend dragged me to her church eight and a half years ago, I was indeed one of you; I was among the "spiritual but not religious." I had been meditating some 50 years and my life was good. I was definitely not conscious of being lonely. And I certainly wasn't craving a religious community. But at some unconscious level I was all of these. I was largely alone on my path. I had friends and connections around the country and world, but few people on whom I could really count to help when things were dicey. And frankly, I also felt a little spiritually stuck. If I told myself the real truth (which I couldn't have until I burst out crying in Mahwah) I really could have used "somebody's help!" I wasn't actively aware of it, but that yearning was there, in my belly, quietly rumbling.

Perhaps you too feel a mite spiritually stuck. Perhaps you too wish you could count more on some broad mystical energy. Perhaps you are just a wee bit lonely and might want a community that doesn't demand conformity. Though you've no doubt developed your own worldview that accepts modern science, perhaps you too wish you had tribe-mates.

If any of this is true for you, you might want to check out a local church. Find one that feels welcoming and that is congruent with your morals; there are lots.

I have seen in my own life and others' how attending a church with the open attitudes we've here highlighted has shown me how self-involved, how cut-off and, well, how spiritually lonely I was, all without realizing it. I've rediscovered the value of soul-to-soul connections.

If you choose to explore it, please hear one bit of advice. If you're like me, you'll want and expect a perfect path and a perfect community. But no community, no church will be even close to perfect! Every church, every tradition has developed a language through which members can meaningfully talk about, sing about, dance about and celebrate the ineffable reality. But, alas, every tradition and every church will also be *in*adequate in how it does so. No tradition, no language, no community *fully* exemplifies the love that blossoms out of the ineffable mystery. No tradition and no community is without its human foibles. As the Zen aphorism has it, every tradition offers but a finger pointing to the moon, but *isn't* the moon.

In other words, if we approach it as we have here, you may find Christianity's models and language appealingly lovely and helpful. You may find it's developed a perfectly wonderful way to talk of ineffable realities or that it offers some beseeching parables, metaphors and yes, theological theories.

But, alas, you will also find it to be *in*adequate. Its history is rife with interpersonal tensions, misguided people and the whole human catastrophe. Its way of talking about the spiritual realities, its paths and its church communities are all *flawed*. Almost every church board argues.

But in the last analysis, the Christian path is no worse than, and no better than, any other communal spiritual pathway.

In other words, I have found Christianity to be both imperfect and a wonderful part of my life path. It has opened my emotional life and has led me to some delightful comrades. But even to share this path (or any path) in a reimagined way is not the be-all or end-all. It hits me as sometimes frustratingly flawed. Christianity is then, like every spiritual system, an *adequate-inadequate* system.

To productively engage such an *adequate/inadequate* system, or any existing spiritual path, we must hold it lightly. We'll have to reach past some of the hard feelings and trauma left by its history which were caused by some of its more flawed teachers, systems and ministers. We'll have to stop trying to justify its dubious claims and its first-millennium science.

But as we've seen over these pages, the Mystics on the Margins have developed a way to approach Christianity that doesn't demand that we accept anything that in good conscience we can't. It doesn't ask us to undertake anything that seems wrong, cultish or immoral. Again, there *are* many, many churches that *don't* claim to know it all and that *don't* demand that we dress or think in their way. There *are* churches and denominations that encourage wide open and honest questions and interactions. And there certainly *are* lots of churches that are *not* homophobic, misogynistic or anti-science.

I invite you to look carefully and thoughtfully at the churches in your area. If you've not found one already, I invite you to "church shop" for a community in which you feel welcomed and you can be yourself. If you find one that seems to fit, I encourage you to explore it, and hold it with the forgiving and open-minded attitude that the Mystics on the Margins have demonstrated. If your experience is anything like mine, becoming part of and eventually helping such a community thrive might just be a healthy step of learning how to live with others, open our souls to the Infinite and love ever more deeply.

I wish you ever-maturing peace, meaning and love.

---

1. Ian McClaren, writing under the pen name of Rev. John Watson, is said to have written in 1898, "Be pitiful, for every man is fighting a hard battle."
2. Here I'm thinking of Judaism, which struggles with similar issues. But that's for a separate book.
3. Mary Anne Grammar, personal communication.
4. Margareta Stiernspetz, personal communication.
5. Anna Christina Sungren, personal communication.
6. Elizabeth Young, personal communication.
7. From Ask Pastor John, Blog, "What is the Meaning of Life?" https://www.desiringgod.org/interviews/what-is-the-meaning-of-life
8. *Ibid.*

EPILOGUE

I didn't expect to write this, but after eight and a half years, my pilgrimage of tears seems to be ending. I want to tell you how.

Three weeks ago, our Sunday service included a baptism of baby Alexander. A lot of his relatives came, dressed in their Sunday finest, and a whole coterie of cousins. The church was full.

As the baptism portion began, Alexander's parents and godparents stood around the baptismal basin. His parents held him up, like Simba holding up his cub in *The Lion King*, and said aloud, "we present Alexander to receive the Sacrament of Baptism." It was a highly formal "presentation," but I found it incredibly moving.

Then the priest asked the parents and godparents, with a catch in his voice, "Will you be responsible for seeing that you bring Alexander up in the Christian faith and life?" The "Christian" part didn't much work for me, of course. I translated it as, "Will you be responsible to bring this child up to be a decent human being?" And of course, the parents and godparents heartily declared, "Yes!"

At these two lines, I wept. Not just a few tears, mind you, like on so many Sundays. Not just a decent cry. This was intense, uncontrollable. My sobbing became so hard, my shoulders heaving so heavily, that I had to leave the hall and get myself together.

What got to me so much, I've wondered? Those two sentences clearly touched something deep in me.

I've come to think that in holding Alexander up to the priest, to the congregation, to the broader world and to the Divine, the parents were in effect saying, "I see this child and he is not me. Here is a human being. We present him as complete in his own right." Through their very body language, holding him skyward and away from their own bodies like that, they were presenting him as whole unto himself, ultimately separate from themselves, a full being. They were showing that they recognized him as his own person.

In effect, they were saying to Alexander, "I see you!"

At the depths, I don't think I ever felt that as a kid. As mentioned before, my parents were decent people, but I always thought that they really noticed me only when I had done something impressive, something that they could brag on or be proud of: when I got excellent grades, became popular, learned guitar or achieved some sort of glory. If I did something they could show off to their friends, they could brag on me. It was as if I were an appendage to them, a reflection of them. Frankly, I was not at all sure that I existed for them (or in my own eyes) independently of my successes. I'm certainly sure that my parents didn't recognize me in all my introvertive peculiarity, in all my sensitive and ruminative individuality. Yet here were Alexander's parents, who were (in theory of course) announcing to themselves his independent existence, his value, whoever he turned out to be. Somehow seeing those parents and godparents "present" him, I felt as if I myself was being "presented." In seeing them I was as if seeing my own parents (or me myself) recognize me in all my individuality. And I was also seeing myself as a father, and how I more or less recognized my own children as discrete beings.

As I told you, the priest then asked, "Will you be responsible for seeing that Alexander is (brought up well)...?" What I understood was, "Will you raise him to be the best Alexander that he can be?" When he asked Alexander's parents to take responsibility for their child like that, I felt he was asking the same thing of me and of every parent and grandparent in the audience. He was asking us all to promise that we have or will take responsibility for our children's lives. As he was to the parents, he was asking *us* to raise our offspring to become *their* best selves. He was reminding us all to *always* take responsibility for our offsprings' development.

When I was younger, I never had the sense that there was "anyone there for me." Oh, my parents were good people and no doubt tried their best. But they were practical people, busily trying to build a business and get ahead, and had no idea how to support their highly sensitive, philosophical son. My four grandparents were the same, happy to have grandchildren but not really able to connect with me. Nor was there an aunt or uncle who saw me for who I was. I was alone at the depths.

In a conversation with Krista Tippets, Father Greg Boyle said that what he was about, what Christianity is about, is what psychologists call "attachment repair":

> *Mom was frightening or frightened and you cannot calm yourself down if you have never been soothed by that significant caretaker. So, for us as adults we need to learn soothing and sometimes it takes*

others to soothe us. There is a task that needs to be attended to and this is <u>the</u> task for so many of us that needs to be attended to (Tippett, 2019).

Father Boyle named my dilemma well. My mother *was* frightening. In part as a result, I didn't grow up with the sense that who I was was OK, that I counted, that someone really had my back. I didn't feel loveable just as I am. The monkey has been forever on my back, yearning constantly to be seen, valued, worthy. You know, if at first you don't succeed, work even harder!

I've struggled with feeling as alone as Sisyphus. No wonder I felt I had to do it all on my own. Filling this hole became the unrecognized agenda for my lifetime of soul-rebuilding. And no wonder that these two lines—that the parents recognized their child and that they promised to raise him to be the best Alexander that he could be—touched me so deeply!

Doing all this sounds so simple! These parents were to notice and take care of their child: just what parents are *supposed* to do! But hearing it that morning, feeling the love in the space, I was somehow able to receive this—being noticed and cared for—into my own heart. However it happened, *something* registered! Somehow, I came to feel that I was seen and valued for just being me. That I too am welcome. That I too was loved.

No wonder I sobbed so hard!

While I was getting myself together and coming back into the room, the mass had continued. It came to the section in which we're invited to think about any moments during the past week in which we had felt grateful. Generally, we do this privately, but occasionally someone comes up to the podium to speak.

EPILOGUE

That morning, I was feeling so moved that I got up and walked slowly to the mic.

"I have a two-minute-old moment of gratitude," I began...

I want to thank Alexander's parents and godparents here. The line that got to me this morning was "will you be responsible for seeing that the child you presented will grow up as a decent human being." I am so moved by the fact that you're doing what you can to help him grow up well, to help him become the best Alexander he can be. I am so inspired that you've taken on this task.

Then I turned to the congregation and, through tears, continued,

I am also grateful for all the parents and grandparents in this space as well. As flawed and inadequate as we each are, I want to thank each of you for doing your best to help your children and grandchildren grow up and turn into decent people as well. I thank you too.

As I sat down, the place applauded. In our church this rarely happens. When I motioned that I wasn't looking for applause, it stopped. But truth be told, I was moved. It meant that I had touched them, that we had connected, and that they had felt my gratitude with me.

That short talk was cathartic for me. In expressing all this through my tears, in saying what I sincerely appreciated about the parents and grandparents there, I was saying my truth vulnerably. And I felt seen. I wasn't seen as a performer or someone who was showing off. I felt seen in who I am, with all my blubbering emotional tenderness. I felt seen not for my accomplishments or intelligence, but rather seen for who I am.

I was moved by the connection I was seeing between Alexander and his parents, and moved as well by the connection I was sensing with my congregation. I was also recognizing that I *have* tried my best as a father and grandfather. I felt that I was a parent among parents, a part of this congregation and connected with these people. I didn't have to earn my membership. I felt welcomed in who I am, welcomed in all my tearful feelings. I am safe. I don't have to prove anything to be welcomed here. I too count. It was as if some sort of veil fell away and I could see that I no longer had to hide behind it. I *am* part of the human story.

In this context, I'm coming to understand why I've been crying all these Sundays. When it started happening, I thought I cried because in seeing folks singing, processing down the aisle two by two or gracefully setting the alter table together, it reminded me of what I never had. I thought I was grieving my lack of cooperative togetherness, crying about being so damn self-sufficient all my life. I thought that in seeing the mutual respect with which an acolyte gave the plates and chalices to her priest or seeing people greeting one another so warmly, it highlighted all that I never had. When that female cantor in Mahwah sang "pray for us," and I said to myself "Lord knows I can use *some*body's help!" I thought that I was weeping over exactly that, that I needed help.

But today, I think I had it backwards. I have come to see my tears have all been about *connecting* and *being seen*. I weep not because I am mourning my losses, but rather because I'm *finding* connections! When the priest and I lock eyes and he places the little Eucharistic wafer in my hands, what enchants me is not a lack but a gift. I feel seen. When I allow the music to percolate into my chest and belly, it's because I feel so *full* that I weep. Even in that ejaculation in the Mahwah church that began this journey—"Lord knowns I can use someone's help"—I was moved not by an absence but rather by the possibility that someone will see me and help. I was *connecting* with that cantor, with the chanting congregation and with the mysterious energy. I've come to see that what I've been weeping about has not been my loneliness but rather its opposite:

EPILOGUE

connecting with my churchmates. I *am*, we *are*, together and worth saving.

In fact, I have come to think that, ever since this began, my tears have *all* been about feeling seen and connected: I am recognized, accompanied and welcomed here. My tears have all been about feeling and offering love. As I gave that short talk in the church, standing so naked, I was in effect saying, "I am here. Through all my emotional tenderness, see me. Love me for who I am as I love you."

Two days after the baptism, I had a scheduled video call with Mary, my spiritual advisor. As I told her this story, she said, "In those tears and in your seeing the other parents and grandparents, you felt seen." When she said this, I again teared up. She not only saw me in all my rawness, but she helped make the process and my feelings *conscious*.

It's as if over all these years I have been digging a well. Every week I have touched into some of the healing water down below. But that day, that week, it was as if I'd hit the motherload and a geyser had erupted. The tears that baptismal week were the finale.

I say this because since those events—weeping so hard, giving my little talk and talking with my spiritual advisor—things actually have changed. And dramatically.

First, I stopped crying. For eight and a half years of Sundays I cried so regularly in church that I came to count on letting out whatever deep pain was down there. But the Sunday after the Baptism moment, nary a tear. And I have not cried any Sunday since! I haven't even sensed that I'm about to cry. The impulse just hasn't been there! My eyeballs have remained dry as a bone. Honestly, I'm stunned!

A second change has had to do with my emotional life. For many, many years I have woken up slightly depressed. It would lift after I got up and going, but it was serious and annoying enough that I got a prescription for an antidepressive (though I stopped taking it because of its side effects). But since that baptismal Sunday, I have never felt that old morning depression. Nothing. I've even been waking up a little optimistic, glad to be alive!

I am genuinely perplexed about all this! My first thought is that all my adult life I have been trying to fill the hole that was left by my upbringing. As I told you, I never felt really seen as a kid, never sensed that I was enjoyed as a human being with all my intense feelings. So, all my life I've been craving to be seen for who I am. Over the years I tried every which way to get noticed—being silly or funny, playing sports, getting good grades—but I never felt actually seen or welcomed. Even after I published book after academic book, I've still never felt quite seen or valued. I became quite well-known in my field and was even awarded an honorary Doctorate, but still never felt quite seen or valued. But there I was, standing in front of my church congregation, naked, vulnerable and tearful, with all my gratitude. I was myself with nothing added. This was a whole different kind of being seen. Or perhaps in feeling really recognized, really seen like that, I was able to get beyond my longings to be seen. Yes, I am here. Yes, this is who I am.

No doubt all my years of psychotherapy, meditation and yearly retreats helped. My endless ponderings and self-analysis, all attempts to fill that ancient hole, probably helped too. But none of them quite did the trick. Being with others on the path and going through all those crying jags seemed to have added something crucial.

However it happened, something seemed to complete itself that day. I hesitate to say that that lifelong issue was "cured." Few psychological issues actually get "cured." Much more common is that we "work on our issues" (and work...and work). A psychiatrist friend once told me that we can never cure our issues but only hope to lessen our problems' intensity from a 7 on the Richter scale to a 3. So, I'm wary of saying this issue has

EPILOGUE

actually been resolved. But seeing those parents hold that baby and seeing that a parent can indeed recognize and support their child...seeing that I too, despite my inadequacies, have cared for my children and my grandchildren...seeing that parents can actually notice who their kids are... My lifelong struggle actually seems to have lifted. Though my parents may not have seen me as discrete, here I was seeing Alexander—and I myself—as discrete. And in giving that little talk and talking with Mary, I felt seen not as a successful professional nor as a charming friend, but as just a human being. In seeing Alexander's parents recognize and support him, I felt recognized and supported.

This process, though, has been damned painful. It's been hard to admit to myself what I have always lacked and been longing for throughout my life. It's been hard to own up to all my failings as a friend and as a parent. But in going through all this, I've come to recognize that *this* is what it is to be this human being. The pain has been a critical part of this process. My vulnerable and intense longings and feelings are some of what makes me what I am. And in writing this, I am telling myself and showing you who I am. Here I stand.

If we continue the analogy with digging a well, I'd point to a wider aquifer that's also here. I think that facing courageously into the truth of our failings, "our sins," in letting them go in order to come to openness, is at the core of the whole Christian enterprise. We have imposed so much theology, ritual and institutional structure on it. But at its heart rests this simple realization: that I'm OK, that I am connected, that I too am loved. There is nothing more intangible, yet nothing more important. The whole of the religion is about this miracle, the baptism of the soul that can only come from "grace."

If we peel away the centuries of theologizing, mythmaking and sermonizing, it comes down to something as simple as this: a tousle-haired teenage boy holding a shiny, wobbling emblem longing to know deep down to his orange sneakers that he is loved.

One final step in this epilogue: Over the past years, my son and I have often struggled. Many a tense phone call, many an angry text. But that Friday, when we spoke on the phone, he shared that around the same time, completely independently of what was happening to me, he had had an important therapy session. He had made a huge step of progress, and had begun to resolve his side of our struggles. He was unmistakably softer than he'd been! His frustration and anger with me had clearly lifted! He had turned a corner, as if becoming a different person. And I too was ready: it was such a joy to be with him! Our conversations ever since, have been wonderfully sweet and connected. That old residue of anger has lifted!

I asked him later when he had had his breakthrough. It turned out that his ah-ha moment had happened on *virtually the same day, virtually the same hour,* as had my baptism breakthrough!

Now, I'm not big on the claim of some cosmically orchestrated "synchronicity." But these two dots just beg to be connected! Did my son feel some calmness coming from me over the soul-to-soul telegraph wires? Did I feel something emanating from him that helped me get beyond my own struggles? Was there some kind of supra-personal agency at work here? Or should we note that the Quantum Vacuum Field or the Ground of Being at the foundation of all reality connects all things, especially family members? Or that my son and I have been entangled like a pair of quantum quarks?

Whatever the explanation, *something* seems to have led us both to virtually simultaneous breakthroughs!

Here again, we must leave great mysteries mysterious.

EPILOGUE

But whatever the cause, for this mysterious process I am profoundly grateful. Grateful for my son. Grateful for meditation and therapy. Grateful for the tears and the pain and the church that provoked this wonderful journey. Grateful for the resolutions. And grateful for the hope.

I wish you a similarly magical pilgrimage!

GRATITUDE

I am grateful to all of my interviewees and contacts. Several were especially helpful. I had repeated and extended conversations with Stephanie Bradbury, Doug Kruschke, Elizabeth Young, Anna Christina Sundgren, Mary Meader, Ted Harris and others. Many others, especially Melissa West, Chris Schaefer, Livingston Van De Water, Martin Rutte and Beth Sutton helped as readers, reviewers, all-around supports. Melanie Wald-Fuhrmann and Jacob Melancon were even co-authors and co-workers. I am also especially grateful for the insights and wisdom of Anne Marie O'Farrell, agent *par excellence*, who was so generous with her thoughts and time. And of course, I am profoundly grateful to my amazingly insightful, beloved and long-suffering wife, Yvonne Kraus-Conrad Forman.

I can't express my appreciation enough to:

Melissa West, Kerry Gordon, Yvonne Forman, Margareta Stiernspetz, Inger Gustafsson, Elizabeth Young, Colin Greer, Patricia Maguire Smith, Christopher Schaefer, Phil Goldberg, Kathy Clausen, Ted Harris, Doug Kruschke, Pennie Curry, Rolland Vasin, Mary Ellen Washienko, Rev. Bill Weinsenbach, Sue Gore, Anna Christina Sundgren, Beth Sutton, Jack Brown, Veronica Cunningham, Bengt Johansen, Anne Andrews, Brian Farrell, Peter Feltman-Mahan, Stephanie Bradbury, Dan Lemons, Cristina Rathbone, Mary Anne Grammer, Jennifer Clark, Patricia Tudor Stendahl, Jon Geldert, Lee Cheek, Igal Harmelin, Kenzo An, Rodrigo Tarrazza, Sr. Gail Worcelo, Marc Roberts, Jacob Melancon, Meredith Haider, Melanie Wald-

Fuhrmann, Anne Marie O'Farrell, Mary Meader, Greg Darling, Robert Pohl, Livingston Van De Water, Mati Engel, Laura Jordan, Zachary Carl, Channing Carl, Nathan Ingalls, Chelsey Warren, Rochelle Willingham, Matt Lewis, Stacy Lewis, Elenor Parkins.

Thank you, thank you all!

WORKS CITED

Adams, James Rowe. "So You Think You're Not Religious: a Thinking Person's Guide to the Church." *ProgressiveChristianity.org*, 2 Aug. 2024, progressivechristianity.org/resources/so-you-think-youre-not-religious-a-thinking-persons-guide-to-the-church-2nd-edition/.

Adey, Peter. *Levitation: The Science, Myth and Magic of Suspension.* Reaktion Books, 2017.

Alexander, Eban. *Proof of Heaven: A Neurosurgeon's Journey into the Afterlife.* Simon & Schuster, 2012.

Alper, Becka A., Michael Rotolo, et. al. "Spirituality Among Americans," *Pew Research Report*, December, 2023. https://www.pewresearch.org/wp-content/uploads/sites/20/2023/12/PR_2023.12.7_spirituality_REPORT.pdf.

Anders, S, et. al. "Pseudo-hyperscanning shows common neural activity during face-to-face communication to be associated with shared affective feelings but not mere emotion recognition," PII: S0010-9452(20)30279-3 DOI: https://doi.org/10.1016/j.cortex.2020.06.015 .

Aslan, Reza. *God: A Human History.* Random House, 2017.

Association of Religious Data Archives. "US Charity Work?—Belief Statistics Topic." https://www.thearda.com/us-religion/statistics/beliefs?qsid=44 .

Astin, J.A. et al. "The efficacy of "distant healing": a systematic review of randomized trials. *Ann Intern Med.* 2000 Jun 6;132(11):903-10. doi: 10.7326/0003-4819-132-11-200006060-00009.

Azhari, A. et al. "Parenting Stress Undermines Mother-Child Brain-To-Brain Synchrony: A Hyperscanning Study." *Scientific Reports*, vol. 9, no. 1, 6 Aug. 2019, https://doi.org/10.1038/s41598-019-47810-4.

Bass, Diana Butler. *Grateful.* HarperOne, 2019.

Battersby, Stephen. "It's Confirmed: Matter Is Merely Vacuum Fluctuations." *New Scientist*, 20 Nov. 2008, www.newscientist.com/article/dn16095-its-confirmed-matter-is-merely-vacuum-fluctuations/.

BBC News. "*Resurrection Did Not Happen, Say Quarter of Christians.*" BBC News, 8 Apr. 2017, www.bbc.com/news/uk-england-39153121.

Beck, Richard. *Hunting Magic Eels.* Broadleaf Books, 2024.

Benson, Herbert et al. "Study of the Therapeutic Effects of Intercessory Prayer (STEP) in cardiac bypass patients: a multicenter randomized trial of uncertainty and certainty of receiving intercessory prayer." *Am Heart Journal*, vol. 151, no. 4, 2006.

Borg, Marcus, "Re-Visioning Christianity: The Christian Life." A transcript of a speech delivered at the National Forum of the Center for Progressive Christianity, Irvine, California, June 1-3, 2000.

Borg, Marcus, *The Heart of Christianity*. HarperOne, 2003.

Borg, Marcus. *The God We Never Knew: Beyond Dogmatic Religion to a More Authentic Contemporary Faith*. HarperOne, 1998.

Brach, Tara. "The Winds of Love: Taking Refuge in Conscious Relationship." *Garrison Institute*, 9 Jan. 2018, www.garrisoninstitute.org/blog/the-winds-of-love/.

Brooks, David. "The Nuclear Family Was a Mistake." *The Atlantic*, March 2020.

Brown, Daniel James, *The Boys in the Boat: Nine Americans and Their Epic Quest for Gold at the 1936 Berlin Olympics*. Penguin, 2014.

Bruce, Marino A. "Church attendance, allostatic load and mortality in middle aged adults," *PLoS ONE*, 12(5): e0177618. May 16, 2017, https://doi.org/10.1371/journal.pone.0177618 .

Buzsáki, G. *Rhythms of the Brain*. Oxford University Press, 2006.

Carmichael, Joel. *The Death of Jesus*. MacMillan, 1962.

Carroll, Sean, California Institute of Technology. C-SPAN broadcast of Cosmology at Yearly Kos Science Panel, Part 1, June 22, 2006.

Carter, Joe. "Survey: Majority of American Christians Don't Believe the Gospel." *The Gospel Coalition*, 9 Aug. 2020, www.thegospelcoalition.org/article/survey-a-majority-of-american-christians-dont-believe-the-gospel/.

Cha, KY et al. Does prayer influence the success of *in vitro* fertilization-embryo transfer? Report of a masked, randomized trial. *J Reprod Med.* 2001;46:781–7.

Chabin, T. et al. Audience interbrain synchrony during live music is shaped by both the number of people sharing pleasure and the strength of this pleasure. *Frontiers in Human Neuroscience*, 2022. https://doi.org/10.3389/fnhum.2022.855778.

Coruh, Başak et al. "Does Religious Activity Improve Health Outcomes? A Critical Review of the Recent Literature." *Explore*, 1:3, May, 2005, pp. 186–191. https://doi.org/10.1016/j.explore.2005.02.001.

"Csíkszentmihályi, Mihály—FLOW PSYCHOLOGY." *FLOW PSYCHOLOGY*, 2024, sidhere.wordpress.com/category/mihaly-csikszentmihalyi.

Csikszentmihalyi, Mihaly, *Flow: The Psychology of Optimal Experience*. (NY: Harper Perennial, 1990).

Czepiel, A. et al. "Synchrony in the periphery: inter-subject correlation of physiological responses during live music concerts." *Scientific Reports*, 11(1), 1-16, 2021. https://doi.org/10.1038/s41598-021-00492-3 .

Dennett, Preston. *Human Levitation*. Schiffer Publishing, 2007.

Dikker, S. et al. "Crowdsourcing neuroscience: Inter-brain coupling during face-to-face interactions outside the laboratory." *Neuroimage*, 227, 2021. Article 117436. https://doi. org/ 10. 1016/j. neuro image. 2020. 117436 .

Dikker, S. et al. "Brain-to-Brain Synchrony Tracks Real-World Dynamic Group

Interactions in the Classroom." *Current Biology*, 27(9), 1375–1380, 2017. https:// doi. org/ 10. 1016/j. cub. 2017. 04. 002 .

Dossey, Larry. *Healing Words: The Power of Prayer and the Practice of Medicine*. HarperSanFrancisco, 1993.

Dossey, Larry. "Prayer: Interview with Dr. Larry Dossey." *Tricycle: The Buddhist Review*, Mar. 2000, tricycle.org/magazine/interview-with-dr-larry-dossey/.

Eckhart, Meister, *The Essential Sermons*. Paulist Press, 1981.

Emerson, Ralph Waldo. "Gifts." *Essays: Second Series (1844)*, http://www.emersoncentral.com/gifts.htm.

Emmons, Robert. "The Psychology of Gratitude." *Thanks! How the New Science of Gratitude Can Make you Happier* (Boston: Houghton Mifflin, 2007) pp 130-131.

Fincham, Frank. "What Can Science Say about the Study of Prayer?" *John Templeton Foundation*, Sept. 18, 2024. www.templeton.org/news/what-can-science-say-about-the-study-of-prayer.

Finley, Jim. "An Interview With James Finley," *Progressive Christianity*, April 13, 2023. https://progressivechristianity.org/resource/an-interview-with-james-finley .

Forman, Robert K.C. *The Problem of Pure Consciousness*. Oxford: Oxford University Press, 1990.

Forman, Robert K.C. *Meister Eckhart: The Mystic as Theologian*. Dorset England: Element Books, 1991.

Forman, Robert K.C., ed. *The Innate Capacity*. NY: Oxford University Press, 1998.

Forman, Robert K.C. "Introduction," *Mystical Consciousness, the Innate Capacity and the Perennial Philosophy*. NY: Oxford University Press, 1998.

Forman, Robert K.C. *Mysticism, Mind, Consciousness*, SUNY Press, 1999.

Forman, Robert K.C. *Enlightenment Ain't What It's Cracked Up To Be*. London: O Books, 2011.

Forman, Robert K.C. and Melanie Wald-Fuhrmann. "The Body of 'the Body of Christ': An Introduction to Hyperscanning Research and a Discussion of Its Possible Implications for Understanding Social Experiences During Religious Gatherings." *Pastoral Psychology* (2024) 73:379–394. https://doi.org/10. 1007/s11089-024-01142-x .

Funane, T. et al. Synchronous activity of two people's prefrontal cortices during a cooperative task measured by simultaneous near-infrared spectroscopy. *Journal of Biomedicine*, 7, Article 077011, 2011. https:// doi. org/ 10. 1117/1. 36028 53 .

Gallagher, Michael and S.J. Paul. *The Human Poetry of Faith*. Paulist Press, 2003.

Gendlin, Eugene. *Focusing*. New York: Bantam, 1981.

Grosso, Michael, *The Man Who Could Fly: St. Joseph of Copertino and the Mystery of Levitation*. Rowman & Littlefield, 2015.

Haidt, Jonathan. *The Righteous Mind*. Vintage Books, 2013.

WORKS CITED

Hameroff, Stuart and Roger Penrose. "Consciousness in the Universe: A review of the "Orch OR theory," *Physics of Life Reviews* 11(2014):39–78. https://doi.org/10.1016/j.plrev.2013.08.002.

Hanson, Rick. *The Enlightened Brain: The Neuroscience of Awakening.* Sounds True, 2014. www.sooundstrue.com/products/the-enlightened-brain-online-course.

Harris, William S. et al. "A Randomized, Controlled Trial of the Effects of Remote, Intercessory Prayer on Outcomes in Patients Admitted to the Coronary Care Unit," *Arch Intern Med.* 2000; 160(12):1877-1878. https://jamanetwork.com/journals/jamainternalmedicine/article-abstract/525428?resultClick=1. To see responses: *Arch Intern Med.* 1999;159(19):2273-2278. doi:10.1001/archinte.159.19.2273.

Harvey-Wilson, Simon. "Human Levitation," *Australian Journal of Parapsychology*, June 2006, pp. 21-34.

Heimlich, Russell. "Mystical Experiences." *Pew Research Center*, www.pewresearch.org/fact-tank/2009/12/29/mystical-experiences/.

Hirsch, Joy, et al. "Frontal temporal and parietal systems synchronize within and across brains during live eye-to-eye contact." *NeuroImage*, Volume 157, 15 August 2017, pp. 314–330. https://doi.org/10.1016/j.neuroimage.2017.06.018 .

Hutchings, Dawn. "Progressive Christianity," *Pastordawn BEYOND CHURCH*, 2012, Accessed Oct 21, 2022.

James, William. *The Varieties of Religious Experience: A Study in Human Nature.* Library of American Paperback Classics, 2009.

Jiang, Jing, et al. Neural Synchronization during Face-to-Face Communication. *Journal of Neuroscience* 32 (45), 2012. 16064-16069; DOI: https://doi.org/10.1523/JNEUROSCI.2926-12.2012 .

Kalra, Aarat P., et al. "Electronic Energy Migration in Microtubules." *ACS Central Science*, vol. 9, no. 3, 12 Jan. 2023, pp. 352–361, https://doi.org/10.1021/acscentsci.2c01114.

Kelsen, B. A et al. "What has social neuroscience learned from hyperscanning studies of spoken communication? A systematic review," *Neuroscience and Biobehavioral Reviews 132*, 2022, pp. 1249–1262.

Khullar, Dhruv. "How Social Isolation Is Killing Us." *The New York Times*, 22 Dec. 2016. www.nytimes.com/2016/12/22/upshot/how-social-isolation-is-killing-us.html.

Krieg, Carl. "The Deconstruction and Reconstruction of the Historical Jesus—Part 1." *ProgressiveChristianity.org*, 19 Nov. 2023, progressivechristianity.org/resource/the-deconstruction-and-reconstruction-of-the-historical-jesus-part-1.

Krieg, Carl. "The Deconstruction and Reconstruction of the Historical Jesus—Part 2." *ProgressiveChristianity.org*, 19 Nov. 2023, progressivechristianity.org/resource/the-deconstruction-and-reconstruction-of-the-historical-jesus-part-2/.

WORKS CITED

Kristof, Nicholas. "Opinion | Pastor, Can White Evangelicalism Be Saved?" *The New York Times*, 19 Dec. 2020, www.nytimes.com/2020/12/19/opinion/sunday/christian-evangelical-christmas.html.

Lange, E.B., et al. "In Touch: Cardiac and respiratory patterns synchronize during ensemble singing with physical contact." *Frontiers in Human Neuroscience 16*. (2022) https://doi.org/10.3389/fnhum.2022.928563 .

Leder, D. "'Spooky actions at a distance': Physics, psi, and distant healing." *J Altern Complement Med*. Vol. 11, 2005, pp. 923–30.

Leibovici, L. "Effects of remote, retroactive intercessory prayer on outcomes in patients with bloodstream infection: randomised controlled trial. BMJ, 2001; vol 323, no. 7327), 2001, pp. 1450–1451. DOI: 10.1136/bmj.323.7327.1450 .

Leon Festinger, et al. *When Prophecy Fails*. NY: Harper-Torchbooks,1956.

Levertov. Denise. "The Avowal." *Oblique Prayers*, 1984. Also found at *Art and Theology*, https://artandtheology.org/2021/03/16/the-avowal-by-denise-levertov/

Ligonier Ministries. "The State of American Theology: Theological Awareness Benchmark Study," *Lifeway Research*, October 28, 2014. https://research.lifeway.com/stateoftheology.

Lindenberger, U. et al. "Brains swinging in concert: cortical phase synchronization while playing guitar." *BMC Neurosci* 10, 22 (2009).

Lipka, Michael. "U.S. Religious Groups and their Political Leanings." *Pew Research Report*, Feb 23, 2016.

Liu, Ning, et al. "NIRS-Based Hyperscanning Reveals Inter-Brain Neural Synchronization during Cooperative Jenga Game with Face-To-Face Communication." *Frontiers in Human Neuroscience*, vol. 10, 8 Mar. 2016, https://doi.org/10.3389/fnhum.2016.00082.

Longhurst, Christine. "Call to Worship Litany: Psalm 32." *Blogspot.com*, 2024, reworship.blogspot.com/2013/02/call-to-worship-litany-psalm-32.html.

Marshall, L. *Nyae Nyae !Kung Beliefs and Rites*. Peabody Museum Monographs 8:63-90.

McKay, Brett and Kate. "Via Negativa: Adding to Your Life by Subtracting." *The Art of Manliness*, Sept 21, 2015. https://www.artofmanliness.com/character/advice/via-negativa-adding-to-your-life-by subtracting/#:~:text=But%20downside%20can%20create%20a,doing%20something%20is%20much%20simpler.

McLeod, Saul. "Erik Erikson's Stages of Psychosocial Development" *Simply Psychology*, January 25, 2024. https://www.simplypsychology.org/erik-erikson.html .

Meisenhelder, Janice Bell, and Emily N. Chandler. "Frequency of Prayer and Functional Health in Presbyterian Pastors." *Journal for the Scientific Study of Religion*, vol. 40, no. 2, June 2001, pp. 323–330, https://doi.org/10.1111/0021-8294.00059. Accessed 26 Nov. 2021.

WORKS CITED

Montague, P. R. et al. Hyperscanning: Simultaneous fMRI during linked social interactions. *NeuroImage, vol. 14, no. 4, 2002, pp* 1159–1164.

Moody, Raymond. *Life After Life.* Harper, 2015.

"Mortal Sin," *Wikipedia*, s.d. See also, "List of Mortal Sins Every Catholic Should Know—St. Mary of the Seven Dolors." *Stmaryofthesevendolors.com*, stmaryofthesevendolors.com/prayers-2/list-of-mortal-sins-every-catholic-should-know.

Müller, V. et al. Complex networks emerging during choir singing. *Annals of the New York Academy of Sciences* 40, 1–17, 2018.

Müller, V. and U. Lindenberger. "Hyper-brain networks support romantic kissing in humans." *PloS ONE* vol. 9, no.11, 2014.

Müller, V. and U. Lindenberger. "Dynamic orchestration of brains and instrumentals during free guitar improvisation." *Frontiers in Integrative Neuroscience 13,* 2019.

Müller, V., et al. (eds.) "Neuronal synchrony and network dynamics in social interaction." *Frontiers in Human Neuroscience,* 2022.

"MultiVu: Multimedia Production & Strategic Distribution." *MultiVu: Multimedia Production & Strategic Distribution,* 2024, www.multivu.com/players/English/8294451-cigna-us-loneliness-survey/docs/IndexReport_1524069371598-173525450.pdf.

Newberg, Andrew and Mark Robert Waldman. *How God Changes Your Brain: Breakthrough Findings from a Leading Neuroscientist,* 2010, Ballantine Books.

Newport, Frank. "Religion and Wellbeing in the U.S.: Update." *Polling Matters,* February 4, 2022. https://news.gallup.com/opinion/polling-matters/389510/religion-wellbeing-update.aspx.

Norris, Gunilla. *Inviting Silence: Universal Principals of Meditation.* BlueBridge, 2004. Quoted in GoodReads Quotes: https://www.goodreads.com/quotes/9925216-within-each-of-us-there-is-a-silence-a-silence.

Office of Planning, Research and Evaluation, U.S. Department of Health and Human Services. "NSECE Snapshot: The Role of Faith-based Organizations in Center-based Child Care and Early Education," 2019. https://www.acf.hhs.gov/opre/report/2019-nsece-snapshot-role-faith-based-organizations-center-based-child-care-and-early .

Pas, Heinrich, *The One.* Basic Books, 2023.

Paul, Ian. "Do Christians Really Not Believe in the Resurrection? | Psephizo." *Psephizo,* 13 Apr. 2017, www.psephizo.com/life-ministry/do-christians-really-not-believe-in-the-resurrection.

Pérez, Alejandro et al. (2017). "Brain-to-brain entrainment: EEG interbrain synchronization while speaking and listening." *Sci Rep* 7, 4190 (2017). https://doi.org/10.1038/s41598-017-04464-4

Pew Research Center. "Spirituality among Americans." *Pew Research Center's*

WORKS CITED

Religion & Public Life Project, 7 Dec. 2023, www.pewresearch.org/religion/2023/12/07/spirituality-among-americans/.

Pfeiffer, U.J. "Towards a Neuroscience of Social Interaction." *Frontiers*, 2024, www.frontiersin.org/research-topics/211/towards-a-neuroscience-of-social-interaction#overview.

Physics Notes. https://www.ldolphin.org/studynotes/relativ/quantum.htm .

Plumer, Fred. *Drink From the Well*. St. Johann Press, 2016.

Plumer, Fred. "On the Christian Movement and Jesus." *ProgressiveChristianity.org*, 2014, https://progressivechristianity.org/resource/fred-plumer-on-the-christian-movement-and-jesus . Accessed March 2023.

Plumer, Fred. "Progressive Christianity and God by Fred Plumer." *YouTube*, 15 June 2012, youtu.be/ppmDw9iGjNA.

Radin, Dean. *The Conscious Universe: The Scientific Truth of Psych Phenomena*. Harper One, 1977.

Rathbone, Christina. *The Contemplative Imperative*, no publisher, no date.

Ray, Christopher. *Time, Space and Philosophy*. Routledge, 1991.

Real, Terrence. *I Don't Want to Talk About It: Overcoming the Secret Legacy of Male Depression*. Schribner, 1998.

Rhine, J.B. and J.G. Pratt, "A review of the Pearce-Pratt distance series of ESP tests, *Journal of Parapsychology*, vol. 18, 1954, pp 165-177.

Rohr, Richard. *Falling Upwards*. Jossey Bass, 2011.

Sänger, J., Müller, V., and U. Lindenberger. "Directionality in HyperBrain networks discriminates between leaders and followers in guitar duets." *Frontiers in Human Neuroscience* 7, 2013.

Sänger, J., Müller, V., and Lindenberger, U. Intra- and interbrain synchronization and network properties when playing guitar in duets. *Frontiers in Human Neuroscience* 6, 2012.

Schmälzle, R. and C. Grall. "An investigation of the collective brain dynamics of an audience watching a suspenseful film." *Media Psychology 32(4)*, 2020. https://doi.org/10.1027/1864-1105/a000271.

Seltzer, Leon F. "Trauma and the Freeze Response." *Psychology Today*, Jul 08, 2015.

Stevenson, Ian. *Children Who Remember Previous Lives: A Question of Reincarnation*. McFarland, 2000.

Struckmeyer, Kurt. "A Conspiracy of Love: Following Jesus in a Postmodern World." *ProgressiveChristianity.org*, 17 Oct. 2023, progressivechristianity.org/resource/a-conspiracy-of-lovefollowing-jesus-in-a-postmodern-world/.

Sullivan, Andrew. "America's New Religion," *New York Magazine*, Dec 7, 2018.

Targ, R. and H. Putoff. *Mind Reach: Scientists Look at Psychic Ability*. Delacorte Press, 1977.

WORKS CITED

Tarrants, Thomas A. "Discovering God's Purpose for Your Life" *C.S. Lewis Institute*, 15 Jan. 2024, www.cslewisinstitute.org/resources/discovering-gods-purpose-for-your-life/?gclid=CjwKCAjw7c2pBhAZEiwA88pOF2wnsRcvU8I1KDDS6HGc-HTcGNkdHEpEMCgJhH8iJhu1PCQnYGjEiEB0Ci9UQAvD_BwE.

Tart, Charles T. *The End of Materialism: How Evidence of the Paranormal is Bringing Science and Spirit Together*. New Harbinger Books, 2009.

Thielen, Martin. "Do You Think I Am Still a Christian?" *ProgressiveChristianity.org*, 9 Jan. 2024, progressivechristianity.org/resource/do-you-think-i-am-still-a-christian/.

Thompson, Derek. "The True Cost of the Churchgoing Bust." *The Atlantic*, 3 Apr. 2024, www.theatlantic.com/ideas/archive/2024/04/america-religion-decline-non-affiliated/677951/.

Thornhill, Ted. "Praise Be! The more often you attend church services the happier you'll become, says survey," *Mail Online, Daily Mail*, 26 Mar. 2012, http://www.dailymail.co.uk/sciencetech/article-2120595/Going-church-makes-happy-says-Gallup-poll.html#ixzz54SY2Q8VF.

Tippett, Krista. "Greg Boyle with Krista Tippett." *Apple Podcasts*, 19 Dec. 2019, podcasts.apple.com/us/podcast/unedited-greg-boyle-with-krista-tippett/id150892556?i=1000460178309.

Tippett, Krista. "How to Be Grateful in Every Moment (but Not for Everything)." *The On Being Project*, onbeing.org/programs/david-steindl-rast-how-to-be-grateful-in-every-moment/.

Tschacher, W. and D. Meier. "Physiological synchrony in psychotherapy sessions," *Psychotherapy Research*, 30(5), 558–573. 2020. https://doi.org/10.1080/10503307.2019.1612114 .

Tschacher, W. et al. Physiological synchrony in audiences of live concerts (Advance online publication). *Psychology of Aesthetics, Creativity, and the Arts*. 2021. doi:10.1037/aca0000431.

Tschacher, Wolfgang and Deborah Meier. "Physiological Synchrony in Psychotherapy Sessions." *Psychotherapy Research*, 6 May 2019, pp. 1–16, https://doi.org/10.1080/10503307.2019.1612114.

Underhill, Evelyn. *Mysticism*. E.P Dutton, 1961.

The U.S. Surgeon General's Advisory on the Healing Effects of Social Connection and Community. "Our Epidemic of Loneliness and Isolation." 2023 https://www.hhs.gov/sites/default/files/surgeon-general-social-connection-advisory.pdf .

van Lommel, Pim. *Consciousness Beyond Life, The Science of Near-Death Experience*. Harper, 2011.

Wang, Xinyue, et al., "Dynamic Inter Brain Networks Correspond with Specific Communication Behaviors: Using Functional Near-Infared Spectroscopy Hyperscanning During creative and non Creative Communication. *Frontiers Hum Neurosci*, 16, 2022.

WORKS CITED

West, Louis Jolyon. "A Psychiatric Overview of Cult-Related Phenomena." *Journal of the American Academy of Psychoanalysis*, vol. 21, no. 1, Mar. 1993, pp. 1–19, https://doi.org/10.1521/jaap.1.1993.21.1.1.

Wilczek, Frank. "Nobel Lecture: Asymptotic Freedom: From Paradox to Paradigm." *Reviews of Modern Physics*, vol. 77, no. 3, 7 Sept. 2005, pp. 857–870, web.mit.edu/physics/people/faculty/docs/wilczek_nobel_lecture.pdf, https://doi.org/10.1103/revmodphys.77.857. Accessed 4 Sept. 2020.

Wiltshire, T. J., et al. Interpersonal coordination dynamics in psychotherapy: A systematic review. *Cognitive Therapy and Research*, vol. 44, no. 4, 2020, pp. 752–773. https://doi.org/10.1007/s10608-020-10106-3.

Wink, Walter. *My Struggle to Become Human*, Fortress Press, 2017.

Witters, Dan. "Loneliness in U.S. Subsides from Pandemic High." *Gallup.com*, 4 Apr. 2023, news.gallup.com/poll/473057/loneliness-subsides-pandemic-high.aspx.

Yogananda, Paramahamsa. *Autobiography of a Yogi*. Philosophical Library, 1946.

www.ingramcontent.com/pod-product-compliance
Lightning Source LLC
Chambersburg PA
CBHW030104170426
43198CB00009B/483